Marie Engemann
Paradigm uniformity in inflectional stems

Marie Engemann

Paradigm uniformity in inflectional stems

Durational differences in production and perception

düsseldorf university press

D 61 Düsseldorf

Original title of the thesis: "Paradigm uniformity effects in inflectional stems: Durational differences in production and perception"

ISBN 978-3-11-101293-3
e-ISBN (PDF) 978-3-11-101775-4
e-ISBN (EPUB) 978-3-11-101809-6
DOI https://doi.org/10.1515/9783111017754

This work is licensed under the Creative Commons Attribution-NonCommercial-NoDerivatives 4.0 International License. For details go to https://creativecommons.org/licenses/by-nc-nd/4.0.

Creative Commons license terms for re-use do not apply to any content (such as graphs, figures, photos, excerpts, etc.) not original to the Open Access publication and further permission may be required from the rights holder. The obligation to research and clear permission lies solely with the party re-using the material.

Library of Congress Control Number: 2022948384

Bibliographic information published by the Deutsche Nationalbibliothek
The Deutsche Nationalbibliothek lists this publication in the Deutsche Nationalbibliografie; detailed bibliographic data are available on the internet at http://dnb.dnb.de.

© 2023 with the author(s), published by Walter de Gruyter GmbH, Berlin/Boston.
This book is published with open access at www.degruyter.com.

d|u|p düsseldorf university press is an imprint of Walter de Gruyter GmbH

Cover image: Debopre / iStock / Getty Images Plus
Printing and binding: CPI books GmbH, Leck

dup.degruyter.com

Acknowledgements

This dissertation would never have been possible without the help of a number of amazing people, therefore I would like to use this opportunity to express my gratitude to everyone who has accompanied me on this journey for the past 5 years.

First of all, I would like to thank my supervisor Ingo Plag who offered me the incredible opportunity to become part of this research unit and pursue a PhD. You believed in me (even when I didn't believe in myself), and your passion for the project kept me going even when my results were less than straightforward. You were always available when I needed feedback, and working together was always a pleasure. You are the best supervisor I could have imagined and I will always be grateful to you for having given me this chance.

Thanks also to Arne Lohmann for being my co-supervisor back when you were still part of our department. You were the best office neighbor Simon and I could have had and we missed you dearly after your departure to Leipzig. Thank you for also being part of my defense committee, and I would also like to thank my additional defense committee members, Heidrun Dorgeloh, Ruben van de Vijver and Ulli Seegers.

Very special thanks go to Simon Stein and Dominic Schmitz, who were awesome 'academic brothers' to me, and without whom I would have drowned in a sea of academic journal articles. Without our Reading Group 2.0, I would have become utterly lost and would not have made the progress on my dissertation that I made in the time that I made it. But also beyond the reading group, both of you have always been an incredible help to me, answering my numerous questions or random ponderings, sharing your insights or just giving thoughtful advice.

Special thanks also go to Dinah Baer-Henney, and again to Ingo, Simon and Dominic for being the VAR / ENG-S Dream Team. Our first incarnation of the reading group and our semi-regular progress meetings were an amazing help in finding a way through the forest of research, in developing my experiments, and in just making progress on my dissertation.

I am also grateful to Lea Kawaletz for initiating the Writing Accountability Group, and to Viktoria Schneider and (again) Simon for being part of it. Our weekly meetings were an incredible help in structuring my working routine and in setting myself manageable goals. And in times of Corona, these meetings were a great substitute for the dearly missed socializing from pre-pandemic times.

Special thanks also go to my current and former colleagues from the Department of English Linguistics and our neighbors, Gero Kunter, Christian Uffmann,

Sonia Ben Hedia, Jessica Nieder, Kathi Sternke, Julia Muschalik, Ghattas Eid, Ulrike Kayser, Jasmin Pfeifer, Kevin Tang, Akhilesh Kakolu Ramarao and everyone else who was always there to answer questions and give advice when needed. My gratitude also goes to Jennifer, Sally, Lisa-Marie, Julika, Ann-Sophie and all the Hiwis who spent countless hours navigating their way through my production experiment data, proofreading, and helped me with whatever I needed help with throughout the years.

Very special thanks go to the research unit FOR2373 'Spoken Morphology', and of course to the Deutsche Forschungsgemeinschaft for funding this research unit. Being part of this research unit was the best possible environment I could have dreamed of – not only did it allow me to fully focus on my dissertation for 4 years, but I also greatly benefited from the experience and advice from the other members of this research unit. The input from everyone in our colloquia was invaluable and I am grateful to everyone who patiently listened to my talks on paradigm uniformity countless times and always giving new insights. Very special thanks go Mel for giving me feedback on my cloze task sentences.

Thank you Scott Seyfarth for writing the article that inspired this, and for giving me the advice to put my research in such a good place. Thanks go to Susanne Gahl for her advice on my project, and for offering me to perform my experiments in Berkeley – even though thanks to Corona, this never happened. Special thanks to Jen Hay for stepping in and giving me and Dominic the opportunity to perform our experiments remotely in Christchurch, with the help of Wakayo Mattingley and Gia Hurring.

I would also like to thank the HHU Open Access Fund of the University and State Library (ULB) at Heinrich-Heine-University for funding the publication of this dissertation, and for helping me contribute to open science by making this research publicly available to everyone.

Thanks also go to all of the people who gave me feedback at the conferences I attended: *DGfS Stuttgart 2018*, *LabPhon16 Lisbon 2018*, *12 Mediterranean Morphology Meeting Ljubljana 2019*, *15. Phonetik und Phonologie Tagung Düsseldorf 2019*, *MoProc Tübingen 2019*, *17. Phonetik und Phonologie Tagung Frankfurt 2021*, *Words in the World Conference 2021* and *Morphology in Production and Perception: Phonetics, Phonology and Spelling of Complex Words Düsseldorf 2022*.

Finally, I would also like to thank the people in my life beyond my research. You are the ones who reminded me that there's more to life than paradigms, homophones and statistical models – Lea, Sarah, Tyna, Simon E., Katja, Melo, Vlad, Sara, and the rest of the GG crew, my brothers Christoph and Heiko and my family, and of course, the biggest thank you goes to Nim and Bifi for always being there for me.

Table of Contents

1	Introduction —— 1	
2	**Replicating paradigm uniformity —— 3**	
2.1	Replicating Seyfarth et al. —— 3	
2.2	The replication crisis in modern linguistics, and other problems of the current research climate —— 7	
2.3	What is paradigm uniformity? —— 11	
2.3.1	Categorical paradigm uniformity —— 15	
2.3.2	Gradient paradigm uniformity —— 16	
2.4	Previous research on effects of paradigm uniformity —— 17	
2.4.1	Phonological approaches of paradigm uniformity: Optimality Theory —— 17	
2.4.2	Paradigm uniformity (and similar effects) as a phonetic phenomenon —— 20	
2.5	Perceiving phonetic properties —— 23	
2.6	Summary and hypotheses —— 26	
3	**Processing phonetic paradigm uniformity effects: The mental lexicon —— 31**	
3.1	The dual-route model: Decomposability and whole word representations —— 32	
3.1.1	Explaining relative frequency and resting activation —— 33	
3.2	Spreading activation —— 37	
3.3	Other aspects of language —— 40	
3.3.1	Frequency —— 40	
3.3.2	Homophony —— 41	
3.3.3	Orthography —— 46	
3.4	Perception —— 47	
3.5	Summary —— 49	
4	**Corpus studies —— 51**	
4.1	Methodology —— 53	
4.1.1	Selection of items —— 53	
4.1.2	Statistical analysis —— 54	
4.1.3	Variables —— 59	
4.2	QuakeBox corpus study —— 63	
4.2.1	Data —— 64	

4.2.2	Variables —— 66	
4.2.3	Analysis —— 67	
4.2.4	Results —— 68	
4.2.5	Summary —— 76	
4.3	Buckeye corpus study —— 77	
4.3.1	Investigation of [s] and [z] —— 78	
4.3.2	Investigation of [t] and [d] —— 92	
4.3.3	Summary —— 99	
4.4	Summary and comparison of QuakeBox and Buckeye results —— 100	
5	**Production experiment —— 103**	
5.1	Methodology —— 105	
5.1.1	Experimental design for elicitation of speech data —— 105	
5.1.2	Selection of items —— 106	
5.1.3	Participants —— 111	
5.1.4	Processing audio recordings —— 112	
5.1.5	Variables —— 113	
5.2	Analysis —— 115	
5.3	Results —— 116	
5.3.1	Categorical paradigm uniformity —— 116	
5.3.2	Gradient paradigm uniformity —— 118	
5.4	Summary —— 122	
6	**Perception experiments —— 123**	
6.1	Same-different task —— 124	
6.1.1	Methodology —— 126	
6.1.2	Data and analysis —— 131	
6.1.3	Signal Detection Theory —— 132	
6.1.4	Summary of the same-different task —— 138	
6.2	Comprehension task —— 139	
6.2.1	Methodology —— 139	
6.2.2	Analysis using QGAMs —— 142	
6.2.3	Variables —— 146	
6.2.4	Results —— 147	
6.2.5	Summary of comprehension task —— 154	
7	**Discussion —— 155**	
7.1	Categorical paradigm uniformity —— 155	

7.2	Gradient paradigm uniformity	**158**
7.3	Perception	**161**
7.4	Summary and outlook	**163**
8	**Conclusion**	**167**
9	**Appendix**	**169**
10	**References**	**173**
11	**Index**	**187**

List of Figures

Fig. 2.1: Visualization of partial gestural scores —— 5
Fig. 2.2: The cyclical evolution of scientific theory —— 8
Fig. 2.3: Illustration of categorical paradigm uniformity —— 15
Fig. 2.4: Illustration of gradient paradigm uniformity —— 16
Fig. 3.1: The dual-route model —— 33
Fig. 3.2: Formula for calculating relative frequency —— 33
Fig. 3.3: Relative frequency calculated for the word *reheat* —— 34
Fig. 3.4: Relative frequency calculated for the word *insane* —— 34
Fig. 3.5: Two theories of the representation of homophones —— 42
Fig. 4.1: Partial effects of the final model testing for categorical paradigm uniformity —— 69
Fig. 4.2: Scatterplot matrix of durations in Quakebox dataset —— 71
Fig. 4.3: Plural word form frequency by bare stem frequency —— 74
Fig. 4.4: Scatterplot matrix of frequency in gpu_pl —— 83
Fig. 4.5: Frequency band without correlation (gpu_pl_freqband) —— 84
Fig. 4.6: Correlation between stem and word form frequency in gpu_pl_freqband —— 85
Fig. 4.7: Interaction between MORPHEMETYPE and WORDFORMFREQ —— 88
Fig. 4.8: Effect of STEMFREQ on the duration of the plural stem —— 90
Fig. 4.9: Frequency band without correlation selected from gpu_past —— 95
Fig. 4.10: Correlation between stem and word form frequency —— 95
Fig. 4.11: Interaction in the model for cpu_past —— 98
Fig. 5.1: Example for a cloze task from the production experiment —— 106
Fig. 5.2: Example of annotation of production items in Praat —— 112
Fig. 6.1: Example for the segmentation of a carrier sentence —— 127
Fig. 6.2: Stem durations by voicing —— 129
Fig. 6.3: Stem durations by voicing and vowel type —— 129
Fig. 6.4: Participant performance in the same-different task —— 132
Fig. 6.5: Visualization of possible participant bias in the same-different task —— 133
Fig. 6.6: Visualization of *a'* for all participants —— 135
Fig. 6.7: Visualization of *a'* in the beta regression model —— 137
Fig. 6.8: Comparison of mousetracking curve and fitted values of quantiles —— 143
Fig. 6.9: Density of mouse movements in relation to the mousetracking curve —— 144
Fig. 6.10: Comparison of QGAM xy plots and a mousetracking plot —— 145
Fig. 6.11: Comparison of mouse tracks for plural and monomorphemic items —— 148
Fig. 6.12: Interaction for complex items between condition and response —— 151
Fig. 6.13: Interaction for monomorphemic items between condition and response —— 153

List of Tables

Table 2.1: Verbal paradigms —— 12
Table 2.2: Nominal paradigms —— 13
Table 2.3: Stem and final sound durations found by Seyfarth et al. (2017) —— 26
Table 4.1: Overview of response and variable of interest —— 58
Table 4.2: Dataset and subsets used in the analysis of the QuakeBox data —— 65
Table 4.3: Variable information for dataset 1 extracted from the QuakeBox corpus —— 66
Table 4.4: Variable information for dataset 2 extracted from the QuakeBox corpus —— 67
Table 4.5: QuakeBox dataset 1: Fixed-effects coefficients and p-values —— 70
Table 4.6: Variables and their importance values in the random forest analysis —— 73
Table 4.7: Correlation matrix for lexical frequency measures —— 75
Table 4.8: Effects of STEMFREQ and WORDFORMFREQ —— 75
Table 4.9: Effect of RELATIVEFREQ on plural stem duration —— 76
Table 4.10: Overview of the subsets of data used for the [s] and [z] investigation —— 79
Table 4.11: Variable information for dataset cpu_pl in the Buckeye corpus —— 80
Table 4.12: Variable information for dataset cpu_3sg in the Buckeye corpus —— 81
Table 4.13: Significant covariates in the final models for stem duration —— 86
Table 4.14: Fixed effects coefficients and p-values in the final model —— 87
Table 4.15: Distribution of stem vowels in the dataset cpu_3sg —— 92
Table 4.16: Overview of the subsets of data used for the [t] and [d] investigation —— 93
Table 4.17: Variable information for dataset cpu_past in the Buckeye corpus —— 93
Table 4.18: Significant variables after applying the step() functions —— 96
Table 4.19: Overview of the presence or absence of paradigm uniformity —— 100
Table 5.1: Example frequencies and frequency ratios for potential target items —— 108
Table 5.2: List of items used for the production experiment —— 109
Table 5.3: Descriptive statistics of the variables in dataset d_h1 —— 114
Table 5.4: Overview of subsets —— 115
Table 5.5: Fixed effects and random effects in the model d_h1_lmerstep1_trimmed —— 117
Table 5.6: Fixed effects and random effects in the model d_h2b_lmerstep_2b_trimmed —— 118
Table 5.7: Fixed effects and random effects in the model d_h2b_lmerstep_2c_trimmed —— 119
Table 5.8: Fixed and random effects in the final model d_h2b_lmer_3 —— 120
Table 5.9: Fixed and random effects in the model d_h2b_lmerstep_2d —— 121
Table 6.1: Stimuli combinations of same and different durations —— 125
Table 6.2: Signal Detection Theory: Stimulus classes vs. responses —— 134
Table 6.3: Parametric coefficients and significance of smooth terms —— 137
Table 6.4: Least Squares Means table —— 138
Table 6.5: Combinations of matched and mismatched spliced forms —— 140
Table 6.6: Significance of variables in the set of QGAMs comparing complex items —— 150
Table 6.7: Significance of variables in the set of QGAMs for monomorphemic —— 152
Table 7.1: Summary of the results for categorical paradigm uniformity —— 156
Table 7.2: Summary of the results for gradient paradigm uniformity —— 159
Table 9.1: Terms used to refer to the different types of "stems" —— 169
Table 9.2: List of target and filler items used in same-different task —— 169
Table 9.3: List of target and filler items used in comprehension task —— 170

1 Introduction

Language is a fascinating, yet infinitely complex subject of research. The production and perception of human speech can be affected by a variety of factors, such as stress and sentence accent (Turk & Sawusch 1997), position in phrase (Oller 1973), overall frequency (Gahl 2008), predictability in context (Bell et al. 2009), sociolinguistic aspects (Labov 1972; Byrd 1994), or morphological structure. A growing amount of research has been conducted on the influence of morphological structure on phonetic properties of speech in the past couple of years, largely with a focus on segmental duration (Plag, Homann & Kunter 2017a; Pluymaekers et al. 2010; Smith, Baker & Hawkins 2012). Several studies have found that morphological structure can affect the phonetic realization of words, for example phonetic differences between geminated consonants (Ben Hedia 2019; Ben Hedia & Plag 2017), decomposability effects on the production of English derivatives (Stein & Plag 2019b; Stein & Plag 2019a), or phonetic differences in word-final S in pseudowords (Schmitz 2022; Schmitz, Plag & Baer-Henney 2020).

However, there still does not seem to be a consensus on possible causes of these influences. Some studies have suggested phonological rules, however, some researchers, such as Seyfarth et al. (2017) have proposed a phonetic paradigm uniformity effect as a cause of possible phonetic differences between some monomorphemic and morphologically complex words. Seyfarth et al. (2017) have investigated stems of homophone word pairs with a monomorphemic and a complex member, and claim that the complex members of these pairs have longer stems due to influence from freestanding related forms (e.g. free influences frees, thus having longer duration that freeze).

What exactly happens phonetically in the production of such stems? Do inflectional stems indeed differ phonetically from monomorphemic words? Can these differences be perceived? Inspired by the study by Seyfarth et al. (2017), I aim to answer these questions by investigating data from two corpora and a production experiment, as well as extending my research with two perception experiments. These studies investigate what happens phonetically in the stems of words that end in homophonous suffixes, in what way the segments to the left of the morpheme boundary are sensitive to that boundary, and whether listeners can perceive these subtle phonetic differences.

With the intent to replicate the paradigm uniformity effect found by Seyfarth et al. (2017), I performed a corpus study using the QuakeBox corpus, which was recorded in Canterbury, New Zealand. I was not able to replicate Seyfarth's findings, but did find some interesting results regarding the influence of stem

ә Open Access. © 2023 the author(s), published by De Gruyter. This work is licensed under the Creative Commons Attribution-NonCommercial-NoDerivatives 4.0 International License.
https://doi.org/10.1515/9783111017754-001

frequency and word form frequency on plural words. To diversify my research, I additionally attempted to replicate my own findings from the QuakeBox corpus using the Buckeye corpus of conversational speech and found mixed results. To not rely solely on corpus data, which usually comes with a number of problems, I also performed a production experiment. Overall, I found mixed results and was not able to conclusively replicate the findings by Seyfarth et al. (2017). This is not necessarily surprising, as quantitative linguistics are currently experiencing a replication crisis. Many effects that have been found in previous research were not replicable in follow-up studies.

While there does not seem to be conclusive evidence for a paradigm uniformity effect in production, I did find that listeners are indeed sensitive to subtle phonetic differences similar to those theorized to be present in paradigm uniformity. I performed two perception experiments to test sensitivity to durational differences, and to test whether listeners behave differently when exposed to words with mismatched stems.

All of these studies; the two corpus studies, the production experiment, and the two perception experiments, will be discussed in detail in their pertinent chapters. But before diving into these studies, I will elaborate on the theoretical background of paradigm uniformity, the necessity for replication studies, and the relation between paradigm uniformity effects and the mental lexicon.

2 Replicating paradigm uniformity

The topic of this dissertation is paradigm uniformity, an effect that has been well-established in previous research. I chose a study by Seyfarth et al. (2017) about paradigm uniformity and attempted to replicate its results in a dual-method approach. But why a replication? Why bother looking at an effect that seems to be firmly established within a discipline? Linguistics is currently experiencing a replication crisis, meaning that many well-established effects are not reproducible in follow-up studies. To further complicate matters, the current publication system is biased towards novelty and confirmatory results, whereas replication studies, null results and exploratory studies rarely reach publication. In sum, there is a lack of replication studies in linguistics, and many 'well-established' effects are seldomly questioned.

In my dissertation, I will attempt to contribute to an established body of research and collect new evidence for (or against) the existence of a paradigm uniformity effect in production. Furthermore, I will explore the perception and comprehension of fine phonetic detail in relation to paradigm uniformity effects, which have thus far been limited to production in most research. It is important to explore whether the durational differences found for production actually serve a purpose also in perception and help listeners distinguish between, in this case, morphologically complex and simple words.

In this chapter I will first explain the study that I am replicating. Then I will briefly introduce the larger context of the replication crisis and its issues, and elaborate on my dissertation as a replication project and its role in the environment of modern science. Finally, I will explain what paradigm uniformity actually is in detail and then I will give an overview of related previous research on this phenomenon.

2.1 Replicating Seyfarth et al.

A growing body of research[1] on the acoustic properties of morphologically complex words, especially in English, provides evidence that morphological complexity may influence the phonetic properties of words (Plag, Homann & Kunter 2017a; Seyfarth et al. 2017; Tomaschek et al. 2019; Plag et al. 2020; Ben Hedia & Plag 2017; Ben Hedia 2019; Lee-Kim, Davidson & Hwang 2013; Mackenzie et al.

---

[1] Parts of this chapter have previously been published in an earlier state of research in Engemann & Plag (2021).

2018; Bell, Ben Hedia & Plag 2021; Schmitz, Plag & Baer-Henney 2020; Stein & Plag 2022; Stein 2022).

Despite these studies (among many others), it is still currently not quite clear how such effects come about. One explanation for effects on the duration of inflectional stems was suggested by Seyfarth et al. (2017): paradigm uniformity. Seyfarth et al. (2017) found that stems of words ending in [s, z] have longer durations if these words are inflected words, whereas the corresponding strings of segments in monomorphemic words ending in [s, z], henceforth 'pseudo-stems', have shorter durations. They propose that this is due to a paradigm uniformity effect: stems of morphologically complex words like *days* are influenced by their morphologically simple paradigm members, in this case *day*. These stems should differ phonetically from the pseudo-stems[2] of monomorphemic homophones such as *daze* (henceforth categorical paradigm uniformity).

In Seyfarth's conceptualization, it is suggested that paradigm uniformity effects come about due to a co-activation of the articulatory plan of related free-standing stems when producing their related forms. To illustrate this with an example, they theorize that the articulatory plan of *day* activates when producing the related word *days*. They suggest that a lengthening effect occurs due to syllable weight – because a bare stem such as *day* has an open syllable and is located at the edge of a prosodic boundary, it is lengthened. This longer duration influences the articulation of its related complex form *days*. A monomorphemic word such as *daze*, on the other hand, does not have an open syllable and the vowel is not at the edge of the prosodic boundary, therefore the pseudo-stem of such a word is not lengthened.

---

[2] A note on terminology: I will use the following terms to refer to the phonetic material that I am interested in in this dissertation. I will refer to the phonetic material such as [deɪ] in the example word day as the 'bare stem'. In contrast to this, I will use the term 'complex stem' to refer to the same phonetic material [deɪ] as part of [deɪz] in the complex word days. Finally, I will use the term 'pseudo-stem' to refer to the corresponding string of sounds in monomorphemic words, so for example to refer to the sounds [deɪ] as the 'stem' of [deɪz] in the word daze. It is important to note that all three terms are used to refer to the same phonological material, albeit in three different types of words. See also the appendix for an illustration.

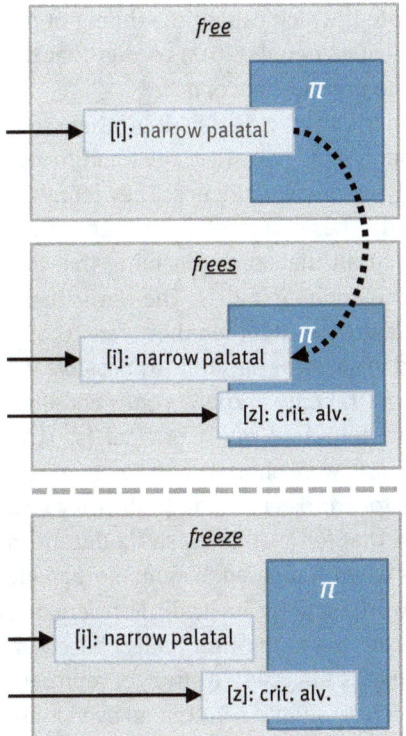

Fig. 2.1: Visualization of partial gestural scores for *free*, *frees* and *freeze* (adapted from Seyfarth et al. (2017)). The two top visualizations show the activation of the prosodic gestures (π) and tongue position from left to right for the rime of *free* and *frees*. The articulation of [i] overlaps with the prosodic gesture, which is activated early due to its relation to the plan of *free*. The visualization on the bottom shows the partial prosodic gestures for the unrelated homophone *freeze*, in which [i] does not overlap with the prosodic gesture.

Aside from syllable weight, Seyfarth et al. (2017) also argue that differences in duration come about due to the differences in prosodic alignment of the gestural scores. This is visualized in Figure 2.1. Different sounds are associated with different constriction gestures of the tongue and articulatory system, which overlap with prosodic gestures. For example, *day* is a prosodic word that ends in a prosodic word gesture and with a tongue-body constriction, this means that the constriction rate is slowed and causes word-final lengthening and elongation of the vowel. However, in *daze*, the prosodic word gesture overlaps with the constriction of the [z], and thus [z] is the most elongated element of this word (as opposed to the vowel being the most elongated in *day*). When producing *days*, the gestural score for *day* is co-activated, which causes the timing of the gesture in days to be elongated. In sum, Seyfarth et al. (2017) predict that the stem of *days* is expected to be longer than the pseudo-stem of *daze*.

Seyfarth et al. (2017) tested their hypothesis in an experiment in which they used 40 monosyllabic simplex-complex homophone pairs (e.g. *frees* and *freeze*) embedded into conversational, phonetically-matched dialogues. They recruited 40 participants who each brought a friend. These pairs of participants were assigned one of four lists containing half of all dialogues (meaning that one participant pair only read out one of the homophone pairs). The participants were given the opportunity to practice the dialogues and then they were recorded 'acting' these out, while being instructed to speak as naturally as possible.

The study conducted by Seyfarth et al. (2017) only partially confirmed their proposed paradigm uniformity effect. They found an effect of final [s, z] in which pseudo-stems of monomorphemic words were shorter than stems of suffixed words, but they did not find an effect for words ending in [t, d]. They also investigated the suffix durations and found that for [s] and [z], suffix durations were significantly longer in inflected words when compared to monomorphemic words. They did not find differences for words ending in [t, d]. Furthermore, they tested another prediction emerging from paradigm uniformity, based on work by Winter & Roettger (2011) and Roettger et al. (2014): a stronger representation of the stem (as indicated by the frequency) should result in an even longer duration of the suffixed stem (henceforth 'gradient paradigm uniformity'). They did not find such a relation between absolute and relative frequency of the bare stem and the duration of the suffixed stem.

However, it is questionable whether Seyfarth et al. (2017)'s hypothesis concerning gradient paradigm uniformity is conceptually on the right track. Based on previous research on frequency effects, it would make more sense that a stronger representation of the bare stem may exert a greater influence on morphologically related forms in the opposite direction of what Seyfarth et al. (2017) predicted: higher lexical frequency usually results in phonetic reduction, rather than enhancement, and thus in shorter articulation. Based on this idea, an alternative hypothesis concerning gradient paradigm uniformity suggests itself: the more frequent a bare stem, the shorter its duration, and as a consequence of the co-activation of the articulatory plan, the shorter the duration of the corresponding inflected stem.

Furthermore, there are some issues with the methodology of the study by Seyfarth et al. (2017) that could be improved upon. Most notably, each participant pair only produced one of the homophones in the pairs that were later compared to each other. For a better comparison, it would be advisable to elicit both homophone pairs from the same speakers. Another problem relates to their analysis of the frequencies of stems, in which they hypothesize that higher frequency stems should result in even longer durations of the suffixed stem. They admit that the stimuli for this hypothesis were not selected to include a broad range of frequency measures, therefore the (null) results of this analysis are questionable.

In sum, there are a number of reasons why a replication of this project is warranted, among them a lack of clear evidence for some of their hypotheses, as well as methodological problems. In this dissertation, I attempted to find more evidence for paradigm uniformity effects, and expanded on the methodological shortcomings of Seyfarth et al. (2017) in two corpus studies and in my own experimental design.

2.2 The replication crisis in modern linguistics, and other problems of the current research climate

Why should one replicate already established research? Quantitative scientific research is subject to the researcher's constant diligence and immense scrutiny, as well as to their peer's vigilant monitoring – this is why the peer review of scientific articles is a well-established process that aims to ensure the quality and validity of scientific research. However, despite all vigilance, for the past 15 years, more and more researchers have pointed out that a lot of scientific research is not reproducible. One notable publication that stirred the discussion was "Why most published research findings are false" by Ioannidis (2005) in a medical journal. This discussion has been coined the 'replication crisis' and has since spread to other disciplines – including linguistics, which has experienced an increasing trend towards empirical and quantitative methods in the past decades (e.g. Sampson 2005; Sampson 2013; Gries 2015; Open Science Collaboration 2015; Roettger, Winter & Baayen 2019; Roettger & Baer-Henney 2019; Sönning & Werner 2021a).

The academic journal *Linguistics* has recently dedicated an entire special issue to the topic of the replication crisis in this field (Issue 59:5, titled "The replication crisis: Implications for linguistics", published September 2021). The editors of this special issue, Sönning & Werner (2021b), aim to raise awareness among linguists towards the replication crisis, and argue that due to linguistics being a relative newcomer to quantitative research, the methodological expertise is still developing, and thus subject to misapplication and misinterpretation.

Some researchers question whether quantitative methods are even useful for the analysis of language, which is by nature characterized by uniqueness, variation and complexity – factors that raise the difficulty level of replication even more when compared to other sciences (Grieve 2021). Other researchers argue that the quantitative turn, in particular also an increased use of language corpora, is for the better. Gries (2013: 361–362) gives a number of reasons for this, most importantly that the quantitative development "situates the field of linguistics more firmly in the domains of social sciences and cognitive science", which have a long tradition of using quantitative methods. Furthermore, he adds that "the quantitative study of phenomena affords us with a higher degree of comparability, objectivity, and replicability".

It seems that researchers currently appear to be at odds with each other (and perhaps with themselves) about the quantitative turn in linguistics. This would mark the "scientific revolution" that Sönning & Werner (2021b) suggest we are approaching at the present time. Citing Kuhn (1962)'s structure of scientific revolutions, they suggest that we are currently in a state of crisis. Kuhn (1962) describes three recurring stages of scientific research: normal science, crisis and revolution. These are repeated in an infinite cycle, as illustrated in Figure 2.2.

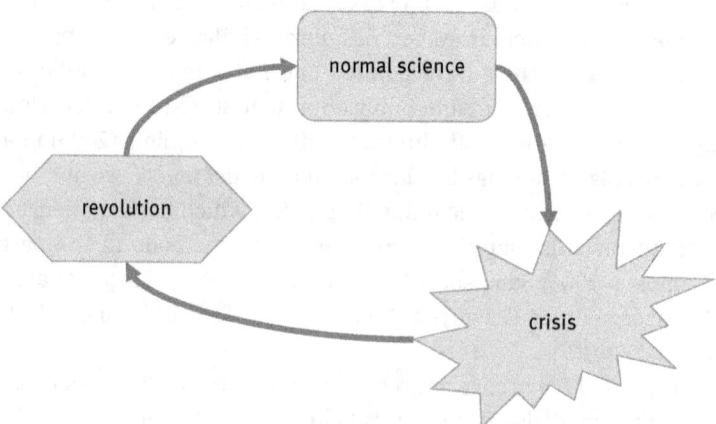

Fig. 2.2: The cyclical evolution of scientific theory according to Kuhn (1962) visualized. Normal science is practiced smoothly for a time, until a crisis emerges, which then leads to a revolution in which all the rough edges of the crises are slowly smoothed out again. After a revolution, a new normal science is practiced until the next crisis.

A period of normal science is characterized by the adoption of commonly used standards within methodological procedures, such as for example experimental setups, particular statistical tools for analyses, etc. However, during a phase of normal science, anomalies may be observed which challenge the commonly used procedures and methods. This leads to a state of crisis and revolution, which will only be resolved once a new set of standards will be adopted by the research community.

A number of issues with quantitative research in linguistics have been discussed in the last couple of years, which led some researchers to the conclusion that we are currently in a state of crisis. A notable issue is that language is an inherently complex research object. That is one reason why any analysis of language is characterized by what some researchers call a "garden of forking paths" (Gelman & Loken 2013) and others call "researcher degrees of freedom" (Simmons, Nelson & Simonsohn 2011). Both of these terms describe the same idea: the decisions that a researcher takes when collecting and analyzing data. A researcher will always have to make decisions throughout their process that could ultimately affect the outcome of the statistical analysis. The parameters chosen to be analyzed, the variables and covariates included (or not included), and the 'cleaning' of data will all determine the outcome. This practice can actually harm science, as researchers may shape and re-shape their data, or use different analytical options for so long until they achieve significant p-values in their analysis, which is the only one reported. Meanwhile, they are not reporting all the options they exhausted which did not result in significant p-values. This is known as p-hacking.

But how did the current research climate end up at a point where p-hacking is a common practice, and which has now thrown us into crisis? Three very significant problems of the current research climate that contribute to the crisis are 1) it favors breakthroughs over replication, 2) it favors certainty over uncertainty, and 3) it favors results over null results. These are causes of another common, harmful research practice: HARKing, which stands for "Hypothesising After Results are Known" (Kerr 1998). In order to understand HARKing, it is necessary to first understand the difference between *exploratory* and *confirmatory* data analysis (see also Roettger, Winter & Baayen 2019). Exploratory and confirmatory are two distinct, but sometimes intertwined, stages of data analysis. The exploratory stage describes a stage at which a researcher observes patterns which can lead to the formulation of new hypotheses, also called the hypothesis-generating process. This is also the stage at which many breakthroughs in science were discovered, and which describes the initial stages of the scientific method. This is followed by the confirmatory stage, also called the hypothesis-testing process, in which the newly formulated hypotheses are tested using new data, for example in controlled experiments.

In present-day academic publishing, confirmatory analyses are regarded as more prestigious than exploratory analysis, which is why these tend to be more 'publishable' and easier to fund. These circumstances have led to the practice of HARKing, in which researchers present exploratory studies as if they were confirmatory studies, even though they did not have clearly formulated hypotheses before analyzing the data. Rather, exploratory indications are framed as if they were the results of a confirmatory study.

To avoid HARKing, *p*-hacking and other harmful practices, exploratory studies should be regarded equally as prestigious as confirmatory studies. This entails that the current research climate will have to, to some degree, embrace uncertainty rather than hunting for "significant" or "robust" effects. Most linguistics papers encourage a binary categorization of their results as either "significant" or "not significant". But how can we say with certainty that a somewhat arbitrarily chosen cut-off point for a *p*-value means that an effect is robust, especially for a research subject as complex and diverse as language?

Significance testing comes with its own problems, which ultimately could mean that even a significant *p*-value does not justify that a decisive claim can be made. A common problem is that many studies have low statistical power, i.e. studies that have a very low number of observations, items, participants, informants, etc. Some 'well-established' effects in linguistics are the result of studies with low numbers of informants and equally low numbers of items, neither of which provide enough statistical power to arrive at any conclusion that speaks for absolute certainty (see also Vasishth & Gelman 2021). Low statistical power is often (but not always) the reason why many significant effects are not replicable. As Vasishth & Gelman (2021) put it, "Power should be seen as the ball in a ball game; it is only a very small part of the sport, because there are many other important components. But the players would look pretty foolish if they arrive to play on the playing field without the ball." – this is one of the reasons why Vasishth & Gelman encourage researchers to embrace uncertainty and accept that variation is part of the nature of language. Simultaneously, they also warn against a possible 'uncertainty overshoot', in which researchers might become overly conservative and careful in drawing conclusions from their data.

In summary, the replication crisis is, as Sönning & Werner (2021b) call it, a "multi-headed hydra". Researchers should generally be more cautious in the interpretation of their empirical contributions and regard them as merely a small part of a larger whole, that cannot be regarded with definite certainty as proof for or against certain features or idiosyncrasies of language.

Sönning & Werner (2021b: 1198) and Kortmann (2021: 1218–1220) provide practical suggestions on which scientific practices to adopt and how to best conduct quantitative research in linguistics in the context of the current crisis. Furthermore, Gelman (2018) suggests general guidelines in how to deal with ethical concerns in quantitative research. In this thesis, I will attempt to apply some of their suggestions to my research. This is, however, only partially possible, as I began working on this project several years before the discussion around the replication crisis intensified, and to complicate matters further, this project experienced disruptions in its methodology and conceptualizations due to the Corona virus pandemic in 2020/2021. Therefore, I will have to fall subject to some of Kortmann's *Don'ts*; for example, parts of my research clearly started out as exploratory without pre-defined hypotheses, and some of my research went through a variety of statistical analyses before finding a suitable method. I will discuss these problems in relation to my research in detail in chapter 7.

However, my research developed out of a replication project, replicating Seyfarth et al. (2017), thereby it may be regarded as addressing the current replication crisis, and it will also meet many of the recommendations and *Do's* by the aforementioned authors. In sum, my research on paradigm uniformity is primarily motivated by gaps in methodology and findings of previously published work and grew beyond that.

2.3 What is paradigm uniformity?

The previous sections have thoroughly introduced the study by Seyfarth et al. (2017) that is subject to replication, as well as the greater context of the replication crisis. But what does paradigm uniformity actually mean? To clarify this question, I will explain the notions of paradigms and paradigm uniformity effects in detail, and establish two different types of paradigm uniformity.

In order to understand paradigm uniformity, it is first necessary to understand what a paradigm is. In inflectional morphology, a paradigm consists of all the word forms that are part of a lexeme (Bauer, Lieber & Plag 2015: 8). The term lexeme is used to refer to different word forms that have the same meaning. For example, the lexeme free can have the different word forms *free, frees, freed* or *freeing*. These word forms are what constitutes the morphological paradigm of the lexeme free.

The term 'paradigm' is generally used to refer to inflectional paradigms which contain forms of the same lexeme, however, it can also be used to refer to the morphological relatedness of derived words and compounds, such as for example *impress, impression, impressive*, etc (Bauer, Lieber & Plag 2015: 518–519) or *worm, wormy, ringworm, woodworm* (Hay & Baayen 2005: 343). As my dissertation deals exclusively with the properties of inflected words, I will use it only in the sense of inflectional paradigms that refer to different forms of the same lexeme.

There are several different subtypes of inflectional paradigms, based on the type of lexeme of which they consist: adjectival, adverbial, nominal, and verbal paradigms. Adjectival paradigms contain word forms of adjectives, such as for example the forms *fast, faster* or *fastest* for the lexeme fast. This also applies to adverbs, such as for example *few, fewer, fewest* for the lexeme few. Adjectives and adverbs are not relevant for my dissertation though, as I only investigated verbs and nouns. In the upcoming sections, I will provide a closer look at verbal and nominal paradigms, as these are relevant to my research.

Verbal paradigms

Verbal paradigms, as mentioned above, consist of the different word forms of a verb. An example of this can be found in Table 2.1, which was taken from Bauer, Lieber & Plag (2015: 65). Regular verbs can be realized in five different forms in English, which can fulfill six different morphosyntactic functions. An example for the lexeme TALK is given in the table. Some irregular verbs behave differently, such as for example GIVE, which has an irregular past tense form *gave*. There are also some verbs that behave in an even more irregular way, such as for example PUT, which only has three different forms: *put, puts, putting* (see also Bauer, Lieber & Plag (2015: 62)).

Table 2.1: Verbal paradigms in detail; terms usually used to refer to the form, examples, and the morphosyntactic categories that are realized by the forms. From (Bauer, Lieber & Plag 2015: 65).

Name of form		Regular verb	Irregular verb	(Morpho-)syntactic category realized by the form
base form	plain form	talk	give	infinitive, subjunctive, imperative
	plain non-past form	talk	give	non-3rd singular non-past tense
3rd singular non-past		talks	gives	3rd singular non-past tense
preterite		talked	gave	past tense
present participle		talking	giving	present participle
past participle		talked	given	past participle

My dissertation concerns only the base form and the 3rd singular non-past in verbal paradigms, as I am investigating words that end in [s] or [z]. In a limited scope, I also investigated words ending in [t] and [d], and thus preterite forms. Reasons for the restrictions to these forms will also be discussed in detail in this and the subsequent chapters.

Nominal paradigms

Nominal paradigms consist of the different word forms of a noun. An example can be seen in Table 2.2, which I created analogous to the verbal paradigm table from Bauer, Lieber & Plag (2015: 65) in the previous section. Nominal paradigms are smaller in English, as there are only between two to four different forms for four different functions, depending on whether the noun is a regularly inflected noun, subject to phonologically conditioned allomorphy, or irregular.

Table 2.2: Nominal paradigms in detail; terms usually used to refer to the form, examples, and the morphosyntactic categories that are realized by the forms.

Name of form	Regular noun	Regular noun with allomorphy	Irregular noun	(Morpho-)syntactic category realized by the form
base form	day	bus	mouse	singular definite and indefinite
plural	days	buses	mice	plural definite and indefinite
genitive	day's	buses	mouse's	possession (singular)
genitive plural	days'	buses'	mice's	possession (plural)

Regarding nominal paradigms, my dissertation concerns the base form and plural forms of nominal paradigms, as due to genitive alternation and the infrequency of genitive in English, it is difficult to find useful material in corpora for genetive forms. While they can be investigated in a more reliable manner in experiments, such as for example in Plag et al. (2019), for the purposes of my dissertation it is more economic to limit the scope to certain types of words, which allows for a better comparison and analysis of both the corpus data and the experiments I performed. My studies were all concerned with paradigm uniformity effects across the stems of select members of nominal and verbal paradigms.

So what does paradigm uniformity actually mean? I will establish the necessary terminology in the following sections.

Establishing paradigm uniformity terminology

The term *paradigm uniformity* originates from within the domain of phonology, and first appeared in Paul Kiparsky's work (Kiparsky 1978), along with the equivalent terms *paradigm coherence* and *regularity*. Previously, paradigm uniformity effects were also discussed under the term *analogy* or *paradigm levelling* in historical linguistics (Antilla 1977). Since then, the phenomenon of paradigm uniformity has also been referred to as 'stem selection' (Raffelsiefen 2004: 95), 'multiple correspondence' (e.g. Burzio 1998), the 'split-base' effect (Steriade 2000), or 'paradigm levelling' (Kenstowicz 1995; Albright 2004).

A paradigm uniformity effect arises if two or more forms that are members of the same morphological paradigm influence each other. For example, a morphologically complex form such as *days* may be influenced in its phonetic characteristics by its related simplex form *day*. However, it is also possible that the opposite may be the case, for example the complex form *days* may influence the simplex form *day*, especially if the complex form is used more frequently than the simplex form. The idea of paradigm uniformity in which stems influence complex forms was proposed by Seyfarth et al. (2017)'s hypothesis that a stronger representation of stem (as indicated by the frequency) should result in an even longer duration of the suffixed stem – which they did not find in their investigation, possibly as their data was not optimized for such an investigation.

While paradigm uniformity effects have presently been well-established in phonological theory (as will be discussed also in the subchapter following this), I am interested in investigating whether such effects can also be investigated on a phonetic level, namely in how paradigm uniformity effects arise phonetically, and how paradigm members influence each other phonetically – do they become more similar or less similar? If they become more similar, then this would provide evidence for a phonetic paradigm uniformity effect.

I performed a series of studies to investigate paradigm uniformity effects, based on a number of assumptions made from Seyfarth et al. (2017)'s study, as well as the larger body of literature concerning paradigm uniformity. As I both replicated previous work, as well as expanded on it on a methodological level, it was necessary to establish new terminology for the different types of paradigm uniformity that I investigated.

In the following, I will give my own definitions for the two types of paradigm uniformity effects which I will investigate in this dissertation. Traditionally, paradigm uniformity is a somewhat binary phenomenon, typical for its field of origin, phonology. Therefore, I will henceforth refer to this traditional version of paradigm uniformity as *categorical paradigm uniformity*.

In addition, I investigated the role of frequency in relation to paradigm uniformity, based on research by Seyfarth et al. (2017). I will henceforth refer to this type of paradigm uniformity as *gradient paradigm uniformity*. I will explain both types of these effects in the following.

2.3.1 Categorical paradigm uniformity

The general paradigm uniformity effect that has been investigated by many previous researchers[3] is what I will refer to as *categorical paradigm uniformity*. This type of paradigm uniformity is typically investigated by comparing complex with structurally similar simplex words, and is illustrated in Figure 2.3.

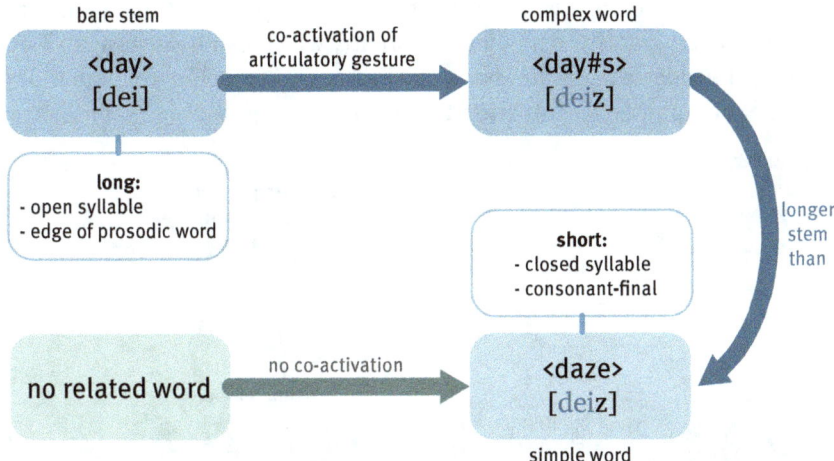

Fig. 2.3: Illustration of categorical paradigm uniformity. Complex words (e.g. *days*) are influenced by their paradigm members (e.g. *day*) due to a co-activation of the articulatory gesture of *day* for the articulatory plan of *days*. Due to the open syllable and position on the edge of the prosodic word of *day*, the stem of *days* has a longer stem than a comparable monomorphemic word such as *daze*, which is pronounced shorter since it is consonant-final and has a closed syllable.

---

3 Previous research on paradigm uniformity will be discussed in detail in 2.4.

In a categorical paradigm uniformity effect, morphologically complex forms are influenced in their articulation by their morphologically simple paradigm members. For example, in the nominal paradigm {day, days}, the plural form *days* is influenced by the bare form *day*. This effect can be seen when comparing the plural example *days* to a monomorphemic word with the same or similar phonetic structure, such as *daze*. This effect has been observed in many previous studies, including my subject of replication Seyfarth et al. (2017).

2.3.2 Gradient paradigm uniformity

Due to the numerous problems that arise around frequency effects (see also 3.1), it is advisable to take frequency into account when investigating paradigm uniformity effects. Therefore, I will investigate a second type of potential paradigm uniformity effect; gradient paradigm uniformity, which can be investigated by comparing frequencies and durations of simplex and complex words that are part of the same paradigm. This effect is illustrated in Figure 2.4.

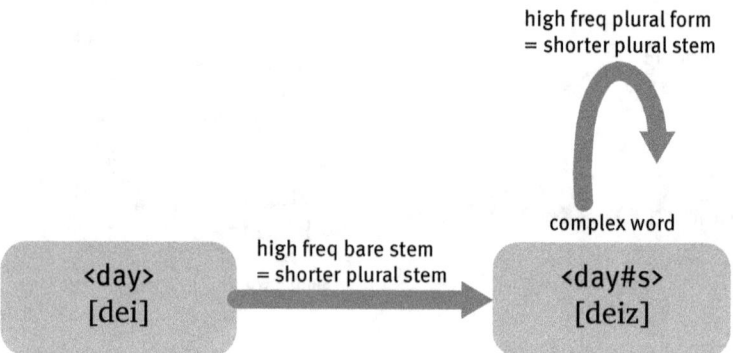

Fig. 2.4: Illustration of gradient paradigm uniformity. Complex words such as *days* are influenced by their paradigm members (e,g. *day*) due to the frequency of the bare form. A higher frequent bare stem *day* will also cause a shorter plural stem of *days* due to the phonetic reduction effect on high frequency forms.

In gradient paradigm uniformity, a high frequency bare stem such as *day* will cause a phonetic reduction effect on its morphologically complex paradigm member *days*. Furthermore, a high frequency complex word such as *days* should have a shorter duration than low frequency complex words of similar structure.

2.4 Previous research on effects of paradigm uniformity

In order to better understand paradigm uniformity effects, I will provide an extensive literature review on paradigm uniformity and similar effects, ranging from the phonological roots of paradigm uniformity to a number of phonetic phenomena that are closely related to paradigm uniformity. These are presented in the following subsections.

2.4.1 Phonological approaches of paradigm uniformity: Optimality Theory

Paradigm uniformity has its roots in phonology and has been established among phonologists as a set of constraints within Optimality Theory (OT). Optimality Theory is a grammatical framework developed by Smolensky & Prince (1993) and McCarthy & Prince (1993a,b) which acts as a universal grammar for phonology and focuses on phonological phenomena and the interface between phonology and morphology. As paradigm uniformity is so well established in relation to Optimality Theory, it is impossible to establish a discussion about paradigm uniformity without introducing its origins in OT. I will introduce some of the most pertinent studies that are mainly phonological in nature and that focus on paradigm uniformity in Optimality Theory here.

Paradigm uniformity and the phonetics-phonology boundary by Steriade (2000: 314) has been established as one of the most influential papers on paradigm uniformity. It aims to show that paradigm uniformity "is enforced through conditions that govern both phonological features and properties presently classified as phonetic detail" and argues that phonological and phonetic features are treated identically and cannot be studied separately. Part of the study examines paradigms that share contextually invariant morphemes. It includes a production experiment with 12 speakers of American English investigating *-istic* derivatives. Steriade (2000) found that bases with a flap were always flapped in the derivative, whereas bases with a stressed [t] were usually realized as [t], rather than with a flap. Additionally, she also investigated elision of schwa between consonants in French. She argues that the realization of phonetic detail such as the presence or absence of t-flapping in English or schwa in French are subject to the same principles as phonological or contrastive features, as the evaluation of paradigm uniformity constraints requires grammar to establish these distinctions.

While the basis of Optimality Theory is well-suited for categorical analysis, critics of generative grammars such as OT have continuously pointed out that generative linguistics is much fuzzier, and often language cannot be assigned to strict categories. This was addressed by Hayes (2000) in his paper *Gradient and well-formedness in optimality theory*. Rather than ranking constraints against each other, as in OT, he used so-called Strictness Bands to rank constraints. These were enhanced to also include fringes in cases of overlap, marked by question marks.

Hayes (2000) used a ranking of such Strictness Bands to demonstrate that paradigm uniformity as a constraint requires derived forms to possess the vowel quality of their bases. He investigated clear and dark /l/ based on previous research by Sproat & Fujimura (1993), who found that clear and dark /l/ are not categorical, but a gradient phonetic continuum. Hayes (2000) argues that there is a categorical distinction which is partially obscured by free variation and near-neutralizing lenition, and to investigate this, did a survey with 10 native speakers of American English, half of which were linguists. The participants rated acceptable pronunciations of words with clear or dark /l/.

The results of this survey were used to establish constraints to evaluate the status of clear and dark /l/ in certain environments, such as in onset position, in coda position, at a morpheme boundary, or at a word boundary. These constraints state that morphologically derived forms may not deviate from their bases in property X, which is conversed across paradigms. The paradigm uniformity constraints require morphologically derived forms to possess the vowel quality of their bases, which indirectly regulates the distribution of clear and dark /l/.

The analysis has found that different environments produce different levels of darkness in /l/, some of which cannot be categorized. Thus, darkness of /l/ should be regarded as gradient, in line with the gradient analysis using strictness bands. In onset position it can with some certainly be said that /l/ is always light, while in coda position, it is with some certainty always dark. However, any cases in between are gradient, such as on morpheme boundaries (both with /l/ in coda and onset of the respective morpheme), in proper names, or across word boundaries. Of relevance for paradigm uniformity is the finding that morphologically complex words seem to inherit the darkness of /l/ from their bases. A complex word such as *mailer* (consisting of the morphemes {mail}{er}) is perceived to have a darker /l/ than a morphologically simple word such as the proper noun *Mailer*.

Another paper investigating paradigm uniformity using both OT and experimental data is *Output-Output Faithfulness to Moraic Structure* by Frazier (2006). She found that vowels in complex words ending in /d/ are longer than in homophonous monomorphemic words due to the influence of the prosodic structure of the base. Frazier set out to answer the question of how long the vowel of a dimorphemic monosyllable like *passed* is, by using OT. She specifically examines moras, which determine syllable weight and are here assumed to be a timing unit; segments attached to two moras are longer than segments attached to one. Frazier claims that polymorphic outputs in English are sensitive to the moraic structure of their bases, indicating a paradigm uniformity effect. Two production experiments were performed to investigate such an effect; an experiment using triplets such as *pass – passed – past*, and an experiment using homophone word pairs such as *banned* and *band*. The results showed that dimorphemic words contain longer vowels than monomorphemic words, and that the vowels of dimorphemic words were not as long as the vowels of the bases. For comparison, Seyfarth et al. (2017) found a null result for words ending in /d/ and /t/ in their study.

In addition, a perception experiment was performed in which the vowel lengths of stimuli were manipulated. Participants were more likely to select a dimorphemic word as the vowel got longer. These results indicate that the difference in vowel length between mono- und dimorphemic words is used by speakers and recognized by listeners. The results were used to rank OT constraints, creating a grammar that guarantees that monomorphemic monosyllables will be attached to two moras with mora-sharing, ensuring that all rime segments are attached to mora.

To summarize, the paper finds that the prosodic structure of polymorphemic words can be influenced by the prosodic structure of the base, as in a paradigm uniformity effect. However, the results of the experiment should be treated with caution, as there was a very small number of target items in the experiments, as well as a very small number of participants.

Studies on phonological approaches to paradigm uniformity are not limited to English. In a paper on vowel reduction in Russian, Bethin (2012) proposed that blocking of a vowel reduction process is subject to a constraint on paradigmatic contrasts within inflectional paradigms. In a study on Greek dialects of East Lesvos, Gafos & Ralli (2002) found evidence that paradigms play a key role in the phonological realization of noun-clitic clusters. Kenstowicz & Sohn (2008) investigated paradigm uniformity constraints in Korean, while Rebrus & Törkenczy (2005) looked at paradigm uniformity in Hungarian verbs. These given examples are few among many studies on paradigm uniformity within OT.

To summarize, paradigm uniformity is a firmly established effect within the domain of phonology. However, paradigm uniformity has also been adopted into the domain of phonetics. A number of phonetic studies have been conducted on paradigm uniformity (or similar effects, titled differently) – among them also my subject of replication, Seyfarth et al. (2017), which I introduced in section 2.1. In the following, I will introduce other pertinent phonetic studies.

2.4.2 Paradigm uniformity (and similar effects) as a phonetic phenomenon

While the previous section introduced studies that were mainly phonological in nature, there are a number of studies on paradigm uniformity and similar effects that focus mainly on phonetics. Caselli, Caselli & Cohen-Goldberg (2016) investigated the relationship between inflected words suffixed with *-ing*, *-ed* or *-s* and their roots, as well as a novel measurement called inflected neighborhood density, in which they defined the number of inflected words that differ from a target word by one phoneme. Based on their results, they argue for both whole-word and morpheme-based representations in the mental lexicon. They found that both root and word frequency influence the production of inflected words, an important finding that I will aim to replicate with my experimental data (see Chapter 5). They conclude that inflected words are included in the lexicon for spoken production, that inflected words have whole word representations and that both simplex and complex words influence spoken word production.

Losiewicz (1992) did a production experiment in which she tested whether morphological structure plays a role in acoustic reduction. She hypothesized that a segment should be less reduced if it forms an affix by itself than if it is positioned at the end of a longer morpheme. She tested this on homophonous words ending in /t/ and /d/, such as for example *swayed* and *suede*. A set of 12 homophones were placed in lists and read out loud by 16 participants. Analysis of the items showed that on average, the past tense /t/ or /d/ was about five milliseconds longer than the monomorphemic /t/ or /d/. This suggests that a segment's duration is affected by the morphological status of the word. There are a number of problems with this study, most notably the low statistical power with only 12 items and 16 participants. Also, the stimuli were selected based on their frequency in Francis & Kucera (1971) and Carroll, Davies & Richman (1971), which are rather small corpora, rendering these frequencies unreliable. Thus, it is possible that the durational differences found by Losiewicz (1992) are likely due to a general frequency effect.

Cohen (2014) investigated particular kinds of final [s], such as for example third person singular [s], which can vary phonetically based on morphological properties such as paradigmatic probability. She differentiates between contextual probability, which is the likelihood of a unit being used in a particular context, and paradigmatic probability, which describes the likelihood of a particular form being selected from a set of related units. Higher contextual probability has been well established to cause phonetic reduction, whereas paradigmatic probability may either reduce or enhance. In her study, Cohen has found that higher paradigmatic probability causes longer suffixes, as well as shorter stem durations. This effect was mainly carried by the relative frequency of the singular vs. the plural form. Increased relative frequency yields longer suffix durations, as well as shorter stem durations, i.e. the suffix is enhanced and the stem is reduced.

Several studies have been conducted on /l/ darkening in relation to the morphological context of the /l/. Mackenzie et al. (2018) found that /l/ darkening and lightening depends on the morphological context and on vowel reduction. They investigated items like *jail owner* and *jay loaner*, and found that a preceding morpheme boundary or a stressed vowel have a lightening effect on /l/, whereas /l/ following unstressed vowels tends to be darker. Both morphological status as well as vowel stress play a role in the darkness of /l/, making final morphological darkening harder to detect when there already is darkening due to a reduced vowel, as well as making morphological lightening harder to detect when /l/ is followed by an unreduced high vowel. The results of this study provide evidence for both final darkening as well as initial lightening.

Another study on the darkness of /l/ in relation to morphological structure was performed by Lee-Kim, Davidson & Hwang (2013). They did an ultrasound investigation of 6 participants in which they compared stem-final /l/ in pre-boundary positions (e.g. *tall-est*), word-internal positions (e.g. *coolest*), and post-boundary positions (e.g. *flaw-less*). They found evidence for the presence of morphological effects on the darkness of /l/: it is darkest in pre-boundary, word-final position, lighter in word-internal positions, and lightest in word-internal, morpheme-initial positions.

Studies on effects related to paradigm uniformity have also been conducted on languages other than English. Dąbrowska (2008) investigated the effects of frequency and neighborhood density in Polish dative inflections. Using written cloze tasks in which participants had to write the correctly inflected dative form of nonce and real words, she found an effect of neighborhood density, because nouns from high density neighborhoods were inflected more reliably than nouns from sparsely populated neighborhoods. She also found that gender plays a role, as masculine and feminine nouns were inflected more reliably than neuter nouns. Lastly, she argues that education also plays a significant role in participants' ability to correctly produce dative inflection, as more educated participants produced correct endings more reliably than less educated participants. However, there are some issues with this study, most notably the measurement used for neighborhood density, which here was measured by counting the number of nouns sharing the same ending rather than more traditional definitions.

A well-researched language more similar to English in structure is Dutch. Pluymaekers et al. (2010) investigated the duration of the /xh/ cluster in the Dutch suffixes -*igheid*, as well as -*ig* + -*heid*, and found that the duration of this cluster is affected by its morphological informativeness. This suffix occurs in three types of derived words; words in which –*igheid* is a single suffix, words in which there is a boundary before –*heid*, and words in which either boundary is possible. They found that this cluster is shorter in words in which –*igheid* is not a single suffix, and longer in words in which it is a single suffix. They conclude that the duration of this cluster is affected by its morphological informativeness in relation to the word's paradigmatic neighborhood. Thus, words with lower paradigmatic neighborhoods, i.e. fewer related forms, cause shorter durations, meaning that speakers save effort on uninformative units.

An effect that can be described as paradigm uniformity is incomplete neutralization, which appears in languages such as Catalan, Dutch, German, Polish, Russian and Turkish (Kenstowicz 1994). Incomplete neutralization in German, for example, occurs as a result of final devoicing of word-final consonants. In German, word-final obstruents are devoiced, e.g. *Rad* 'wheel' is pronounced [ʁaːt] and therefore homophonous with *Rat* 'council'. However, *Rad* has phonetic cues associated with following voiced consonants due to influence of the paradigm member *Räder* ([ʁɛːdɐ]), which is the plural form of *Rad*. Roettger et al. (2014) conducted production and perception experiments on incomplete neutralization in German, and found evidence for such an effect based on the duration of the preceding vowel. They found that vowels tend to be longer before voiced stops and shorter before voiceless stops. Regarding perception, they found that listeners were able to perceive the differences between final voiceless and 'devoiced' stops (e.g. between *Rat* and *Rad*), but barely above chance level (55%). They argue that listeners and speakers access related forms rather than extract subtle phonetic differences.

Incomplete neutralization in Dutch was investigated in a study by Ernestus & Baayen (2006) in which they found a significant difference in vowel duration for vowels preceding underlying voiced obstruents. These were on average 3.5ms longer. They propose that incomplete neutralization is mainly an artifact of orthography, but also affected by lexical analogy. Similar to the German *Rad* and *Räder*, Dutch speakers also co-activate related forms. When they have to realize *verwijd* 'widen' [vɛrvɛit], inflectionally related words such as *verwijden* 'to widen'/ plural [vɛrvɛidən] are activated, resulting in the final obstruent of *verwijd* to be slightly voiced (rather than completely devoiced).

2.5 Perceiving phonetic properties

Paradigm uniformity is an effect that has primarily been observed in production. However, it also suggests itself to consider the domain of perception. There have been no perception studies on paradigm uniformity itself, but there have been studies on similar and related phenomena. A large body of research has been performed to find out whether listeners are able to perceive differences between morphologically simple and morphologically complex words, a few select of which I will introduce in the following.

In a comprehension study on plural dominant nouns in Dutch, Baayen et al. (2007) found that high information paradigms are harder to access. They performed a picture naming paradigm, in which they found that plural dominance leads to slowed picture naming latencies for both singular and plural forms. In additional experiments, they ruled out a reversed dominance effect and replicated their first experiment with a new design. Their stimuli were balanced for frequency, and they found that the greater the relative frequency, the more accessible an inflected form is in its paradigm.

Shatzman & McQueen (2006) performed an eye-tracking study to investigate the processing of word boundaries in Dutch. They investigated phrases that have identical segments across different types of boundaries, such as for example *een spot* 'a spot' vs. *eens pot* 'one pot'. They found that this prosodic difference is articulated most on the /s/, which either belonged to the first word's coda, in which case it was shorter, or the second word's onset, in which case it was longer. Shatzman & McQueen (2006) then used this finding to manipulate recordings by splicing the target word (e.g. *pot*) and the preceding /s/ from another token into the carrier sentence (the 'identity-spliced version'). To contrast that, they also spliced a version in which in the target and preceding /s/ came from the cluster-initial recording (e.g. spot), which they called the 'cross-spliced version'. They performed two experiments. In the first experiment, they found that targets in the identity-spliced condition were fixated significantly more often than targets in the cross-spliced condition. They assume that this is due to a number of acoustic differences of the /s/ in both conditions, such as /s/ duration, closure duration and word duration. To further investigate this, they conducted another experiment in which they created stimuli in which the /s/ was artificially lengthened or shortened. Participants took longer to fixate on the target in the longer /s/ condition of the ambiguous sequence. Contrary to the first experiment, this effect appeared almost immediately after the point of disambiguation, thus the authors assume that the duration of /s/ plays a critical role in the disambiguation of the ambiguous sequence. These findings clearly show an effect of the duration of the segment /s/. In my perception experiment, I investigated words ending in /s/, but focused on the stem duration. My perception experiment expands on Shatzman & McQueen (2006)'s findings by considering the segments preceding the word-final /s/, albeit it is methologically different.

Previous research has found that listeners are able to distinguish phonemically identical onsets of embedded words, which constitute segmental strings such as the word *cap* and the *cap* part of *captain* (Davis, Marslen-Wilson & Gaskell 2002). In multisyllabic words, the vowel of such embedded words is shorter in duration, which listeners are able to perceive in cross-splicing tasks. Such cross-splicing tasks, where the first syllable of a word such as *hamster* was replaced with a recording of the monosyllabic *ham* and similar pairs, were performed in English and Dutch for monomorphemic words (Salverda, Dahan & McQueen 2003).

Research on embedded words was expanded to multimorphemic words by Blazej & Cohen-Goldberg (2015) who investigated embedded words in morphologically complex contexts, such as *clue* and *clueless*. They found that listeners are able to recognize disambiguating cues due to the realization of prosodic boundaries that follow monosyllabic words. Blazej & Cohen-Goldberg (2015) performed 4 experiments. In Experiment 1, they tested whether participants can distinguish between suffixed and unsuffixed words, i.e. sequences such as *clue* (freestanding word) or *clue-* from *clueless*. They found that participants were able to distinguish these. Experiment 2 was a forced choice task in which they also controlled for coarticulation. Using the same word pairs from Experiment 1, they created carrier sentences in which the freestanding word was followed by a word similar to the suffix of the suffixed word, i.e. "*there was a clue left to find*" vs. "*clueless*". Again, participants reliably identified the different words correctly. Experiment 3 was a mouse-tracking experiment with real words, in order to clear up any possible misgivings about the artificiality of experiments 1 and 2. Mouse-tracking is an implicit measure, which adds another layer of possible analysis. Participants listened to unsuffixed and suffixed words and were asked to click on the word that they heard. The trajectory was subsequently analyzed. They showed that the response trajectories for the shortened stimuli veered closer to the suffixed response button than for the unshortened stimuli, indicating that listeners make early use of the durational information. They also found that participants took longer to click on the target in the shortened condition.

Finally, experiment 4 was a mouse-tracking experiments with non-words. They extracted 100 non-words from the ARC Nonword Database and assigned suffixes to these randomly (-*ly*, -*less* and -*ness*). These were then recorded and the experiment was performed identically to experiment 3. In this experiment, Blazej & Cohen-Goldberg (2015) did not find a statistically significant result. While the trajectories showed the same pattern as in experiment 3, it appears that nonwords behave differently from real words. In summary, Blazej & Cohen-Goldberg (2015) found significant evidence for the influence of subsegmental information within the mental lexicon. Listeners were able to identify morphological structure in advance for real words, and durational information appears to be sufficient to distinguish suffixed from unsuffixed words. Extrapolating from these findings, it is likely that listeners would also be able to perceive acoustic differences that relate to paradigm uniformity, such as durational differences between monomorphemic and morphologically complex words.

Research on the perception of morphologically complex words was performed in several experiments by Kemps, Wurm, et al. (2005) and Kemps, Ernestus, et al. (2005) on Dutch and English inflected words. In Dutch, plural is formed by adding -*en* to a noun, (which is usually realized as only a schwa, e.g. *boek* [buk] 'book'—*boeken* [bukə] 'books') and as a result of this, the stem of the plural form differs in duration and intonation when compared to the stem of the singular form. This prosodic information can also be found in other types of morphologically complex words in Dutch and English. Kemps, Ernestus, et al. (2005) investigated this by performing a cross-splicing task, in which the stems of morphologically simple words were spliced onto morphologically complex words and vice versa. To rule out an effect of the splicing, they performed additional experiments in which all items were spliced, either as matched or mismatched splice. They found that listeners are sensitive to the acoustic differences between uninflected and inflected forms, as they exhibit a processing delay when exposed to a form in which the prosodic information mismatches the segmental information. In particular, duration and intonation play important roles in the distinguishing of singular forms from the stems of their corresponding plural forms.

In a follow up replication study Kemps, Wurm, et al. (2005) also performed this for comparatives and derivation in Dutch and English. For Dutch, they selected monomorphemic comparatives and agent nouns, as well as similar pseudo-words. When adding the comparative or agent noun suffix -*er* [əʀ], these are resyllabified. Both stems and complex forms were recorded and subsequently cross-spliced, so that the constructed stem's prosodic information was mismatched and was significantly shorter. This process was very similar for the

English agent nouns and comparatives. Items were selected to be matched with the Dutch words and pseudo-words and spliced according to the same principle. They found further evidence that listeners had significantly shorter reaction times when presented with a mismatched spliced form and additionally found that Dutch and English listeners are equally sensitive to prosodic cues that signal whether a stem will be followed by one or more unstressed syllables.

What does this mean for the perception of phonetic properties, such as those found in paradigm uniformity? Paradigm uniformity assumes that the stems of morphologically simple words affect the stems of their related morphologically complex relatives and vice versa. As an example, if a particular noun is plural-dominant, one would expect the plural noun to be reduced, while the corresponding singular form would show less reduction. In terms of spreading activation, related forms should be activated when accessing a particular form. This means that if listeners are exposed to a mismatched stem, such as those presented to participants in the studies conducted by Kemps, Wurm, et al. (2005) & Kemps, Ernestus, et al. (2005), they should be affected by the mismatched information in their behaviour.

2.6 Summary and hypotheses

To summarize, a large body of research has been published that presents effects related to paradigm uniformity, and effects of morphological complexity on perception. Some of the previously presented studies provide evidence for effects of morphology on the duration of words, while others can directly be assigned to the domain of paradigm uniformity effects, such as for example incomplete neutralization in Dutch and German. What does this mean for paradigm uniformity in English though? Clearly, morphology plays a role when investigating stem duration. But to what extent this is due to paradigm uniformity has yet to be investigated.

Table 2.3: Stem and final sound durations found by Seyfarth et al. (2017).

	Monomorphemic words		Complex words	
	stem	final sound	stem	suffix
final [s, z]	shorter	shorter	longer	longer
final [t, d]	null result	null result	null result	null result

As I am interested primarily in replicating the findings for stem durations by Seyfarth et al. (2017), I will focus primarily on the effects they found, which are listed in Table 2.3. Based on these previous findings by Seyfarth et al. (2017), I formulated a number of different hypotheses which can be categorized either as confirmatory or exploratory. Regarding categorical paradigm uniformity, I would like to find out what happens phonetically in the stems of inflected words, how these differ from homophonous monomorphemic words, and whether words that are part of a morphological paradigm are being influenced by the properties of their paradigm members. In particular, I am looking at duration, i.e., whether morphologically complex words like *days* are longer or shorter in duration than monomorphemic homophones like *daze*. This directly replicates Seyfarth et al. (2017).

Regarding gradient paradigm uniformity, I would like to find out whether these durational differences are significant even on the account of frequency effects, i.e., how the frequency of a bare stem affects its paradigm members (e.g., how does the frequency of *day* affect *days?*). In particular, I would like to investigate whether low frequency bare stems cause longer durations of their paradigm members, and vice versa, whether high frequency bare stems cause shorter durations on inflected forms. This is something that was suggested by Seyfarth et al. (2017), but they did not choose their stimuli to balance for frequency, therefore I am expanding on their research. Aside from investigating complex words by predicting their duration with the bare stem frequency, I also investigated this by using relative frequency. Relative frequency will be explained in more detail in section 3.1.1. In addition to bare stem and relative frequency, I also investigated whether a general frequency effect affects these stem durations as a reality check.

Finally, in one of my experiments I expanded my research to the domain of perception and investigated the perception and comprehension of phonetic properties similar to those found in paradigm uniformity. Here I would like to find out whether listeners can perceive possible durational differences between complex and simplex words. This is tested in two different ways; first, by testing whether listeners perceive differences between a word and an artificially lengthened version of the same word that has been lengthened by 10, 25, 50 or 75 milliseconds. Second, by investigating whether listeners are slowed in their reaction time when they are exposed to a form with a mismatched stem, e.g. when they expect to hear *days*, but they hear the pseudo-stem of *daze* with an added plural *s*. This is an exploratory study inspired by previous research, in which I would like to investigate whether the phonetic properties similar to paradigm uniformity effects found by Seyfarth et al. (2017) can also be perceived, and I used studies by Kemps, Wurm, et al. (2005) and Kemps, Ernestus, et al. (2005) for methodological inspiration. These hypotheses are summarized here.

H1: Categorical paradigm uniformity

a) Stems of inflected words have longer durations than the pseudo-stems of monomorphemic words.

H2: Gradient paradigm uniformity

a) The higher the frequency of the bare stem, the shorter the duration of the inflected stem (gradient paradigm uniformity).
b) The higher the relative frequency (inflected word form / bare stem frequency) and the higher the decomposability of the inflected word, the longer the duration of the inflected stem.

H3: General frequency effect

a) The higher the absolute frequency of the inflected word form, the shorter is its duration and the duration of its stem (general phonetic reduction effect).

R1: Perceiving phonetic paradigm uniformity

a) Can listeners perceive possible durational differences between the same strings in complex and simplex words? More specifically, can listeners perceive differences between a word and an artificially lengthened version of the same word (lengthened by [10, 25, 50, 75] milliseconds)? Which of these durational differences can they perceive?
b) Are listeners slowed down in their lexical processing when they are exposed to a form with a mismatched stem, e.g. when they expect to hear days, but they hear the pseudo-stem of daze with an added plural s?

The hypotheses developed here were investigated in five different studies: two corpus studies and three experiments; or: three production studies and two perception experiments. In the context of the ongoing replication crisis in quantitative linguistics, a multi-method approach is an excellent way to find evidence for or against an effect that has been claimed to exist, such as paradigm uniformity in Seyfarth et al. (2017). Furthermore, investigating different types of speech, such as careful speech and casual speech, can have different implications. Some researchers, such as Tucker & Ernestus (2016: 376), argue that "in order to truly understand the cognitive processes underlying communication, psycholinguistic research requires a concerted shift to more casual, spontaneous types of speech". To summarize, they argue that there should be more focus on whether hypotheses that were supported by careful speech also hold up in casual speech. This would allow for more solid evidence on establishing theories on speech cognition and processing. In my studies, I aimed to replicate the careful speech elicited by Seyfarth et al. (2017) using casual speech, i.e. corpus data, and then further aimed to replicate my own corpus findings with careful speech (while attempting to elicit careful speech that imitates natural speech). In the production studies, I investigated the phonetics of inflectional stems and compared these to pseudo-stems, while in the perception studies, I investigated the reactions of participants to the phonetics of monomorphemic and complex words.

Before diving into the investigation of my hypotheses, I will provide some theoretical background on how one can explain these effects in terms of psycholinguistic theories, such as the dual route model and spreading activation. These will be discussed in the next chapter.

3 Processing phonetic paradigm uniformity effects: The mental lexicon

In this chapter, I will explore how paradigm uniformity effects can be explained through the means of psycholinguistic theories. There are different branches of morpho-phonetic and morpho-phonological theories; formal, phonological theories of a mostly generative nature, and psycholinguistic theories that tend to be focused more on phonetics and tend to be gradient and probabilistic in nature. Formal linguistic theories, such as for example Optimality Theory (e.g. Prince & Smolensky 1993) or Word and Paradigm Morphology (Matthews 1974; Blevins 2003) usually do not allow for a direct morpho-phonetic interface, as phonetic detail is not seen as an indicator of morphological structure. Rather, in these theories phonological entities are regarded as abstract. Thus, they are not particularly well suited to explain phonetic effects such as those found by Seyfarth et al. (2017) and will not be further discussed.

Psycholinguistic approaches, on the other hand, tend to expect gradient, probabilistic effects of morphological structure on phonetic detail, as opposed to categorical differences. Thus, they are well-suited to predict phonetic paradigm uniformity effects. Psycholinguistic approaches also differ from formal phonological theories in that they have a tendency to be based on empirical research. Psycholinguistic studies tend to focus on how the properties of individual words can explain a particular theoretical concept. For example, Cohen (2014) conducted an experiment to determine the contextual and paradigmatic probability of verb suffixes and found that higher paradigmatic probability causes longer suffixes as well as shorter stem durations.

In this chapter, I will focus on two frequently discussed psycholinguistic approaches revolving around the mental lexicon. The mental lexicon is defined as a mental dictionary as part of the human brain in which all information relating to a word is stored, such as for example phonetic, phonological, morphological and syntactic information (Jackendoff 2002). The two theories of the mental lexicon that I will focus on are decomposability and spreading activation. Furthermore, I will discuss a number of other aspects of language that may significantly influence the production and perception of spoken language, such as frequency, homophony and orthography.

3.1 The dual-route model: Decomposability and whole word representations

Theories of decomposability[4] and whole word representation have stood in contrast to each other until the introduction of dual-route models of morphological processing. While theories of decomposability argue that the constituents of morphologically complex words are stored separately in the mental lexicon and are assembled during retrieval, whole word models argue that morphologically complex words are always stored and retrieved in their entirety (cf. Chomsky & Halle 1968; Prasada & Pinker 1993; Marcus et al. 1995; Clahsen 1999; Pinker & Ullman 2002; Taft & Ardasinski 2006). Decompositional models assume that semantically opaque complex words are stored as a whole, but all regular, transparent words are stored in their constituents. These approaches have been deemed problematic through empirical investigation, leading to the introduction of dual-route models. Dual-route models assume that morphologically complex words, such as derivatives and inflected forms, are stored as a whole and in their separate constituents (cf. Frauenfelder & Schreuder 1992; Baayen & Schreuder 1999; Hay 2001; Hay 2003; Schreuder & Baayen 2015; Caselli, Caselli & Cohen-Goldberg 2016).

Dual-route models combine these two opposing approaches of decomposability and whole word storage models (Schreuder & Baayen 1995; Levelt, Roelofs & Mayer 1999). This idea was also taken up by Hay (2001; 2003), who proposed that the competition between the decomposition route and the whole word route in the dual-route model is determined, among other things, by the frequency of the base in relation to the complex form[5]. She argues that a word is more decomposable if its base is more frequent than its assembled form, and vice versa, that a very high frequent complex form with a low frequency base is more likely to be stored as a whole in the mental lexicon. Examples of these routes are visualized in Figure 3.1.

---

[4] In the literature, morphological *decomposability* is also known as morphological *segmentability*. For consistency, I will use the term *decomposability*.
[5] Hay also mentions other factors that influence decomposability, such as for example semantic transparency. I will not discuss semantic transparency or similar factors, as these are only relevant for derivatives and not applicable to my area of research, inflected words.

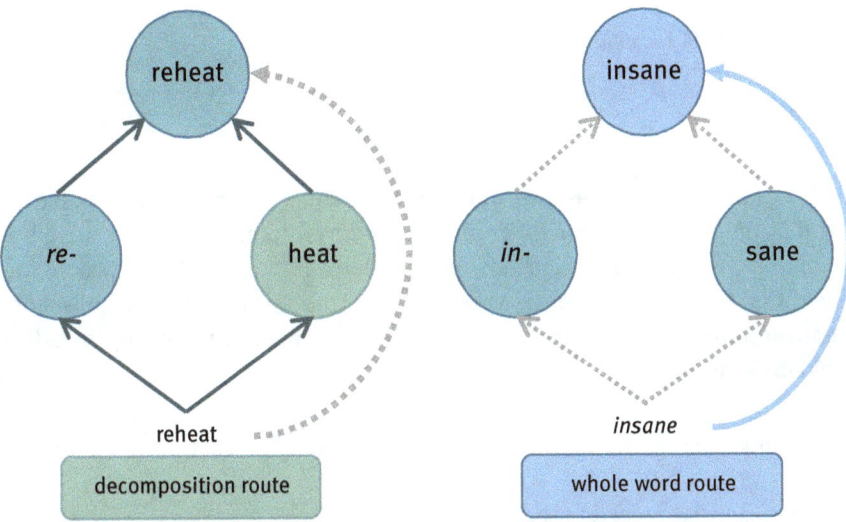

Fig. 3.1: The dual-route model, visualization adapted from Hay (2001), to show an example of the decomposition route (left) and the whole-word route (right). If a complex word's base, such as *heat* in *reheat* is more frequent than the derivative, the decomposition route is chosen (left, indicated by green arrows). If a complex word is more frequent in itself, such as *insane*, and has a low frequent base, the whole word route is chosen (right, indicated by the blue arrow).

3.1.1 Explaining relative frequency and resting activation

A measurement to determine the decomposability of words is relative frequency, as proposed by Hay (2001; 2003). Relative frequency is calculated by dividing the frequency of the word form and the bare stem [6], as illustrated in Figure 3.2.

$$\text{relative frequency} = \frac{\text{word form frequency}}{\text{bare stem frequency}}$$

Fig. 3.2: Formula for calculating relative frequency

An example of this is the relative frequency of the word *reheat* as found in the Corpus of Contemporary American English (Davies 2008), which is calculated in Figure 3.3:

---

[6] It is also possible to divide the bare stem frequency through the word form frequency. In that case, higher relative frequency means higher decomposability.

$$\text{relative frequency of } reheat = 0.0084 = \frac{746}{87774}$$

Fig. 3.3: Relative frequency calculated for the word *reheat*[7]

In this example, *reheat* has a very low relative frequency (smaller than 1), meaning that the base is more frequent than the derived form. A higher relative frequency, on the other hand, means that the derived form is relatively more frequent that the bare form. An example of this is the word *insane*, which is more frequent in the derived form, hence it has a higher relative frequency, as calculated in Figure 3.4.

$$\text{relative frequency of } insane = 3.1939 = \frac{16056}{5027}$$

Fig. 3.4: Relative frequency calculated for the word *insane*

In regards to decomposability, a derivative that is more frequent than its base, i.e., having a high relative frequency, is less decomposable and therefore more likely to be accessed as a whole. This relationship between relative frequency and lexical processing is explained by *resting activation*. Generally, the higher the frequency of a word, the higher the resting activation of a word. For example, *insane* being a very frequent word, has a high resting activation, whereas *sane* has a much lower frequency, and therefore also a lower resting activation. As *insane* has a higher resting activation, it is faster accessed via the whole word route. On the other hand, a low frequent derivative such as *reheat* has a low resting activation, whereas its base *heat* has a high resting activation, therefore in this case the decomposition route is faster.

How is the dual-route model relevant to the investigation of phonetic paradigm uniformity? The choice of decomposition route vs. whole word route is generally assumed to have an effect on its phonetic realization. Words that are accessed via the whole word route are more likely to show phonetic reduction than words that are assembled via the decomposition route. Previous research has shown that morphologically complex words show less phonetic reduction than monomorphemic words (cf. Cho 2001; Sugahara & Turk 2009; Smith, Baker & Hawkins 2012), confirming that morphologically complex words are more resistant to phonetic reduction. Using relative frequency as a measurement, Hay

---

7 In practice, these values are often log-transformed.

(2003) and other researchers following in her footsteps have shown that also different morphologically complex words behave differently accordingly to their degree of decomposability.

For categorical paradigm uniformity, this means that inflected forms such as plural or past tense forms should show less phonetic reduction than monomorphemic words. For gradient paradigm uniformity, this means that inflected words with a high relative frequency, such as plural-dominant nouns, are less decomposable and should therefore show more phonetic reduction than inflected words with low relative frequency. While these predictions seem straightforward, there are also a number of issues with the approach of using relative frequency as a measure for decomposability, which have been pointed out by numerous researchers. Results of studies using relative frequency have been unreliable and contradictory, as they are often not easily replicated. While many studies have found relative frequency effects (e.g. Hay 2001; Hay 2003; Plag & Ben Hedia 2018; Engemann & Plag 2021), others have not been able to find any effects (e.g. Hay 2003; Hay 2007; Schuppler et al. 2012; Ben Hedia & Plag 2017; Plag & Ben Hedia 2018; Stein & Plag). This unreliability may have a number of causes similar to what has been mentioned in section 2.2 regarding the ongoing replication crisis in quantitative linguistics.

First, a lot of these studies have differing methodological approaches, making comparability harder. For example, some studies looked at word duration, some at segment duration, and some at average durations. Second, these studies look at different affixes. Different affixes may behave in different ways, which could explain these discrepancies. Third, one should differentiate also between inflection and derivation. A large amount of these studies focused primarily on derivation, which generally is more prone to grammaticalization, to derivates losing their semantic transparency, and to being integrated into the prosodic word. However, as my focus is on inflection, it is important to determine the usefulness of relative frequency as a measure for the decomposability of inflected forms rather than derived forms. Often, other aspects besides relative frequency are mentioned in relation to the decomposability of words, such as for example semantic transparency. In the case of inflection, semantic transparency does not play a role at all, as inflected words are generally semantically transparent. Similarly, in derivational processes the part of speech of the base and of the derivative can play a role in decomposability as well, which also does not apply to inflection, as the part of speech never changes in inflection. In the following paragraphs, I will discuss the usefulness of relative frequency and possible problems that come with it by looking at a number of studies that used relative frequency.

Hay (2003) pioneered research using relative frequency by comparing the phonetic realization of base-final /t/ in derived words suffixed with -*ly* (e.g. *softly*, *swiftly*). She tested whether /t/ is more reduced in words that are less decomposable, i.e. words with a higher relative frequency. As pointed out by Hanique & Ernestus (2012), Hay's methodology is problematic, as only 6 speakers produced items. Furthermore, Hay compared durations calculated from the averages of segment durations rather than word or segment durations, which do not accurately represent articulatory duration.

Ben Hedia & Plag (2017), Plag & Ben Hedia (2018) and Stein & Plag (2022) investigated derivational affixes and theorize that the usefulness of relative frequency is directly related to the prosodic structure of a word. While Plag & Ben Hedia (2018) found that for certain prefixes relative frequency does predict decomposability, for other prefixes and suffixes it does not. Stein & Plag (2022) investigated a large number of derivational prefixes and suffixes across three different corpora, and have found that relative frequency and prosodic structure of derived words do not interact, and that effects of relative frequency do not emerge in a consistent manner. They argue that for affixes that are phonologically integrated into a word, it is harder for a relative frequency effect to arise. Furthermore, they found that relative frequency effects only occur together with general word frequency effects, and argue that due to this, relative frequency should be discarded as a predictor of duration.

Studies on other languages have also failed to deliver convincing results for relative frequency as a measure of decomposability. In an investigation of Dutch derivational affixes, Pluymaekers, Ernestus & Baayen (2005b) did not find significant effects of relative frequency for three affixes, they did however find an effect in the opposite direction to what Hay (2001; 2003) predicted for the prefix *ge-*. According to the authors, this might be due to the fact that monomorphemic words in Dutch are stressed on the first syllable, and speakers may perceive words prefixed with *ge-* as such.

As these studies show, there is no consistent evidence for relative frequency as a measure to predict decomposability of derived words. Most previous research has focused on derivation. However, a number of studies have also used relative frequency to investigate inflection. Schuppler et al. (2012) have investigated Dutch inflected words and found that the final [t] marking past tense undergoes enhancement; they found that less decomposable derivates show less reduction – the opposite of what was predicted by Hay (2003). This finding appears to be similar to the findings on *ge-* by Pluymaekers, Ernestus & Baayen (2005b).

For second- and third-person singular past tense verbs in German, Zimmerer, Scharinger & Reetz (2014) also did not find an effect of relative frequency. Their investigation focused on /t/-deletion in inflected words, which they performed by constructing a corpus of recordings of ten German native speakers. In this dataset, relative frequency did not significantly affect the rate of /t/-deletion.

English appears to be rather lacking regarding experiments conducted on relative frequency effects on inflected words. Seyfarth et al. (2017) tested an effect of relative frequency for their experimental data, but they did not find an effect of relative frequency on stem duration or suffix durations. I explored relative frequency as a predictor in my studies and evaluated its usefulness to determine decomposability of plural, past tense and third person singular words in English. To preview my results, I have not found solid evidence for relative frequency, neither to predict stem duration nor as a measure for decomposability. For the QuakeBox study, I found an effect of relative frequency (also published as Engemann & Plag 2021), but for the Buckeye study, I did not find an effect of relative frequency for plural, third person singular or past tense words. In sum, in my experiments, relative frequency was not a significant variable in the prediction of stem duration for gradient paradigm uniformity (for categorical paradigm uniformity, relative frequency is not applicable as it cannot be calculated for the monomorphemic words).

3.2 Spreading activation

Spreading activation is the second psycholinguistic approach that I will discuss in relation to paradigm uniformity. It refers to the process that happens in a speaker's mind (i.e., the mental lexicon) when a certain lexical concept, lemma or morpheme is activated and retrieved (Collins & Loftus 1975; Dell 1986; Roelofs 1992). As suggested by Seyfarth et al. (2017), spreading activation can be used to explain phonetic paradigm uniformity. In Seyfarth's approach, they theorize that paradigm uniformity emerges through the activation of stored articulatory gestures, as described in 2.1.

There are several theoretical approaches to explain spreading activation. One of the most cited models is the 'Levelt model' by Levelt, Roelofs & Mayer (1999), a speech-processing model in which there are several processing stages of speech production during which activation may spread. In an initial stage, the conceptual preparation of a speech item leads to the activation of a lexical concept. At this conceptual stage, the selection of a lexical concept such as *horse* may also activate related semantic concepts, such as *gallop, mare, rider*, etc. Levelt et al. presume a feed-forward activation spreading network, which means the results of each stage of the process are passed on to the next stage, with no option for feedback between the stages.

Spreading activation occurs not only on the conceptual level, but also on the lemma and the formal level. On the lemma level, morphosyntactical information such as person, number, gender, tense, aspect or form are activated, i.e., when selecting the verb *to gallop*, activation spreads to progressive *galloping*, past tense *galloped*, etc. On the word form level, morpheme and segment nodes are activated, which may spread to related nodes. When activating *cat*, for example, related words such as *rat* may be activated based on being a phonological neighbor, but also based on the semantic relation (both are animals). The items *cat* and *rat* have a strong connection within the mental network, due to this double link. Activating *cat* may also activate weaker links, such as phonological neighbors like *cap*.

What is the significance of the Levelt model for the investigation of phonetic paradigm uniformity? Based on the process of spreading activation, it can be assumed that activating a word such as *days* would also activate its related word form *day* (and its phonological twin, *daze*). However, the Levelt model is a strictly feed-forward model, and does not really account for the phonetic paradigm uniformity effects that I am investigating, in which the phonetic realization of a plural form such as *days* may affect the phonetic realization of its related form *day* and vice versa. While the Levelt model allows for some degree of self-monitoring of a speaker's internal speech, it does not really account for the feedback loops that would be necessary to explain phonetic paradigm uniformity, and is also fairly vague on the actual articulation processes of speech.

A recent revision of the Levelt model has been presented by Roelofs & Ferreira (2019). In addition to the empirical evidence from production and perception studies that was presented to justify the Levelt model in Levelt, Roelofs & Mayer (1999), Roelofs & Ferreira (2019) also take into account evidence on speech production and processing collected from neuroimaging. This revised model consists of three major phases of speech processing which are further subdivided into smaller phases. The three major phases are conceptualization, formulation and articulation, with formulation being the core of the model, while conceptualization and articulation are not particularly fleshed out.

During the conceptualization phases, a message is being generated based on visual or auditory input. After the concept has been identified, the message is being passed onto the formulation phases, which is the heart of the model. Here, there are two major stages that proceed one after another, while being subject to internal self-monitoring. During these stages, the lexical network is accessed via spreading activation in the form of *if-then*-rules selecting pertinent nodes in the mental lexicon. In the first of these major stages, lemma retrieval, the lemma is retrieved from the mental lexicon. Syntactic encoding happens at this stage, and the sentence function is being assigned. The next stage is word-form encoding, during which morphological, phonological and phonetic encoding take place. If these stages pass the internal self-monitoring, they are passed on to the articulation phase via the phonetic plan. The articulation stage is subject to external self-monitoring via overt speech, meaning that during this stage the speaker may correct any detected speech errors.

Contrary to the original Levelt model, this revised model also attempts to account for sentence production rather than merely word production. Sentences are produced through a content stream very similar to the lemma retrieval process, and through a structure stream which assigns syntactic functions. However, this sentence production model is unclear on how prosody is computed. All over, this revised model is an improvement over the original, strictly feed-forward Levelt model, in that it also allows for feedback loops between the different phases and stages. However, it is unclear as to how suitable these models are to explain phonetic effects such as paradigm uniformity, as they do not really take into account post-lexical processes very well.

Cohen-Goldberg (2013) addresses this lack of research on the post-lexical processing of multimorphemic words by establishing the "heterogeneity of processing hypothesis" (HPH). The idea is that multimorphemic words are processed differently from monomorphemic words, and multimorphemic word processing can be subject to variation. Multimorphemic words differ from monomorphemic words in that they contain boundaries, which can cause structural weaknesses at the point of the boundary where phonemes from different morphemes clash. Furthermore, phonemes of multimorphemic words will inherit the properties of the morpheme to which they belong. To summarize, the HPH entails two predictions: first, post-lexical processes should be weakened by a morphological boundary (leading to less phonological integration of the boundary), and second, post-lexical processes should be influenced by the properties of each lexical morpheme (meaning that phonemes may inherit certain characteristics of their parent morphemes).

Cohen-Goldberg (2013) performed three studies to test the HPH, two of which confirmed the HPH. He concludes that phonemes across different morphemes are subject to less competition than phonemes within the same morpheme. This suggests that post-lexical processing is weaker for heteromorphemic than tautomorphemic sequences, and that post-lexical processing varies according to the morpheme's lexical properties. The HPH suggests inferences about lexical processing of multimorphemic words to be made on the basis of post-lexical data in future research. For the investigation of duration, the HPH would suggest that words with stronger boundaries should be subject to longer durations, or show less reduction.

To summarize, a number of theories are concerned with spreading activation, but there is still a certain lack of accounting for complicating matters such as morphological structure. Numerous studies have found that monomorphemic words as roots play a role in the processing of multimorphemic words. Caselli, Caselli & Cohen-Goldberg (2016) have found that inflected words also play a role in the processing of monomorphemic words through their influence as inflected neighbors.

What does this mean for paradigm uniformity? One can assume that related items, such as members of the same paradigm (e.g. *days* as a paradigm member of *day*) spread through the mental lexicon, activating related forms and influencing them in their phonological properties. However, morphology is not the only matter that might complicate things. Two other possible areas of complication are frequency effects beyond relative frequency, and homophones.

3.3 Other aspects of language

Aside from the two previously presented theories of the mental lexicon, there are several other aspects of language that can have a significant influence on how language is produced and processes within the mental lexicon. These are frequency, homophony and orthography, which some of which may also be subject to spreading activation. These aspects will be explained in more detail in the following subsections.

3.3.1 Frequency

Frequency has been well-established as having an effect on duration, in that higher lexical frequency words tend to have shorter durations (Bell et al. 2003; Pluymaekers, Ernestus & Baayen 2005b; Aylett & Turk 2006; Gahl 2008; Bell et al. 2009; Gahl, Yao & Johnson 2012). This has been demonstrated for both lemma frequency (e.g. Jurafsky et al. 2001; Bell et al. 2009; Gahl 2008; Lohmann 2018) and for word form frequency (Caselli, Caselli & Cohen-Goldberg 2016; Lõo et al. 2018). Beyond surface frequency effects and investigating the relationship between frequency and morphological composition of words, Caselli, Caselli & Cohen-Goldberg (2016) found that the stem frequency of words inflected with *-ed* and *-ing* negatively correlates with the duration of these words in speech, while Winter & Roettger (2011); Roettger et al. (2014) found that highly frequent paradigm members have a stronger phonetic influence on their morphological relatives. Clearly, frequency seems to always be an important factor in the analysis of words and word durations.

How do frequency and spreading activation relate to each other? It is plausible to assume that higher frequency words would spread activation more easily than low frequency words. In regards to paradigm uniformity, in particular gradient paradigm uniformity, this is an interesting research question, mirrored in my hypothesis H2 (see 2.6). H2 states that the higher the frequency of the bare stem, the shorter the duration of the inflected stem. Additionally, the higher the relative frequency, the longer the duration of the inflected stem. In particular for gradient paradigm uniformity, this implies that activation of *days* would spread to its bare stem *day*, and therefore the frequency of *day* might affect the phonetic realization of *days*.

3.3.2 Homophony

Beyond frequency effects on paradigm members, I am also interested in how simplex-complex homophone pairs behave, and what complications homophonous words may bring to spreading activation. A word such as *days* may not only be affected by its own word form frequency or its stem frequency, but also by its relation to its monomorphemic homophone twin, *daze*.

The representation of homophones in the mental lexicon has been a subject of debate in the literature. Some researchers propose models in which homophones share a phonological form, such as the model by Levelt, Roelofs & Mayer (1999), while others propose that there are independent phonological representations for homophones, as in the Independent Network model by Caramazza (1997). These two approaches are illustrated in Figure 3.5.

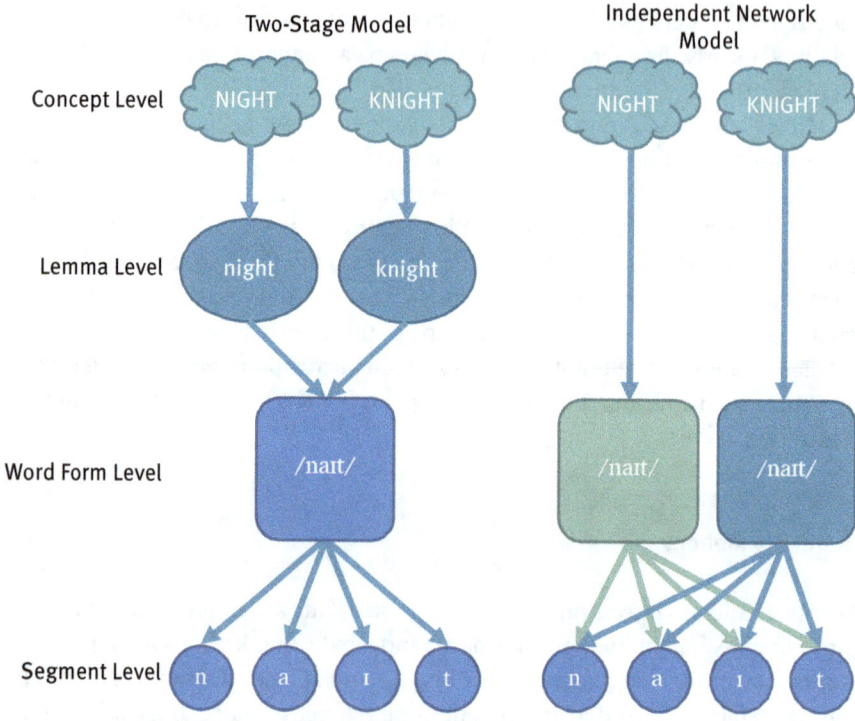

Fig. 3.5: Two theories of the representation of homophones for speech production adapted from Biedermann & Nickels (2008); the left illustration shows the Two-Stage model (aka 'Levelt model') (Levelt, Roelofs & Mayer 1999), in which homophones share one phonological representation. The right illustration shows the Independendent Network model (Caramazza 1997), in which each homophone has its own phonological representation in the mental lexicon.

In the Levelt Model, homophones have different representations at the semantic (concept) level and at the syntactic (lemma) level, but they share the same phonological form at the word form level, which is passed on to the phonemic level. This is also referred to as the 'Shared Representation' view in the literature.

The Independent Network model stands in direct contrast to the Levelt Model. In the Independent Network model, each homophone has its own representation at the concept level, but also at the word form level. This means that homophones do not share the same phonological form, but are different in their phonological realization.

Both these models assume a strictly feed-forward processing. However, in later papers, Levelt, Caramazza, and colleagues have adjusted their models to allow feedback links between different levels. These adjustments were made to allow for effects such as the frequency inheritance effect that homophones may be subject to, however, this effect has subsequently been dismissed in the ground-breaking study on *time* and *thyme* by Gahl (2008). She compared homophone word pairs in which usually one item of the pair has a low frequency and the other a high frequency, such as *thyme* and *time*. On average, *thyme* had a longer duration than its high frequency homophone counterpart *time*.

The study attempted to replicate findings on frequency inheritance effects, but found evidence disproving these. Research on frequency inheritance effects was pioneered largely by Jescheniak & Levelt (1994) and Jescheniak, Schriefers & Hantsch (2003), who claimed that word frequency is encoded at the level of the phonological form rather than at the lemma level. This implies that whenever a phonological form is activated, all words associated with that form are also activated. In other words, if the phonological form [deɪz] is activated, this form would activate both *daze* and *days*. Crucially, however, items sharing the same phonological form behave as though they have the same, cumulative frequency. This means that regardless of whether *days* or *daze* is accessed, both words behave as if they have the same frequency. Therefore, the low frequent word *daze* should show the same phonetic reduction as the high frequent word *days*. It is generally agreed upon that more frequent words have shorter durations, therefore, these shorter durations should be observable also in homophone word pairs that are affected by frequency inheritance.

Gahl (2008) tackled this problem by looking at durations of heterographic homophone word pairs such as *time* and *thyme*. She found evidence against a frequency inheritance effect. In her study, high frequency words like *time* were significantly shorter than their low frequency counterparts, as in this case *thyme*. This result is consistent on account of covariates controlling for speech rate, contextual predictability, syntactic category, proximity to pauses, and orthography.

The results of this study challenge a number of theories such as frequency inheritance, but most notably also the Levelt model, which establishes that word frequency is a property of the phonological form rather than of the lemma. Furthermore, the role of orthography might play a significant role in Gahl's findings – previous research on frequency inheritance was based on homographic homophones, whereas Gahl excluded those in her study and only examined heterographic homophones. Gahl controlled for orthography by using m-scores (phoneme-grapheme probability), which was a significant predictor. It is possible that the importance of orthography has been underestimated and may explain the discrepancy between Gahl's results and previous studies on frequency inheritance effects.

Gahl's results are widely regarded as a milestone. Her results were further confirmed in a follow-up study using a more sophisticated modelling approach (Gahl 2009). However, in a reanalysis of both of Gahl's papers, Lohmann (2018a) pointed out a number of issues with her methodology. Gahl used average durations of high frequency words as the dependent variable, and average duration of the low frequency words as a covariate. Using average durations is problematic especially for the low frequency words, making them very unreliable, but also using both frequencies in the same model is methodologically questionable due to possible collinearity effects. The model delivers evidence for differences between the high frequency words, not between the homophones. Also worth noting is that in Gahl's dataset, the titular *thyme* occurs only once, and as part of the compound *lemon thyme*. This is the case with many of the low frequency homophones and renders them extremely problematic as candidates for comparison to a high frequency twin. Generally, the dataset has a very unbalanced type-token ratio, as is often the case with corpus data. This makes the results subject to scrutiny.

Lohmann addressed these issues in a reanalysis, and discovered that the cumulative frequency of the high and low frequency homophone pair is extremely close to the frequency of the high frequency twin. This indicates that the result found by Gahl is a general frequency effect of only the high frequency twin. Lohmann reanalyzed the dataset using a new variable that calculates a frequency ratio between the high and low frequency homophone pairs, and finds evidence that confirms Gahl's hypothesis.

A different approach to addressing the problem of homophones in the mental lexicon was developed in the theory of homophone dominance established by Dominiek Sandra and collaborators (e.g. Sandra & Van Abbenyen 2009; Verhaert 2015; Verhaert, Danckaert & Sandra 2016; Sandra 2010; Sandra, Frisson & Daems 1999). In several experiments on spelling errors and proofreading in Dutch regular verb forms, Sandra and collaborators found that high frequency homophones exert influence on low frequency homophones in a process called homophone intrusion.

Regular verb forms in Dutch are spelled according to descriptively simple rules, yet are subject to persisting spelling errors. This is especially the case for verbs that have a homophone in their inflectional paradigm (i.e. homophones that are grammatical variants of the same lexeme, such as the heterographic homophones *vind* and *vindt*; as in *ik vind* 'I find' and *hij vindt* 'he finds'). Sandra and collaborators theorize that this is due to the cognitive process involving the retrieval of these words when exposed to the phonological form. More spelling errors were made when participants were exposed to the lower frequency homophone than when they were exposed to the higher frequency homophone. Thus, participants are inclined to write down the high frequency form when they cannot directly map the sounds of a verb form onto its corresponding graphemes.

These experiments suggest that Dutch verb homophones with a high frequency paradigm member are stored in the mental lexicon and thus accessed via the whole-word route, as opposed to the decompositional route – despite being fully regular. Accessing the whole word route is often faster than using the computational process of composing root and inflectional morpheme, causing the emergence of homophone dominance.

While Sandra and collaborators focused on homophones that are part of the same inflectional paradigm, research on lexical homophones has also shown similar effects. White et al. (2008) and White, Abrams & Zoller (2013) performed experiments similar to those by Sandra, in which participants had to write down sentences containing homophones. These experiments tested whether high frequency homophones would intrude on low frequency homophones. They found that participants made more substitution errors, i.e. intrusions, on the low frequency homophone member of the pair than on the high frequency member (i.e. *beach* was more often substituted for *beech* than vice versa). Furthermore, in a proofreading task they found that homophone intrusions for high frequency homophones tended to go unnoticed more often than those for low frequency homophones.

Research on homophone dominance provides further evidence disproving the idea of frequency inheritance and demonstrates that high frequency homophones intrude on low frequency homophones. This may potentially play an important role in phonetic paradigm uniformity as well. As high frequency goes hand in hand with phonetic reduction, a phonetic implementation of homophone dominance would suggest that the high frequency phonological form is accessed when a speaker or listener is exposed to a low frequency homophone.

However, an application of homophone dominance to phonetic paradigm uniformity is not as straightforward as it seems, as in my research I am primarily interested in the phonetics of inflectional stems. Thus, the homophone pairs that I investigate in my experiments (see chapters 5 and 6.2) always consist of a morphologically simple word and a morphologically complex word (e.g. *daze* and *days*). Previous research on homophone dominance focused on grammatical homophones that are part of the same lexeme, or on lexical homophone pairs that are both simplex.

3.3.3 Orthography

Another aspect that might be of concern regarding homophones is orthography. Differences in the behavior of heterographic vs. homographic homophones have already been mentioned; Gahl (2008) for example conducted her ground-breaking study on heterographic homophones, while the frequency inheritance effect that her study was based on focused exclusively on homographic homophones. This discrepancy came to the attention of other researchers, who conducted research specifically geared towards discovering whether heterography or homography plays a role in the phonetic realization of homophones and the differences that have been found between them.

One such study was conducted by Biedermann & Nickels (2008), who investigated the processing of homophones in individuals with aphasia. They tested the Shared Representation view of the Two-Stage Model and the Independent Representation model (see Figure 3.5 on page 42 for a comparison of the models), motivated by previous research which has shown an effect of homophone generalization. Homophone generalization refers to the effect that by naming one homophone meaning, the other homophone meaning also improves in picture naming tasks. This was found especially for homographic homophones (Biedermann, Blanken & Nickels 2002; Biedermann & Nickels 2008). Biedermann & Nickels (2008) also pointed out that the theory of frequency inheritance effects was based exclusively on homographic homophones, whereas Caramazza et al. (2001) used both hetero- and homographic homophones and found no such effect.

Biedermann & Nickels (2008) found evidence suggesting a shared representation of homophones, meaning that homophones share the same phonological form. Their results did not show any differences between heterographic and homographic homophones, therefore they assume that regardless of spelling, the same phonological form is accessed when processing a homophone. Lohmann (2018), on the other hand, has found evidence that homographic noun-verb homophone pairs such as *cut* (n) and *cut* (v) have distinct entries in the mental lexicon. However, noun-verb homophones are a special case, as these are the result of conversion and also play different roles within a sentence, as they are different parts of speech. Furthermore, they are semantically closely related.

There does not appear to be a consensus on the lexical processing of homophones; some researchers have found evidence for a shared phonological representation, while others argue for entirely different phonological representations. Additional complications are the frequency of occurrence, the orthographic status (heterographic or homographic), and the morphological structure of homophones.

For the investigation of categorical paradigm uniformity, however homophones are ideally suited because they allow for a direct comparison between a morphologically complex and a morphologically simple pair of words, such as *days* and *daze*. Due to their different morphological nature, these types of homophones are almost always heterographic. Homophones are also ideally suited because they allow a three-way comparison of a stem to a complex word, and from a complex word to a simplex word, i.e., a comparison between the [deɪ] part of *day*, *days* and *daze*.

3.4 Perception

Previously presented theories were primarily based on research conducted on production. However, perception is also an excellent testing ground for such models. In my hypotheses, I included exploratory research questions on perception, namely whether listeners can perceive possible durational differences between the same strings in complex and simplex words, and whether they can perceive durational differences in artificially lengthened versions of the same word. Furthermore, I wanted to explore whether listeners show different behaviour when exposed to forms with a mismatched stem.

Listeners have been shown to be able to disambiguate ambiguous segment sequences across junctures, such as *plump eye / plum pie, once paid / one spade* or *play skin / place kin* (Lehiste 1960; Shatzman & McQueen 2006; Lee, Kaiser & Goldstein 2020) in English, or for phrases such as *chat grincheux* (grumpy cat), which contains the word *chagrin* (sorrow) in French (Christophe et al. 2004). Results of studies such as those largely show that listeners are able to distinguish these ambiguities and indicate that phonetic detail might be stored in the mental lexicon.

Similarly, listeners are able to distinguish phonemically identical onsets of embedded words, which constitute segmental strings such as the word *cap* and the *cap* part of *captain* (Davis, Marslen-Wilson & Gaskell 2002). In multisyllabic words, the vowel of such embedded words is shorter in duration, which listeners are able to perceive in cross-splicing tasks. Such cross-splicing tasks, where the first syllable of a word such as *hamster* was replaced with a recording of the monosyllabic *ham* and similar pairs, were performed in English and Dutch (Salverda, Dahan & McQueen 2003) for monomorphemic words. Research on embedded words was expanded to multimorphemic words by Blazej & Cohen-Goldberg (2015), who investigated embedded words in morphologically complex contexts, such as *clue* and *clueless*.

Generally speaking, recognition of spoken words is a constant effort of ambiguity resolution. Speakers have to wait for a certain *uniqueness point* in spoken speech to be able to disambiguate possible candidates that are being selected from the mental lexicon. When hearing the string *can*, for example, listeners have to await the uniqueness point until they can identify whether the speaker is uttering *can*, or a longer word with this embedded sequence, such as *candy*, *candle*, *candor*, etc. While additional information on the meta level, such as part of speech or syntactic constituent, narrow down the possible list of candidates, there is still potential for ambiguity. This can also be said about disambiguation of items related to categorical and gradient paradigm uniformity, such as *day*, *days* or *daze*.

There are several different approaches to explain the processing of speech perception. I will discuss abstractionist models, which assume that phonological representations are the unit of comprehension, feature based models, which assume that in comprehension only marked information is retained, and exemplar-based models, which assume that fine phonetic detail is stored in the mental lexicon.

In abstractionist models, phonetic details of the speech signal are transformed into phonological representations at a pre-lexical stage. Thus, these models assume that subphonemic detail is merely a peripheral process or not considered at all. One of the earliest of these models is the speech perception and lexical access model by Klatt (1979), which also performs time normalisation, meaning that timing and duration are only considered if these perform a discriminative role such as in stress placement. Other examples of abstractionist models are the TRACE model (McClelland & Elman 1986) and the Shortlist and Shortlist B models (Norris 1994; Norris & McQueen 2008). None of these models account for subphonemic detail as part of perception, therefore they cannot account for the perception of fine phonetic detail as part of comprehension.

Feature based models, such as for example the Fuzzy Logical Model of Speech Perception (Massaro 1987), or the model proposed by Lahiri & Marslen-Wilson (1991) assume that features, rather than abstract phonemic representations, are the basis for comprehension. In the model proposed by Lahiri & Marslen-Wilson (1991), non-distinctive information is withheld and listeners do not have access to this information. Lahiri & Marslen-Wilson assume that each lexical item has a single underlying phonological representation, in which only marked information is retained. Similarly, in the Fuzzy Logical Model of Speech Perception, comprehension makes use only of marked sets of features rather than of phonological representations, i.e., sets of features that are nontypical and divergent from broader, more dominant forms[8]. Feature-based models make inconclusive predictions about the perception of subphonemic detail such as durational differences.

In contrast to feature-based models, exemplar-based models of speech perception can in principle account for the perception of subphonemic durational differences (Goldinger 1998; Johnson 1997; Pierrehumbert 2001; 2003). They are also based on features, but they assume that listeners access a multitude of exemplars per word form, all of which are stored in the mental lexicon. The exemplar-based framework by (Pierrehumbert 2001; 2003) adds a probabilistic approach to exemplar-based models. In this framework, phonetic categories have probability distributions over a parametric phonetic space, which consist of exemplars that are accessed and encoded during the speech perception process. As exemplars can store phonetic durational information, exemplar-based models would be suited to explain the comprehension of subphonemic detail.

To summarize, there are a number of different approaches to the interpretation of perception. However, not all of them are well-suited to explain the perceivability of fine phonetic detail. Taking my results into account, I will revisit these in Chapter 7.3.

3.5 Summary

In this chapter, I presented a number of psycholinguistic theories and aspects of language that could be used to explain paradigm uniformity effects. Psycholinguistic approaches such as the dual-route model are suited to explain both categorical and gradient paradigm uniformity effects, as they take into account gradient, probabilistic effects of morphological structure on phonetic detail.

The dual route model unites approaches of decomposability and whole word representation by theorizing that high frequency words take the whole word route, while low frequency words take the decomposability route. These can be determined by analyzing the frequencies of the bases and derivatives.

Spreading activation is a more general term which comprises theories to explain how words are activated within the human brain. There are several models concerning spreading activation, as well as more general aspects of language, that may be suitable to explain categorical and/or gradient paradigm uniformity effects, such as for example the HPH, or theories on homophones. These will be

---

[8] An example from morphology for markedness would be irregular plural forms such as *child – children*, as opposed to the regular plural -s as in *cat – cats*.

discussed in regards to my results in the discussion section (chapter 7). Finally, perception can be explained through a number of different approaches as well, such as abstractionist, feature-based, and exemplar-based models. Their use in explaining my findings in the perception study will be discussed in chapter 7 as well.

4 Corpus studies

I conducted two corpus studies; a study using a dataset from the QuakeBox corpus (Walsh et al. 2013) and a study using the Buckeye corpus of conversational speech (Pitt et al. 2007). Conducting the same study with two different corpora has the advantage that more evidence for the same phenomenon indicates that paradigm uniformity is a robust effect. On the other hand, if the two corpus studies were to disagree, a number of causes could be addressed in future studies. Either way, the more studies are being conducted on a topic, the more evidence can be analyzed and interpreted.

There are a number of advantages and disadvantages that come with using corpus data. Possibly the biggest disadvantage is that corpus data tends to be very noisy, both in a figurative and sometimes literal sense. Some corpora, such as for example the Audio BNC (Coleman et al. 2012) contain recordings that were made under less-than-ideal circumstances, and often contain background noise. This is not the case with either the QuakeBox or the Buckeye Corpus, as both were recorded under adequate circumstances or in sound-attenuated booths.

Corpus data can also be noisy in a figurative sense, meaning that the data may be incorrectly annotated or very inconsistent. Incorrect annotation often happens with audio corpora that have been segmented using a forced aligner. These automatic annotations can be prone to errors such as misaligned segments or incorrect matching of assiged words to phonetic output.

A further complication is the less-than-ideal type/token ratio that is usually found in datasets generated from corpora. In corpora, some words tend to occur with a much higher frequency than others. This was the case in one of my QuakeBox datasets, which had 74 types, and 475 tokens; some tokens occurred over 20 times in the dataset (e.g. *shoes, size, noise, keys*), while many others only occurred once (e.g. *bees, booze, clues, pause, skies*). This imbalance of types and tokens causes a lot of problems, as frequent types may have different phonetic characteristics from less frequent types. Thus, it is necessary to find a way to control for this imbalance, for example by adding local frequency as a covariate in the statistical analysis. Ideally, however, a dataset should have a balanced type/token ratio, in which all types have an equal number of tokens.

Variability can be an advantage and a disadvantage at the same time. While it helps to reflect the range of naturally occurring speech, it can also widen the scope of a study to unmanageable dimensions. This is possibly the case with the Buckeye Corpus, as there were no limitations on the topics discussed in in the interviews. However, the QuakeBox Corpus has a more limited scope as all stories revolve around earthquake experiences.

Variability also occurs in corpora in the sense of prosody, due to sentence structure and varying degrees of fluency. Since I am interested in particular types of words, these may occur at the beginning or end of a sentence or utterance boundary, or in the middle of an utterance. This may be problematic, as prosody and the location of a word within a sentence can have significant effects on its phonetic realization. In experiments, on the other hand, this can be controlled by embedding all target words in very similar carrier sentences.

Finally, the contents of corpora are not tailored to a specific research question, which is arguably their biggest disadvantage. Experiments, on the other hand, can be tailored to a research question, as I will describe in chapter 5.

Despite all their disadvantages, corpora are also ripe with opportunity. Most corpora have the advantage that they are easy to access, as most of them are available on the internet (sometimes after going through a licensing process). Another advantage is that most corpora are already annotated and segmented, which especially in the case of spoken corpora makes it much easier to process the data, as there is no need for any additional annotation. In most cases, a dataset that already contains information such as segment durations can be exported from the corpus, and imported into a statistical analysis software such as R (R Core Team 2015).

Finally, one of the biggest advantages of most corpora is that, especially in the case of spoken corpora, they reflect naturally occurring speech. This is also the case in both corpora that I used; the Buckeye corpus contains interviews about everyday topics such as politics, sports, traffic, schools, etc., and the QuakeBox corpus contains monologues of people retelling their experiences in the earthquakes that happened in and around Christchurch in 2010 and 2011.

The two different corpus studies that I conducted also have the advantage that they provide evidence for paradigm uniformity across varieties and speech situations, thus providing evidence (or not) that paradigm uniformity is a very robust effect in English. The Buckeye corpus is a corpus of conversational General American English recorded in approximately 1999 to 2000, while the QuakeBox corpus is a corpus of New Zealand English monologues recorded in 2010 to 2011. Thus, these corpora cover two decades, two varieties, as well as two different linguistic genres. In the following subchapters I present the general methodology used for the corpus studies, and will describe both corpora and the studies I conducted using them in detail.

4.1 Methodology

4.1.1 Selection of items

In the analysis of empirical data, it is important to narrow down a dataset to an optimal form, as datasets that are too large and too noisy become too problematic, even for multiple regression analysis. Therefore, I set specific criteria for my items. For almost all studies, I used only words that fulfill the following criteria:

Criterion 1: they are either monomorphemic or morphologically complex (plural, third person singular or past tense)
Criterion 2: they end in /s/, /z/, or /t/, /d/[9]
Criterion 3: they are monosyllabic

As indicated, some of these applied to only the experiments. These criteria ensure a homogenous dataset that is relatively convenient to analyze statistically, but there are a number of more complex reasons for each of these decisions, which are explained in detail below.

Criterion 1: Monomorphemic vs. complex words

In order to investigate paradigm uniformity, one requires words that are part of a morphological paradigm. The choice fell to plural, third person singular and past tense forms as target items, which were to be compared to monomorphemic words. These types of words were also used by Seyfarth et al. (2017) in their study, and since my studies are based on theirs, it is logical to use similar forms. The majority of my studies focused on plural forms. Third person singular and past tense forms were only used in the Buckeye corpus study and as filler items in the experiments. These morphologically complex words are contrasted with monomorphemic words, similar to Seyfarth's items.

Criterion 2: alveolar fricative (or plosive) as final sound

The plural and third person singular morphemes in English both end in the alveolar fricative [s] or [z], depending on the allomorph. Incidentally, these two different morphemes are also homophonous and have the same allomorphy pattern; they are subject to phonological conditioning. After voiceless consonants,

---

[9] I investigated [t] and [d] only in the Buckeye corpus study.

the final sound is realized as [z], after voiced consonants or vowels it is realized as [s], and after sibilants, it is realized as [ɪz].

Since plural and third person singular forms end in [z] or [s], it is sensible to restrict the monomorphemic items in the dataset to those that end in [z] or [s] as well, disregarding [ɪz] items. This allows for a better comparison of monomorphemic vs. complex stems, as they all have similar phonetic properties.

In the Buckeye corpus study, I also did an analysis of words ending in [d] or [t], resulting in an investigation of monomorphemic vs. past tense words. However, similar to Seyfarth et al. (2017)'s results, this investigation has shown that this environment is not fruitful, therefore further studies were restricted to final [s] and [z].

Criterion 3: Monosyllabic words

Seyfarth et al. (2017) limited their study to monosyllabic words, therefore I also limited my studies to monosyllabic words. Monosyllabic words are an excellent subject for analysis. They always carry main stress, and they are relatively easy to process and analyze due to their brevity and simplicity.

4.1.2 Statistical analysis

In all of my studies, statistical analyses were carried out using the software R (R Core Team 2015). In both corpus studies and in the production experiment, the main analyses concerned the investigation of the duration of the stem in relation to the morphological structure of the word that is being investigated.

In this section, I will give a general introduction into the statistical methods and models used to investigate stem duration, as well as problems that occur across the models in the different studies.

As a first step, and to get an overview of the data, tables and simple plots were generated to compare the durational values across the different morphological categories. I expect that stem durations of monomorphemic words are longer than those of morphologically complex words (categorical paradigm uniformity), and that the stem duration decreases with increasing relative frequency (gradient paradigm uniformity).

To prepare the data for analysis further, I took a close look at the (log-transformed) durational variables[10], such as STEMDURATION or SPEECHRATE, and

---

10 See section 4.1.3 for an explanation of variables.

checked them for outliers. Outliers are data points that are far greater or far smaller than the majority of data points, thus they are data points that are not typical for the dataset (cf. Draper & Smith 1998: 75). Outliers should be investigated carefully. If a there is a meaningful reason for an outliers' extreme divergence from the rest of the dataset, they may be kept. Generally though, the best practice is to exclude outliers from the dataset, as they might skew the results of the statistical model and do not adequately represent the nature of the dataset.

Outliers were removed by visual inspection of pertinent variables. Using R, a plot was created in which data points were sorted. In this plot, any extreme outliers were easily spotted and were removed by trimming the dataset at a threshold before the outlier was visible. This was done for STEMDURATION and if necessary for SPEECHRATE.

After removing outliers and general clean up of the raw data (e.g. removing any wrongly annotated words from the corpus dataset, or participants that are not native speakers from the experimental data), a more advanced statistical analysis was carried out to investigate paradigm uniformity effects and possible factors influencing the duration of the stem. This was done with regression analysis in the corpus studies and the production experiment.

Linear mixed effects regression analysis

Regression analysis is a method to investigate functional relationships among different variables. With regression analysis, it is for example possible to investigate which effect the variables MORPHEMETYPE (indicating whether the item is complex or monomorphemic) and POSITION (beginning, middle or end of an utterance) have on a variable STEMDURATION. In this example, STEMDURATION would be the response variable, also referred to in the literature as dependent variable. It is the variable that is being predicted by the model by taking into account other variables such as MORPHEMETYPE and POSITION. In the case of MORPHEMETYPE, this variable is the predictor or explanatory variable, which is the main variable of interest. A variable such as POSITION, however, is a variable that can control for noise or inconsistencies within a dataset, which needs to be controlled for in an analysis. This type of variable is interchangeably referred to as control variable, noise variable, independent variable or covariate in the literature[11].

There are several different types of regression analysis. I used linear mixed-effects regression modelling in R (function lmer() from the lme4 package (Bates et al. 2017)). This type of modelling has the advantage that it can investigate one

---

[11] I will mainly use the term covariate.

predictor (the variable of interest) while simultaneously controlling for other predictors, as well as controlling for variation that is introduced into the dataset by randomness, such as the speaker or the word under investigation. This is of particular importance when dealing with corpus data, since many speakers provided only one observation to the dataset, and there was only one token for many word types in the dataset. These variables were included into the model as random effects, while the other variables were included as fixed effects.

Collinearity

Regression analysis also bears some risks and problems, such as for example collinearity. Collinearity occurs when two or more of the variables that are included in the model correlate. Correlation can results in counterintuitive coefficients, making the output of the model uninterpretable. This can for example manifest in suppression or enhancement of certain predictor variables (see also Tomaschek, Hendrix & Baayen 2018).

In the models for my corpus studies, concerns of collinearity are particularly problematic regarding the three different frequency variables that I am interested in; word form frequency, stem frequency and relative frequency. If a word has a high word form frequency, it is likely to also have a high stem frequency, thus there is a correlation between these frequencies.

A vast number of tools and functions are available to investigate problems of correlation and collinearity in R. One such function is pairscor.fnc() in the R package languageR (Baayen & Shafaei-Bajestan 2019), which generates a scatterplot matrix in the upper triable and Pearson and Spearman correlations in the lower triangle. The *r* value displayed gives the Pearson correlation as a value between -1 and 1. The higher this value, the stronger the relationship between the two variables. To avoid problems of collinearity, it is desirable for the *r* value be as low as possible. In addition to listing correlation values, the pairscor.fnc() also has the advantage that it visualizes the relationships between the variables, allowing for a quick preliminary visual inspection that makes highly correlated variables easier to spot.

Another function to test collinearity is the vif() function from the car package (Fox et al. 2020), which is suitable if categorical variables are involved. It lists the variance inflation factor of a dataset. When using this function, a value greater than 5 in the output indicates collinearity problems. When using the vif() function on a linear model that includes all three frequencies that I am interested in, the linear model was rank deficient, and was only able to estimate two of the three coefficients. This is likely due to collinearity between the three frequency values. To solve this problem, only a maximum of two of the three frequencies were included in the linear models, which also led to acceptable `vif()` results. Generally though, I created separate models for the different frequencies and only included more than one frequency in models in which the frequencies did not correlate strongly.

Finally, another method to investigate collinearity is random forests (cf. Tomaschek, Hendrix & Baayen 2018), which allow an assessment of the relative importance of predictor variables. This is particularly useful in the analyses of gradient paradigm uniformity, in which I was interested in finding out which of the three frequency variables can predict the duration of the stem in plural words best. I used a type of random forest analysis using conditional inference trees, which is well-suited to deal with correlated variables, the `cforest()` function from the R package `party` (Hothorn et al. 2020). This function produces a list of variables ordered by estimated importance of the variable.

However, when comparing the results of the random forest analysis with the output of the models, a new problem arose; some variables that are estimated by the random forest analysis to be fairly important were not significant in the regression models (cf. Engemann & Plag 2020a). This can have several reasons; regression models only consider main effects and assume linear effects of the predictor variables, while in random forest analyses also complex interactions are considered, and here no linear effects of the predictors are assumed.

In my production experiment, collinearity was not as problematic, as there the target items were carefully selected to correspond to different frequency constellations as part of my research question (see 4.1.1).

Overfitting

A random forest analysis is also a suitable method to deal with the potential problem of overfitting. Overfitting can occur when the number of variables included in a model is not in an appropriate balance to the number of observations, making data reduction and model validation important (see for example Draper & Smith 1998; Babyak 2004; Harrell 2015; Matuschek et. al 2017). If too many variables are included, the model will not be able to adequately compute the effects of the variables on the response variable and the worth of the model will be exaggerated. Random forests can help with this problem, as they estimate which variables are most important and which are least important, giving an indicator which variables should be included in future models.

General model structure and modelling procedure

The models for all my studies had a very similar structure regarding which variables were used as response variable and as main predictor variable. An overview of the production studies and the pertinent variables is given in Table 4.1, which is fairly straightforward; for all studies, stem duration is the predictor variable. To investigate categorical paradigm uniformity, the variable of interest is morphological structure (monomorphemic or complex) in a dataset containing monomorphemic and complex words, and for gradient paradigm uniformity, the variable of interest is bare stem frequency in a dataset containing only complex words.

Table 4.1: Overview of response and variable of interest in all production studies.

Type of PU	Data	Response Variable	Variable of Interest
Categorical	monomorph. + complex	Stem duration	Morphological structure
Gradient	complex only	Stem duration	Bare stem frequency

The models also included a number of other control variables, which are omitted here for brevity. An overview of the properties of these variables will be laid out in section 4.1.3 and will be discussed in detail in the subchapters specific to the study.

The models were fitted according to established practices in the literature (Baayen 2008); in an initial model, all pertinent control variables were included alongside the variable of interest. Then a step-by-step elimination process commenced, in which new models were created, with each new model having a reduced number of predictor variables based on their predictive power in the models.

A variable had to pass three tests to be included in a successive model. First, it had to yield a t-value greater than 2 (or less than -2). Second, the Akaike information criterion (AIC) of the model including the variable had to be lower than the AIC of the model without it. Third, a likelihood ratio test comparing the model including the factor to a model without it had to yield a *p*-value lower than 0.05. If all of these values were satisfactory, the procedure was repeated including also sensible interactions between variables. Models with interactions underwent the same validation process as those without interactions. Once a final model was reached with this elimination process, the residuals were investigated visually, and the process was determined as complete if both tails of the distribution showed a normal distribution and all remaining variables had a *p*-value of < 0.05.

This process was done using the step() function from the lmerTest package (Kuznetsova et al. 2020).

4.1.3 Variables

All datasets for the acoustic analysis have a similar structure, as the variables of interest are all very similar in the corpus studies and the production experiment. The following subsection will give an overview of the variables present in the datasets and my motivation for including them.

Word and utterance structure
WORD: The variable WORD contains the target word that is being investigated. For example, for words in which the bare stem is subject to investigation, this could be *day*, for the complex stem it would be *days*, and for the pseudo-stem it would be *daze*. This variable is included as a random effect in the statistical analysis.

MORPHEMETYPE describes the morphological structure of the WORD that is being investigated. Possible values of this variable are bare, complex or monomorphemic. As my main research question concerns whether paradigm members have an influence on their related forms, this is one of my key variables of interest.

NUMPHON gives, as the name suggests, the number of phonemes in the WORD. These values can be less than straightforward in English due to the inconsistent spelling conventions and the lack of phoneme-letter correspondence. To illustrate this, the word *freeze* has 6 letters <freeze>, but it has only 5 phonemes /friːz/. The purpose of these variables is to control for possible differences in the phonological makeup of the word on the phonetic production of the word. They were created by counting the number of phonemes that were present in the phonemic transcription of the corpus data or the experimental items.

PARTOFSPEECH is a variable that lists whether the WORD under investigation is a singular noun, plural noun, inflected verb, or uninflected verb. The values of this variable differ slightly across the different studies due to the way it was encoded. The Buckeye corpus provides the variable PARTOFSPEECH, so no further action was necessary. In the QuakeBox corpus and in the experiments, this was manually encoded. Considering the part of speech in an analysis is important, as previous studies have shown that different types of homophonous words can have different durations, such as for example *cut* as a noun has a different duration than *cut* as a verb (Lohmann 2017; 2018b). Part of speech tags are used according to the rules established by the Penn Treebank project (Bies et al. 1995).

PRECEDINGSOUND: The control variable PRECEDINGSOUND contains the sound that occurs before the word final [z] or [s]. For the corpus studies, this is usually a vowel due to the restriction to only [z] as word final element, however, in the experiment it may also be a consonant. This control variable can shed light on whether different kinds of vowels have different effects on the STEMDURATION. As vowels have inherently different lengths, it is presumable that the STEMDURATION will be affected by the particular preceding vowel, diphthong or consonant.

PRECEDINGSOUNDTYPE: In addition to PRECEDINGSOUND, the variable PRECEDING-SOUNDTYPE contains similar information, but instead of the particular sound, it merely encodes the type of sound – i.e. vowel, diphthong or consonant. This can shed light on the possible durational differences between these types of sounds.

POSITION contains the location of the word within the sentence, such as for example utterance-initial, in the middle of an utterance, or utterance-final. This variable controls for possible effects of phrase-final lengthening, which are well established in the literature (e.g. Klatt 1976; Byrd, Krivokapic & Lee 2006). This variable is mostly relevant for the corpus data, as in the production experiment the target word was always embedded into the middle of the carrier sentence. But also, in the case of the corpus data, the vast majority of words were in the middle of an utterance, where we expect shorter durations than before pauses.

PHONNEIGHBORDENSITY & PHONNEIGHBORFREQ: PHONNEIGHBORDENSITY lists the number of phonological neighbors, i.e. words differing in one segment from the item in question, extracted from CLEARPOND (Marian 2012). PHONNEIGHBORFREQ is the mean frequency (per million) of these neighboring words. This control variable is of importance because a number of studies have found that phonological neighbors of words may influence their phonetic production; high phonological neighborhood density often goes hand in hand with reduction (e.g. Gahl, Yao & Johnson 2012; Gahl & Strand 2016).

VOICINGRATIO is a variable that was provided with and only used in the QuakeBox dataset. It contains the number of frames of the word final [z] that show vocal fold vibration divided by the total number of frames of the word final [z]. This accounts for phonetic differences in the duration of voicing. Voiced [z] is shorter than unvoiced [s] (e.g. Klatt 1976), which might also affect the duration of the stem in some way.

Durational variables

STEMDURATION is the response variable for all production studies. It is a numerical variable that contains the duration of the (pseudo-)stem, minus the word-final [s] or [z] (if present), regardless of morphological makeup of the word. This means that for a simplex word *day*, it is the duration of the phonemes [deɪ], for the complex word *days* it is also the duration of the phonemes [deɪ] contained within [deɪz], and for a monomorphemic word *daze* it is also the duration of the phonemes [deɪ] contained within [deɪz]. This value was extracted from the corpus data, or in the case of the production experiment, from the annotated Praat files. This duration was log-transformed, as all durations.

ExpectedWordDur is a variable that controls for individual segment durational differences. Different types of segments differ in duration, for example a plosive differs from a fricative, and a diphthong differs from a short vowel in duration. Therefore, it is helpful to control for these individual differences. I used a procedure analogous to Gahl, Yao & Johnson (2012) and Caselli, Caselli & Cohen-Goldberg (2016). Gahl, Yao & Johnson (2012) kindly provided me with a file of average durations of each segment across the whole Buckeye corpus, which I used to calculate the expected word duration for the Buckeye study. For the QuakeBox study, I first calculated the average duration of each segment across the whole QuakeBox dataset, and then used these average segment durations to calculate the expected duration of a given word.

SpeechRate is used as a control variable to account for intra-speaker or intra-utterance durational differences. Some speakers speak faster than others, and even the same speaker can produce utterances at vastly different speeds, which can greatly affect the durational variables that I am interested in (such as the StemDuration). Including a speech rate variable in the statistical model will take this variation into account. Speech rate measures differed slightly in the different studies. In the QuakeBox corpus it was provided as metadata and adopted as it came with the dataset; here it was calculated in syllables per second for each utterance. In the Buckeye corpus it was calculated in a similar fashion by dividing the numbers of syllables from up to four words to the left and right of the target word through the total duration of these up to 9 words. Finally, in the production experiment it was calculated as syllables per second within the entire carrier sentence.

Frequency variables

StemFreq, WordFormFreq, RelativeFreq: I included three different frequency variables that relate to the frequency of the Word and its paradigm members. These are WordFormFreq, which is the frequency of the word form, e.g. the plural frequency of the word *days*; StemFreq, which is the frequency of the stem of a complex word, e.g. the frequency of *day* for the target word *days*; and RelativeFreq, which is calculated by dividing the WordFormFreq and the StemFreq (for more information about relative frequency, see also section 3.1.1). Frequency values are important because they give an approximate measurement of how often a word is used within a language. More frequently used words have a tendency to be phonetically reduced (cp. e.g. Gahl 2008), and one of my main research questions concerns the effect of frequency on a word's related forms.

All frequency values were extracted from a pertinent corpus, such as COCA (Davies 2008) for American English in the Buckeye corpus or BNC (BNC Consortium 2007) for New Zealand English in the QuakeBox corpus. COCA is one of the largest corpora on American English and includes a variety of different genres (spoken and written). It is also continually updated. The frequencies extracted from COCA for this dissertation were extracted using the Corpus query tool Coquery (Kunter 2017b) using downloaded copies of COCA from 2012 and 2020. The BNC is one of the largest corpora of British English. Unlike COCA it is not continually updated, but only includes data until the early 1990s. It was used for the frequency values for New Zealand English, as NZE is linguistically and culturally closer to British English than to American English. The BNC frequency values that were used for the QuakeBox dataset came provided with the dataset from Julia Zimmermann.

All frequencies occur in the datasets both as untransformed variables, as well as log-transformed variables (prefixed with Log, e.g. LogWordFormFreq). For the statistical analysis, log-transformed variables were used as variables of interest.

LeftBigramProb & RightBigramProb: In addition to frequencies of the target word itself, I also included bigram probabilities as a control variable. A bigram is a sequence of two adjacent elements, in this case, words within an utterance. Bigram probability, which is also referred to as bigram frequency in the literature, is a measurement for a potential factor that can influence the duration of a word within an utterance due to its predictability in context. More predictable words have a tendency to be more phonetically reduced (cp. Jurafsky et al. 2001; Pluymaekers, Ernestus & R. Baayen 2005; Bell et al. 2009; Torreira & Ernestus 2009; Gahl, Yao & Johnson 2012). There are two variables for bigram frequencies, LeftBigramProb, which is the frequency of the preceding word and the target word, and RightBigramProb, which is the frequency of the target word and the following word. These frequencies were extracted from a pertinent corpus in a similar fashion to the word form and stem frequencies mentioned in the previous paragraph. For the Buckeye study, this was the Corpus of Contemporary American English (COCA).

Like all frequencies and durations, the bigram probabilities were log-transformed. As some bigrams did not appear in the corpus (especially those used in the production experiment), these had a value of 0. Log-transforming 0 does not work, therefore all bigrams that did not appear in the corpus were transformed to 0.1, in order to avoid problems due to the log-transformation and in order to distinguish them from the bigrams that had a frequency of 1.

Speaker information

SPEAKER: Each record in a given dataset also includes some information about the SPEAKER (in the corpus data) or the PARTICIPANT (in the experiments), such as a unique identifier of the speaker or participant who uttered the WORD, or who participated in an experiment. This control variable is important because in the case of corpus data or production data, one speaker or participant may have uttered the same target item several times. Being able to identify the speaker is thus very important, as different speakers may have different speech rates or idiolects.

GENDER & AGE: A number of sociolinguistic control variables concerning the speakers or participants were included or collected, in order to check for possible effects of for example Gender or Age. Effects of gender, age or social status on speech production are well established in the sociolinguistic literature (e.g. Labov 1972; Byrd 1994).

In the QuakeBox corpus, the variable for AGE is AGEGROUP, in which age is summarized into different categories ranging from 1 to 7, with 1 corresponding to ages 18-25, 2 to 26-35, 3 to 36-45, 4 to 46-55, 5 to 56-65, 6 to 66-75, and 7 to 76-85.

In the Buckeye corpus, AGE is a categorical variable with the value y (young) or o (old). Young speakers were under thirty, and old speakers were over forty.

INTERVIEWER GENDER: In addition to information about the participant, the Buckeye corpus also provides information about the Interviewer Gender, i.e., the gender of the person who conducted the interview.

4.2 QuakeBox corpus study

The QuakeBox corpus study[12] was conducted with the intention to replicate the results found by Scott Seyfarth and colleagues in their paper "Acoustic differences in morphologically-distinct homophones" (Seyfarth et al. 2017), as described in detail in chapter2.1. This replication was evolved and expanded on with new hypotheses, investigating paradigm uniformity from new angles (see chapter2.3).

---

[12] The dataset used for this study and the script for the statistical analysis are available at https://osf.io/p9rv6/?view_only=d100d29a96f24b78852dd231c7700ef5

The QuakeBox corpus (Walsh et al. 2013) was recorded in several locations in Christchurch and Canterbury, New Zealand in 2012. The name comes from the QuakeBox itself, a mobile recording studio inside a shipping container. This mobile studio was previously used by Tourism New Zealand to record tourist impressions of the country, but was repurposed into the QuakeBox after the heavy earthquakes in 2010 and 2011 that destroyed large parts of the city of Christchurch.

The container was placed in 8 different locations in and around Christchurch from December 2010 until December 2011. Participants who wanted to share their experiences were able to do so in private inside the QuakeBox. Participants cover a wide range of demographics from the population of Christchurch; in age they ranged from 18 to 85, and 44% have grown up in Christchurch. With 25%, a significant number of participants have indicated that they grew up outside of New Zealand. However, for my analysis, only data was used in which participants identified themselves as New Zealand European.

The majority of participants also consented to being filmed. Videos of these stories of those participants who gave full consent to have their stories released can be freely accessed on the website of the UC CEISMIC Website (ceismic.org.nz), and selected stories were displayed publicly in an exhibition in Christchurch. The recordings of the QuakeBox Corpus were transcribed by a transcription team and then integrated into a database that is accessible via a tool called LaBB-CAT (Fromont & Hay 2012).

The QuakeBox corpus contains 722 stories, out of which 697 were recorded in English, for a total of 120 hours of recordings. There is no information about the number of words contained in the corpus. The dataset used for my study included only English recordings.

4.2.1 Data

The dataset for this corpus study was provided to me by Julia Zimmermann, who extracted it from the QuakeBox corpus on site at the University of Canterbury in New Zealand for the analysis of word final [s] and [z] (Zimmermann 2016). She extracted all words that were produced by speakers identifying ethnically as New Zealand European and that end phonemically in a word final /s/ or /z/ not followed by a word beginning in /s/ or /z/, as these tend to merge with the word final /s/ or /z/ of the preceding word. Subsequently, she cleaned this dataset by excluding brand names, proper nouns, and clitics which did not represent *has* or *is*. She also removed words from word classes other than nouns, verbs and pronouns, as well as function words such as *has*, *is*, *was*, etc. To avoid an unbalanced dataset by overrepresentation of certain lexemes, only up to 25 tokens of each combination of base and type of word-final S were randomly sampled. Finally, she excluded items with a word-final /s/ or /z/ that had a duration of 250 milliseconds or more, that had a speech rate faster than 15 syllables per second, and items for which the center of gravity showed obviously false measurements (see Zimmermann (2016) for details). The resulting dataset contained 7073 tokens. Since this dataset (dataset 1) met most of the criteria for my items of interest (see 4.1.1), it is a suitable dataset for the investigation of paradigm uniformity.

For the purpose of investigating paradigm uniformity, the dataset was reduced and filtered to achieve greater homogeneity and better comparability to my other studies (i.e. the Buckeye study). In accordance with the criteria listed in 4.1.1, the dataset was reduced to only contain monosyllabic words with a vowel preceding the word final [s] or [z]. Having only vowel-final stems had the consequence that only [z]-final words occur in the dataset, since stem-final vowels trigger the voiced allomorph of the plural morpheme. This resulted in dataset 1, which was used for the analysis for categorical paradigm uniformity.

Dataset 1 was further filtered for the analysis of gradient paradigm uniformity by reducing it to only plural words, resulting in dataset 2. Finally, dataset 2 was further reduced to include only words in which word form and stem frequency do not correlate, resulting in dataset 3.

An overview of the three datasets used in the QuakeBox study is given in Table 4.2, which lists which types of words are included, and how many types and tokens occur in each dataset.

Table 4.2: Dataset and subsets used in the analysis of the QuakeBox data with token and type counts, and which paradigm uniformity (PU) they were used for (C = categorical, G = gradient).

Dataset	PU	Description	Types	Tokens
dataset 1 (sublmer3)	CPU	monosyllabic, monomorphemic words and plural words ending in [z]	38	431
dataset 2 (data2)	GPU	monosyllabic plural nouns ending in [z] (subset of dataset 1)	20	295
dataset 3 (freqband-words)	GPU	selection of monosyllabic plural nouns ending in [z] in which word form and stem frequency do not correlate (subset of dataset 2)	10	159

4.2.2 Variables

The variables used in this dataset are explained in 4.1.3. Table 4.3 gives an overview of the descriptive statistics of the variables that are used in dataset 1 alongside their summaries and distributions. Table 4.4 does the same for dataset 2. As dataset 3 is a subset of dataset 2, an overview of this dataset is not necessary.

Table 4.3: Variable information for dataset 1 extracted from the QuakeBox corpus, which was used for the analysis of categorical paradigm uniformity.

Variable	N	Mean	St. Dev.	Min	Max
Dependent variable					
STEMDURATION	431	-1.246	0.310	-1.966	0.511
Numerical variables					
WORDFORMFREQ	431	8.521	1.180	4.700	10.373
SPEECHRATE	431	1.393	0.162	0.806	1.859
VOICINGRATIO	431	0.390	0.245	0.000	1.000
NUMPHON	431	3.181	0.487	2	4
EXPSTEMDUR	431	-1.613	0.260	-2.549	0.984
LEFTBIGRAMPROB	431	4.253	2.483	0.000	8.567
RIGHTBIGRAMPROB	431	3.942	2.493	0.000	8.787
AGEGROUP	422	4.123	1.562	1.000	7.000
PHONNEIGHBORDENSITY	427	26.166	10.716	8.000	50.000
PHONNEIGHBORFREQUENCY	427	127.073	318.906	4.796	33.183
Categorical variables					
WORD	431	38 levels			
SPEAKER	431	196 levels			
POSITION	431	pause: 54; falsestart: 3; final: 19; hesitation: 7; middle: 325; nearfinal: 11; nearpause: 21			
PARTOFSPEECH	389	AJ0: 4; NN1: 71; NN2: 292; VVB: 22			
MORPHEMETYPE	431	monomorph.: 136; plural: 295			

Table 4.4: Variable information for dataset 2 extracted from the QuakeBox corpus, which was used for the analysis of gradient paradigm uniformity.

Variable	N	Mean	St. Dev.	Min	Max
Dependent variables					
STEMDURATION	295	1.218	0.301	1.966	0.511
Numerical variables					
WORDFORMFREQ	295	8.535	1.087	5.517	10.373
STEMFREQ	295	9.429	1.416	6.455	11.936
RELATIVEFREQ	295	0.894	1.210	6.418	1.134
SPEECHRATE	295	1.390	0.160	0.842	1.859
VOICINGRATIO	295	0.368	0.230	0.000	1.000
NUMPHON	295	3.176	0.505	2	4
EXPSTEMDUR	295	1.627	0.216	1.987	0.984
LEFTBIGRAMPROB	295	4.461	2.468	0.000	8.567
RIGHTBIGRAMPROB	295	3.793	2.263	0.000	8.121
AGEGROUP	287	4.118	1.549	1.000	7.000
NEIGHBORDENSITY	295	25.580	8.997	9	44
NEIGHBORFREQUENCY	295	154.585	377.098	11.066	1,687.658
Categorical variables					
WORD	295	20 levels			
SPEAKER	295	164 levels			
POSITION	295	pause: 30; falsestart: 2; final: 11; hesitation: 3; middle: 227; nearfinal: 8; nearpause: 14			

4.2.3 Analysis

The datasets were analyzed using the modelling procedure described in 4.1.2, using mixed-effects regression modelling and a step-wise elimination process. In addition, a random forest analysis (Tomaschek, Hendrix & Baayen 2018) was performed to investigate collinearity issues.

4.2.4 Results

The results of the analysis will be presented in this subsection. Section 4.2.4 and all its subsections have previously been published in Engemann & Plag (2021).

4.2.4.1 Categorical paradigm uniformity

In a comparison of the durations of the pseudo-stems of monomorphemic words with the stems of plural words, there was a difference in duration of 30 ms, with plural stems being longer than monomorphemic pseudo-stems.

To control for confounding variables, a mixed linear effects model was fitted. In the presence of these other variables, the difference in stem duration was no longer significant, as the variable MORPHEMETYPE was eliminated during the step-process. Table 4.5 gives the output of the final model containing only remaining significant predictors, and Figure 4.1 plots the partial effects. The fixed effects explain 23 percent of the variance, the entire model 46 percent (based on pseudo-R-squared for Generalized Mixed-Effect models, using the function r.squaredGLMM() from the MuMIn package (Barton 2009)). None of the interactions of the covariates with MorphemeType were significant.

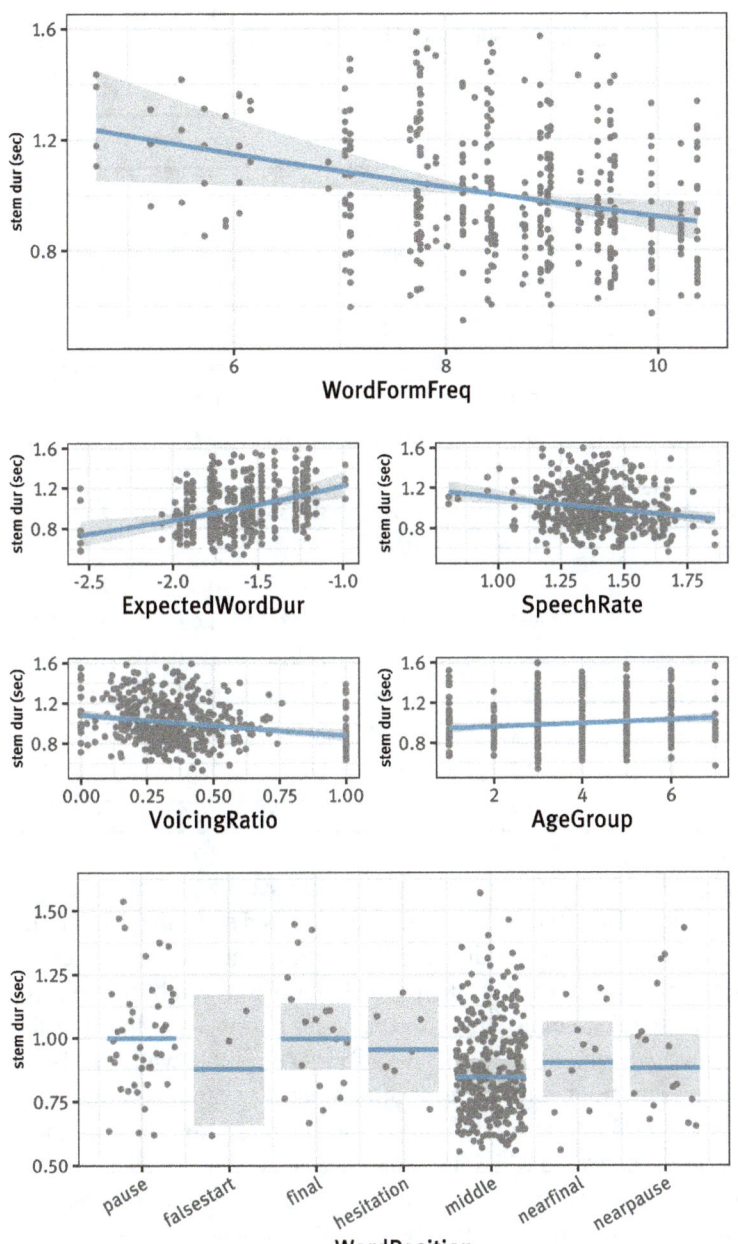

Fig. 4.1: Partial effects of the final model testing for categorical paradigm uniformity.

Table 4.5: QuakeBox dataset 1: Fixed-effects coefficients and p-values in the final model testing the categorical paradigm uniformity effect. (Significance codes: 0 '***' 0.00.1 '**' 0.01 '*' 0.05)

Random effects

Groups	Name	Variance	St. Dev.
WORD	(Intercept)	0.023	0.15
Residual		0.056	0.24

Fixed effects

	Estimate	Std. Error	df	t value	Pr(>|t|)	
(Intercept)	0.25	0.27	56.42	0.95	0.35	
WORDFORMFREQ	-0.06	0.02	35.63	-2.60	0.01	*
EXPWORDDUR	0.33	0.09	37.56	3.52	0.00	**
POSITION: falsestart	-0.13	0.15	394.38	-0.89	0.38	
POSITION: final	0.00	0.07	388.84	-0.04	0.97	
POSITION: hesitation	-0.05	0.10	390.48	-0.47	0.64	
POSITION: middle	-0.17	0.04	394.70	-4.08	0.00	***
POSITION: nearfinal	-0.10	0.08	385.14	-1.23	0.22	
POSITION: nearpause	-0.13	0.07	395.23	-1.78	0.08	.
SPEECHRATE	-0.26	0.08	400.47	-3.33	0.00	**
VOICINGRATIO	-0.21	0.05	397.66	-3.90	0.00	***
AGEGROUP	0.02	0.01	394.35	2.12	0.03	*

All covariates behave as expected. The higher the WORDFORMFREQUENCY, the shorter the duration of the stem – this is a well-established effect in the literature: the more often a word is used within a language, the shorter its duration becomes, as it is subject to phonetic reduction. A similarly well-established effect is that of phrase-final lengthening, which occurs in this dataset as well; words that occur in mid-speech (POSITION: middle) have a shorter duration, while words that occur in word final position have a longer duration. Other variables are also unsurprising; the faster the speech rate of the speaker, the shorter the duration of the stem (SPEECHRATE), words with longer phonemes have longer stem duration (EXPWORDDUR), the more voicing is present in the final /z/, the shorter the duration of the stem (VOICINGRATIO), and finally, the older the speaker, the longer the duration of the stem, as older speakers tend to speak slower (AGEGROUP).

4.2.4.2 Gradient paradigm uniformity

Seyfarth et al. (2017) tested for gradient paradigm uniformity by assuming strength of activation as the responsible mechanism that drives the magnitude and direction of the effect. The higher the strength of activation, the stronger the lengthening of the morphologically related form. They devised two different models, each with only one type of frequency as the predictor of interest. That is, in one model bare stem frequency was included as the sole predictor of interest, in the other model relative frequency was included as the sole predictor of interest. Plural word form frequency was not included in their models, although word form frequency has been shown to influence word duration, and thus, presumably, stem duration.

For my research questions (see 2.6), all three frequencies are of interest, as I am testing alternative hypotheses to those established by Seyfarth et al. (2017). The three frequencies may correlate, therefore possible collinearity needs to be investigated. Figure 4.2 presents a correlation matrix of the three variables, with Pearson and Spearman correlations in the lower triangle.

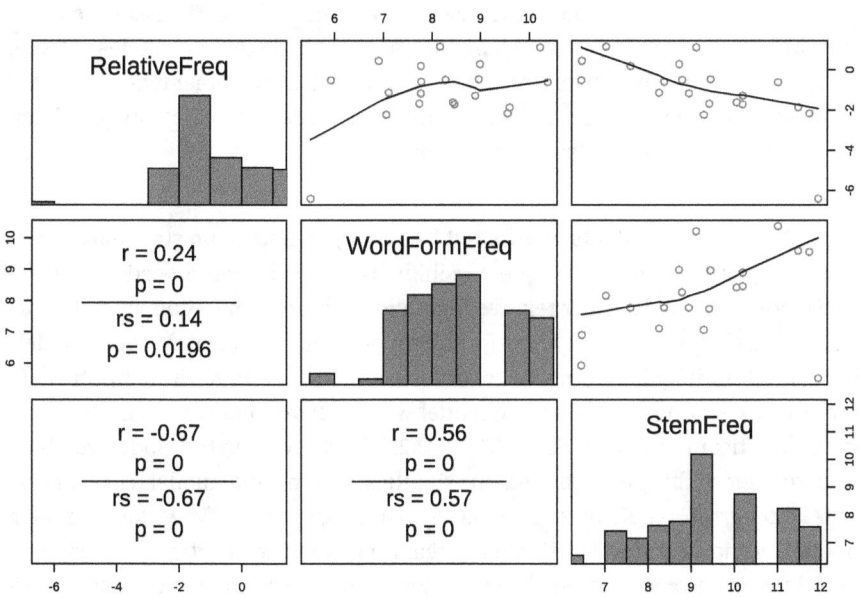

Fig. 4.2: Scatterplot matrix of log-transformed durations in dataset 2 of the QuakeBox study, which was used to investigate gradient paradigm uniformity, with Pearson and Spearman correlations in the lower triangle.

Unsurprisingly there are strong correlations between stem frequency and both word form and relative frequency. Using the condition number as a measure of collinearity danger for these three variables (with the `collin.fnc()` from the languageR package (Baayen & Shafaei-Bajestan 2019)), arrives at an extremely high figure of 19,701,789,290. Values above 30 are considered to indicate harmful collinearity (e.g. Tomaschek, Hendrix & Baayen 2018). Pairwise calculation of condition numbers leads to acceptable values ranging from 18.3 to 20.2.

Additionally, variance inflation factors (VIFs) were investigated (using the `vif()` function of the car package (Fox & Weisberg 2011)). When trying to apply `vif()` to a linear model with all three frequencies, the linear model can only estimate two of the three coefficients. Collinearity is a likely reason why including all three variables as predictors into the regression models leads to rank deficiency, such that only two of three coefficients can be estimated. When including only two of the three frequency variables (in addition to all covariates) in the linear model, the resulting VIFs for the frequency variables are between 2.1 and 3.6. As a rule of thumb, values below 5 are considered acceptable (e.g. Tomaschek, Hendrix & Baayen 2018).

There are different strategies available to address collinearity issues (e.g. Tomaschek, Hendrix & Baayen 2018). In this case, with only three variables at issue, where one of the three is even calculated on the basis of the other two, and where including all three at the same time is impossible, three strategies suggest themselves, as shown in the subsequent sections.

4.2.4.3 Testing the effects of different frequency measures on stem duration

To test Seyfarth's hypotheses, one possibility is to mirror their procedure and devise models with only either relative frequency or bare stem frequency as predictor of interest (i.e., without word form frequency as a covariate). These models were fitted initially including all covariates, and according to the simplification procedure described above. In the model with relative frequency, this predictor is not significant (initial model: $t=1.14$ $p=0.27$). In contrast, in the model with bare stem frequency this predictor remains significant in the final model (*coefficient*=-0.075, *std. error*=0.027, $t=-2.76$, $p=0.015$). The negative coefficient of bare stem frequency shows that with rising bare stem frequency the duration of the stem in plural forms becomes shorter. The direction of this effect is in the opposite direction from Seyfarth's hypothesis and confirms the effect expected based on the considerations underlying the alternative hypotheses (see section 2.6).

These models (like Seyfarth et al.'s) are, however, flawed by not including word form frequency as a covariate. Given the acceptable condition numbers and VIFs for models containing two of the three measures, it seems safe (even if not ideal) to include word form frequency in the two models. This additional variable turns out to be not significant when added to the final model with bare stem frequency (word form frequency: $t=0.047$, $p=0.96$). Bare stem frequency remains significant in this model ($t=-2.37$, $p=0.033$).

In the model with relative frequency and word form frequency, word form frequency is only marginally significant at the point of its elimination ($t=-1.83$, $p=0.09$). At this point, relative frequency is still significant ($t=2.51$, $p=0.023$) and only significant predictors remain in the model (POSITION, SPEECHRATE, NUMPHON, VOICINGRATIO). The direction of the two frequency effects is as predicted by my hypotheses (see 2.6). Higher word form frequency goes together with shorter stem duration (*coefficient*=-0.066, *std. error*=0.036, while higher relative frequency goes together with longer stem durations (*coefficient*=-0.076, *std. error*=0.030).

To address the collinearity issue further, a random forest analysis was conducted (cf. Tomaschek, Hendrix & Baayen 2018) using conditional inference trees [cforest(), R package `party` (Hothorn et al. 2020)]. The results of this analysis are listed in Table 4.6.

Table 4.6: Variables and their importance values in the random forest analyses. Each newly generated random forest has slightly different results, two are shown here. The numbers change slightly with every model, but all-over the ranking is very stable. As here STEMFREQ is ranked higher than RELATIVEFREQ and WORDFORMFREQ, it is a more important predictor.

Variable	Importance	Variable	Importance
WORD	0.0268	WORD	0.0260
EXPWORDDUR	0.0092	EXPWORDDUR	0.0090
STEMFREQ	0.0082	STEMFREQ	0.0079
NEIGHBORDENSITY	0.0047	NEIGHBORDENSITY	0.0046
VOICERATIO	0.0036	NUMPHON	0.0034
NUMPHON	0.0028	VOICERATIO	0.0034
RELATIVEFREQ	0.0028	RELATIVEFREQ	0.0024
WORDFORMFREQ	0.0019	WORDFORMFREQ	0.0019
SPEECHRATE	0.0014	SPEECHRATE	0.0011
POSITION	0.0011	POSITION	0.0010
NEIGHBORFREQ	0.0009	NEIGHBORFREQ	0.0008
LBIGRAMPROB	0.0006	LBIGRAMPROB	0.0003
AGEGROUP	0.0002	AGEGROUP	0.0002
RBIGRAMPROB	-0.0002	RBIGRAMPROB	-0.0003

The random forest analysis showed that bare stem frequency (STEMFREQ) is a more important predictor than relative frequency (RELATIVEFREQ) or word form frequency (WORDFORMFREQ), as STEMFREQ is ranked higher. This supports the conclusions from the analyses presented in the previous paragraphs. Furthermore, bare stem frequency is among the most important predictors, in the same range as the baseline word duration.

4.2.4.4 Controlling for word form frequency: Frequency band analysis

To further disentangle the effects of bare stem frequency and word form frequency, the potentially harmful correlation between bare stem frequency and word form frequency was eliminated by sampling words from a frequency band where there is no correlation between these two frequencies. This also eliminates the danger that the effect of bare stem frequency may be considered as being a hidden word form frequency effect, due to the two being correlated.

This was achieved with the following procedure. Based on the inspection of the distribution of the two frequencies a narrow word form frequency band in the middle of the distribution that had many observations was chosen. Figure 4.3 plots the two variables against each other. The size of the dots reflects the number of observations per word-form, as shown in the legend.

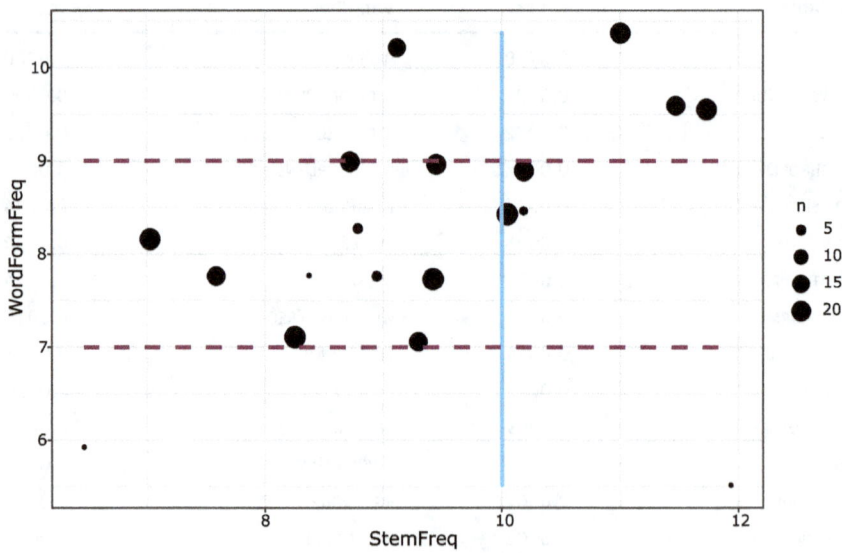

Fig. 4.3: Plural word form frequency by bare stem frequency (dataset 2)

To narrow the range of word form frequency, all observations with log word form frequencies between 7 and 9 were selected, as indicated by the two dotted horizontal lines in Figure 4.3. To reduce the correlation of the two variables the dataset was further restricted by selecting only those observations that had a log bare stem frequency of less than 10 (as indicated by the vertical red line in Figure 4.3). The resulting dataset ('dataset 3') covers the two central quartiles of word form frequency and a few more data points below it (1st quartile: 7.11, median: 7.76, 3rd quartile: 8.62). This reduced dataset still contains 159 observations (as against 295 in dataset 2). The correlation of the three frequency variables in this dataset are given in Table 4.7.

Table 4.7: Correlation matrix for lexical frequency measures in dataset 3 (rho-values, p-values are given in parentheses, Spearman test)

	RelativeFreq	StemFreq
WordFormFreq	0.75 (0.000)	0.02 (0.79)
RelativeFreq		-0.60 (0.000)

In this reduced dataset, bare stem frequency and word form frequency can be safely used in the same model. The final model is documented in Table 4.8.

Table 4.8: Effects of STEMFREQ and WORDFORMFREQ on the duration of plural stems in dataset 3: Fixed-effects coefficients and p-values in the final model. (Significance codes: 0 '***' 0.001 '**' 0.01 '*' 0.05)

Random effects:					
Group	Name	Variance	Std. Dev.		
WORD	(Intercept)	0.0028	0.053		
Residual		0.064	0.25		

Fixed effects					
	Estimate	Std. Error	df	t value	Pr(>|t|)
(Intercept)	-1.92	0.52	5.31	-3.68	0.01
STEMFREQ	-0.10	0.03	4.31	-3.07	0.03
SPEECHRATE	-0.28	0.13	153.95	-2.16	0.03
NUMPHON	0.53	0.10	5.49	5.20	0.00
NEIGHBORDENSITY	0.01	0.01	4.61	2.39	0.07

The model shows a significant effect of bare stem frequency on the duration of the plural stem and no significant effect of word form frequency ($t=1.50$, $p=0.22$ at the point of elimination). The latter was expected due to the narrow range of this variable. The analysis of this subset of data in which word form frequency and bare stem frequency do not correlate thus lends strong support to the hypothesis that low frequency bare stems cause longer durations of paradigm members.

The effect of relative frequency was also tested in this dataset (without also including word form frequency, due to the high correlation of these variables). Relative frequency also had a significant effect on the duration of plural stems: Higher relative frequency goes together with longer duration of the stem. Table 4.9 documents the final model.

Table 4.9: Effect of RELATIVEFREQ on plural stem duration in dataset 3: Fixed-effects coefficients and p-values in the final model. (Significance codes: 0 '***' 0.001 '**' 0.01 '*' 0.05)

Random effects:

Groups	Name	Variance	Std. Dev.
WORD	(Intercept)	0.001542	0.03927
Residual		0.063582	0.25216

Fixed Effects

	Estimate	Std. Error	df	t value	Pr(>|t|)
(Intercept)	-2.19	0.52	5.17	-4.22	0.01
RELATIVEFREQ	0.09	0.02	4.18	3.61	0.02
EXPWORDDUR	0.42	0.21	10.46	2.01	0.07
SPEECHRATE	-0.30	0.13	152.35	-2.32	0.02
NUMPHON	0.51	0.09	4.21	5.44	0.00
NEIGHBOURDENSITY	0.02	0.01	6.93	3.57	0.01

4.2.5 Summary

Using the QuakeBox corpus, I tested for possible effects of categorical and gradient paradigm uniformity, following work on durational effects of paradigm uniformity by Seyfarth et al. (2017). For categorical paradigm uniformity, I found that plural stems are longer than monomorphemic pseudo-stems, but this difference is not significant if other variables are also taken into account by means of statistical modelling.

Regarding gradient paradigm uniformity, there was no evidence for an effect based on Seyfarth et al. (2017)'s idea that greater activation strength of the bare stem leads to a stronger influence on the duration of the morphologically related form. In fact, the QuakeBox study shows the opposite direction of the effects predicted by that approach. The absence of the alleged effect is, however, expected, when taking well-known frequency-related phonetic reduction effects into account – the higher the absolute frequency of the plural word-form, the shorter its duration, and the shorter the duration also of its stem (general reduction effect).

In the larger dataset (dataset 1) there is the predicted effect of word form frequency as a main effect, with no interaction with MORPHEMETYPE. This means that plural words and monomorphemic words are affected by word form frequency in the same way. The subset of the data that only contained the plural forms (dataset 2), did not show a significant word form frequency effect. These two findings together may well be an indication of a lack of statistical power for this rather small dataset.

Due to the lack of statistical power and the somewhat inconclusive results for categorical paradigm uniformity, I attempted to replicate the QuakeBox study using a different corpus, the Buckeye corpus.

4.3 Buckeye corpus study

The QuakeBox study provided promising results for both categorical and gradient paradigm uniformity, and cleared up some misconceptions about these effects that were present in Seyfarth et al. (2017). To provide further evidence for phonetic paradigm uniformity effects, I replicated and expanded the QuakeBox study using another corpus, the Buckeye corpus. The Buckeye corpus (Pitt et al. 2007) was recorded in Columbus, Ohio. It encompasses conversational speech in the form of interviews with 40 different speakers. The data is stratified on age and gender; it contains 20 old (over forty) and 20 young (under 30) speakers, as well as 20 male and 20 female speakers. The recordings were completed in Spring 2000 and subsequently transcribed, aligned and annotated. In total, the corpus contains about 300,000 words and is relatively easy to use for the analysis of duration, as all words are segmented and durational values can easily be extracted.

The dataset provided to me for the QuakeBox corpus was limited to items ending in [s] and [z]. I was not limited to these in the Buckeye corpus, therefore I also separately analyzed items ending in [t] and [d], as Seyfarth et al. (2017) also did in their study. However, like Seyfarth, I did not find any conclusive results for items ending in [t] and [d], which is why these were later disregarded for the production experiment.

4.3.1 Investigation of [s] and [z]

4.3.1.1 Data

Similar to Seyfarth et al. (2017), I investigated the stem duration of monosyllabic words ending in [s] and [z][13]. To investigate these stem durations, I exported a dataset from the Buckeye corpus using the corpus query tool Coquery (Kunter 2017b). This was done by running a query to select all items from the corpus that end in either [z] or [s] in their transcription. In addition to querying data from the Buckeye corpus, I added the English Lexicon Project, short ELP, (Balota et al. 2007) as a reference corpus to this query. The ELP conveniently adds detailed information in the form of additional variables to the dataset, such as for example number of phonemes, number of syllables, number of morphemes, or morphological structure, as well as a variety of frequencies. I also exported frequency information from the Corpus of Contemporary American English (COCA) (Davies 2008) for the words in this dataset. The full list of variables is given in 4.1.3.

The query to select items from the Buckeye corpus ending in [s] and [z] resulted in 32.455 items. These results had to be cleaned and filtered in order to create a dataset that corresponds to my criteria listed in section 4.1.1. To clean up the data from potential problematic items, I excluded all items that were not pronounced canonically. Inspection of the dataset showed that many items were not pronounced canonically, for example very often a word final [z] was devoiced, or eroded completely. In order to have a reliable dataset, I excluded all such items. This was done by comparing the two transcription variables that are provided by the Buckeye corpus using R, the Transcript and the CANONICAL_TRANSCRIPT variable. The QuakeBox corpus data was provided to me in a state that did not require such cleaning, as there, all items were provided as transcribed canonically.

Additional cleaning of the Buckeye dataset was conducted during the generation of the variables. This revealed a lot of items that were annotated incorrectly. Among these were for example all words that are not verbs, nouns or adjectives (e.g. pronouns or function words), and words that are irregularly inflected or unusual in other ways (e.g. *chose, has, his, these, was, whose, close, those*). Additionally, all words with 2 or fewer tokens were excluded, as including (near-)hapaxes[14] in the statistical models could produce correlated errors for word types in a mixed effects regression analysis. After the cleaning process, I created several

---

[13] All files and analyses relating to this subchapter are available in the pertinent subfolder of the repository at https://osf.io/npvx8/?view_only=a1300aa10e0b42aea89557ffeb8bf105
[14] Hapaxes are words that are only attested once within a corpus.

subsets out of the dataset for a thorough analysis into all possible aspects of paradigm uniformity.

The parent datasets were further cleaned by removing outliers after visual inspection of the durational variables, as described in section 4.1.2. Table 4.10 gives an overview of the parent datasets and their subsets that were used for the process of analysis. Datasets beginning with cpu are intended for the analysis of categorical paradigm uniformity, whereas datasets beginning with gpu are intended for the analysis of gradient paradigm uniformity. Datasets ending with _pl contain plural words (and in the case of cpu datasets, monomorphemic nouns), and datasets ending in _3sg contain third person singular words (and in the case of cpu datasets, monomorphemic verbs).

Table 4.10: Overview of the subsets of data used for the [s] and [z] investigation.

Dataset	Description	Types	Tokens
cpu_pl	monosyllabic, monomorphemic nouns and plural words ending in [s] or [z]	95	2072
↳ gpu_pl	↳ subset of cpu_pl with only plural words	60	1043
↳ gpu_pl_freqband	↳ subset of gpu_pl with word form and stem frequency values that do not correlate	20	548
cpu_3sg	monosyllabic, monomorphemic verbs and 3sg words ending in [s] or [z]	32	795
↳ gpu_3sg	↳ subset of only 3sg words	20	477
↳ gpu_3sg_freqband	↳ subset of gpu_3sg with word form and stem frequency values that do not correlate	14	365

4.3.1.2 Variables

The variables used in these datasets have been described in section 4.1.3. Table 4.11 and Table 4.12 give an overview of the descriptive statistics of the variables that are used in cpu_pl and cpu_3sg, respectively.

Table 4.11: Variable information for dataset cpu_pl in the Buckeye corpus, which was used for the analysis of categorical paradigm uniformity in plural forms. Durations, speech rate and frequencies are log-transformed. The gradient paradigm uniformity datasets are a subset of this.

Variable	N	Mean	St. Dev.	Min	Max
Dependent variable					
STEMDURATION	1503	-1.3655	0.344	-2.7029	-0.4132
Numerical variables					
WORDFORMFREQ	95	11.22	1.212	7.277	13.121
STEMFREQ	95	11.57	1.223	6.78	14.02
SPEECHRATE	1609	1.318	0.508	-1.486	2.434
EXPWORDDUR	132	-1.094	0.204	-1.567	0.068
LEFTBIGRAMPROB	592	5.669	3.820	-2.303	11.548
RIGHTBIGRAMPROB	477	4.117	4.410	-2.303	11.206
PHONNEIGHBORDENSITY	36	18.93	9.164	2.00	50.00
Categorical variables					
WORD	95 levels	...			
NUMPHON	4 levels	2: 12; 3: 803; 4: 1129; 5: 128			
SPEAKER	40 levels	...			
AGE	2 levels	old: 1194; young: 878			
GENDER	2 levels	f: 934; m: 1138			
POSITION	11 levels	middle: 1572; beginning: 55; cutoff: 6; disrupted: 158; error: 5; extension: 4; final: 75; hesitation: 1; isolated: 7; laugh: 11; NA: 178			
FINALSOUND	2 levels	s: 1125; z: 947			
MORPHEMETYPE	2 levels	monomorphemic: 1029; plural: 1043			

Table 4.12: Variable information for dataset cpu_3sg in the Buckeye corpus, which was used for the analysis of categorical paradigm uniformity in third person singular forms. Durations, speech rate and frequencies are log-transformed. The gradient paradigm uniformity datasets are a subset of this.

Variable	N	Mean	St. Dev.	Min	Max
Dependent variable					
StemDuration	469	-1.543	0.313	-2.302	-0.711
Numerical variables					
WordFormFreq	32	11.08	0.923	8.223	12.392
StemFreq	32	12.173	1.022	8.223	13.667
SpeechRate	426	1.298	0.446	-1.561	2.137
ExpWordDur	40	-1.153	0.171	-1.737	0.049
LeftBigramProb	170	5.554	4.163	-2.303	10.764
RightBigramProb	210	5.638	.891	-2.303	10.040
PhonNeighborDensity	21	22.61	9.812	8.00	50.00
Categorical variables					
Word	32 levels	...			
NumPhon	4 levels	2: 3; 3: 359; 4: 400; 5: 12			
Age	2 levels	old: 419; young: 355			
Speaker	40 levels	...			
Gender	2 levels	f: 437; m: 337			
Position	7 levels	middle: 665; beginning: 29; cutoff: 5; disrupted: 33; final: 7; isolated: 3; NA: 32			
FinalSound	2 levels	s: 322; z: 452			
MorphemeType	2 levels	monomorphemic: 295; 3sg: 479			

4.3.1.3 Correlations

A number of variables used in the datasets show significant correlations. Therefore, it is necessary to adjust the statistical models accordingly. It is ill-advised to include highly correlated variables into the same statistical models, as this may cause collinearity issues (see section 4.1.2)

Expected durations and number of phonemes

Two variables where correlations are to be expected, are number of phonemes (NUMPHON) and expected word duration (EXPWORDDUR). These variables are similar measures, as they both serve to control for the expected duration of a word – particularly NUMPHON and EXPWORDDUR. The latter was calculated from the average segment duration of all particular segments across the entire corpus (see also 4.1.3). Thus, it is an artificially constructed duration, and therefore doesn't correlate noticeably with any of the other 'real' durations, such as STEMDURATION.

In most subsets, the Pearson correlation of these variables is between 0.40 and 0.60, which is a notable, potentially dangerous correlation. However, in some subsets the correlations are stronger, such as for example in subset cpu_3sg with a Pearson correlation of 0.74.

As NUMPHON and EXPWORDDUR serve the same purpose in a statistical model, these were never included in the same model. Instead, at the beginning of the modelling process I made separate models for these variables, and then determined using an anova() which model is better. Models including NUMPHON were generally better to predict STEMDURATION, therefore I decided to focus on NUMPHON in the modelling process.

Frequencies

Another set of variables that tends to correlate are the different types of frequencies. In this case, the relevant frequencies are log-transformed WORDFORMFREQ and STEMFREQ, which are the word form and the stem frequency from the Corpus of Contemporary American English (COCA), respectively. In the cpu_pl, gpu_pl, cpu_3sg and gpu_3sg subsets, these are highly correlated. Therefore, ideally only one of these frequencies should be included in statistical models. An example of these correlations can be seen in Figure 4.4, which shows the Pearson and Spearman correlations for the dataset gpu_pl in the lower triangle, and a visualization in the upper triangle.

In addition to stem and word form frequencies from the COCA, the dataset also included a local frequency LOCALFREQ. This frequency is the number of times the WORD appears within the Buckeye corpus itself and is thus an additional

WORDFORMFREQ. It correlates with the COCA frequencies, which is encouraging, as this indicates that the Buckeye corpus represents the usage of words in spoken American English well.

The subset gpu_pl also included RELATIVEFREQ, which is calculated by dividing the WORDFORMFREQ and the STEMFREQ. A log-transformed RELATIVEFREQ was not used in the cpu_pl and cpu_3sg datasets (the datasets used to investigate categorical paradigm uniformity), as these include also monomorphemic words, for which the word form and stem frequencies are identical.

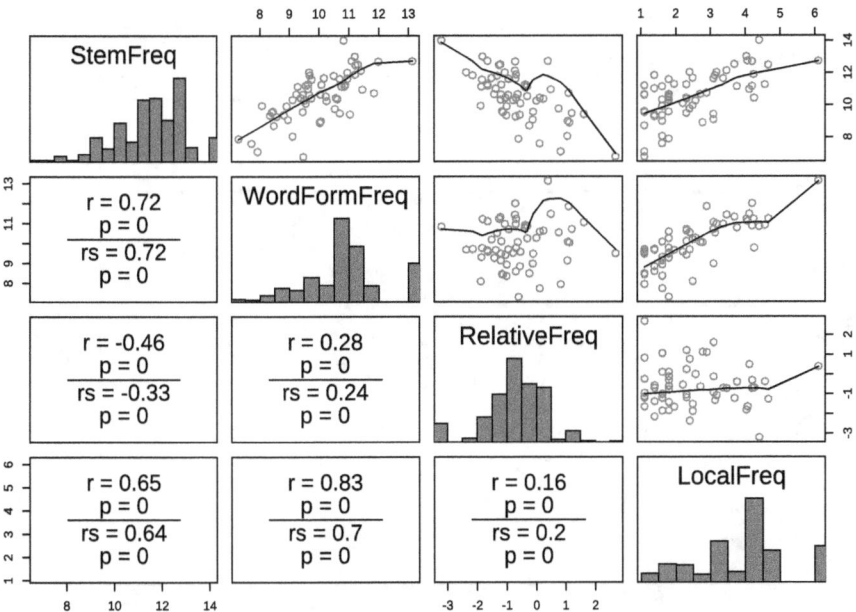

Fig. 4.4: Scatterplot matrix of log transformed COCA frequencies WORDFORMFREQ, STEMFREQ, RELATIVEFREQ, and LOCALFREQ in the subset gpu_pl, with Pearson and Spearman correlations in the lower triangle.

Establishing a frequency band that does not correlate

Due to the nature of my research questions regarding gradient paradigm uniformity, it is necessary to investigate both WORDFORMFREQ and STEMFREQ. However, as these values are highly correlated, they cannot be added to the same statistical model. Therefore, I selected a band from the gpu_pl / gpu_3sg dataset with a high number of observations, in which the frequencies do not correlate. This allowed me to create statistical models in which both frequencies are present, without risking collinearity issues.

The frequency band was selected by visual inspection of the data, as seen in Figure 4.5. Larger dots correspond to a higher number of observations. I selected a band (highlighted by the purple lines) in which there is a high amount of observations, and created a subset gpu_pl_freqband or gpu_3sg_freqband (respective for the plural and the third person singular datasets) from these. Inspection of the resulting subset showed a significant improvement in Pearson and Spearman correlations, as can be seen in Figure 4.6, meaning that the statistical model will be able to more reliably predict STEM DURATION in a model that includes both frequencies.

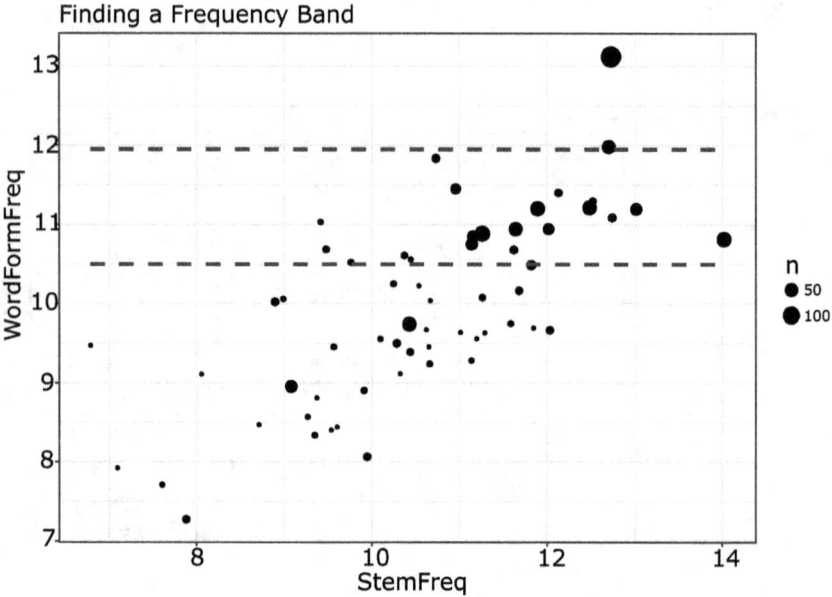

Fig. 4.5: Frequency band without correlation selected from gpu_pl (the selection between the dashed lines would become gpu_pl_freqband). Larger size of the dots corresponds to a higher amount of observations in this range within the dataset.

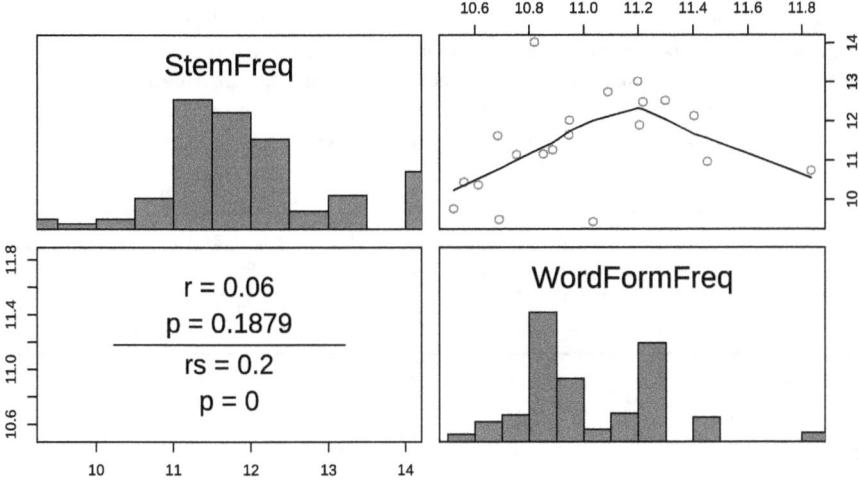

Fig. 4.6: Correlation between stem and word form frequency in the subset gpu_pl_freqband.

4.3.1.4 Results and discussion

To analyze both categorical and gradient paradigm uniformity, I created altogether eight statistical models with STEMDURATION as the predictor variable. These eight models can be further subdivided into four models investigating plural, and four models investigating third person singular, as well as two models investigating categorical paradigm uniformity (with MORPHEMETYPE as dependent variable) and six models investigating gradient paradigm uniformity (with either STEMFREQ or WORDFORMFREQ dependent variables).

Table 4.13 gives an overview of the significant variables in the final model for each dataset, all of which will be discussed in the subsequent sections. From this overview, it becomes immediately apparent that POSITION and SPEECHRATE are highly significant in all models. Other covariates have varying significance in the different models. Rather than going over each of these models individually, I will discuss categorical and gradient paradigm uniformity using examples of these models as a foundation. Detailed model outputs are given only for some exemplary models in the pertinent subchapters. For all model outputs, see the online repository, which is linked in the appendix.

Table 4.13: Significant covariates in the final models for stem duration. Covariates are given in the rows, while the datasets used for the final models are given in the columns. Number of asterisks correspond to significance as reported by the model output (p-value 0 '***'; 0.001 '**'; 0.01 '*'; 0.05 '.'; 0.1 ' ' 1). 'NA' means that this variable was not included or eliminated during the step-analysis, while '*ns*' means that this variable was not eliminated, but is not significant.

	cpu_pl	gpu_pl (STEM FREQ)	gpu_pl (WORD FORM FREQ)	gpu_pl_ freqband	cpu_3sg	gpu_3sg (STEM FREQ)	gpu_3sg (WORD FORM FREQ)	gpu_3sg_ freqband
MORPHEMETYPE	**	NA	NA	NA	NA	NA	NA	NA
WORDFORMFREQ	ns	NA	***	NA	NA	NA	***	**
STEMFREQ	NA	***	NA	*	NA	**	NA	NA
POSITION	***	***	***	***	**	***	***	***
NUMPHON	***	*	*	NA	NA	NA	NA	NA
FINALSOUND	**	NA	*	NA	NA	NA	NA	NA
SPEECHRATE	***	***	***	**	***	***	***	***
LEFTBIGRAMPROB	NA	NA	NA	*	**	NA	NA	NA
RIGHTBIGRAMPROB	*	NA	NA	NA	.	NA	NA	NA
Interaction: MORPHEMETYPE * WORDFORMFREQ	**	NA	NA	NA	NA	NA	NA	NA

4.3.1.4.1 Categorical paradigm uniformity

A categorical paradigm uniformity effect assumes that the stems of complex words differ phonetically from the pseudo-stems of monomorphemic words. I tested for such an effect in the models using the datasets cpu_pl (for plural) and cpu_3sg (for third person singular). Initial models for these datasets included all pertinent covariates, such as MORPHEMETYPE, WORDFORMFREQ, WORDPOSITION, NUMPHON, FINALSOUND, SPEECHRATE, RIGHTBIGRAMPROB, LEFTBIGRAMPROB, PHONNEIGHBORDENSITY, GENDER, as well as SPEAKER and WORD as random effects. Furthermore, an interaction was included between MORPHEMETYPE and WORDFORMFREQ, as it is possible that either complex or simplex words might be more affected by frequency. Using the step() function, the majority of covariates were deemed insignificant by the function and were eliminated. The final model only included covariates that are highlighted in Table 4.13.

Plural

In the final model for plural (Table 4.14), there are significant effects of MORPHEMETYPE, POSITION, NUMPHON, FINALSOUND, SPEECHRATE and RIGHTBIGRAMPROB on the log-transformed STEMDURATION. Most of these effects are to be expected and are well established effects within the literature (cf. 4.1.3).

Table 4.14: Fixed effects coefficients and p-values in the final model testing the categorical paradigm uniformity effect. (Significance codes: 0 '***' 0.001 '**' 0.01 '*' 0.05)

Random effects						
Groups	Name	Variance	St. Dev.			
WORD	(Intercept)	0.02700	0.1643			
SPEAKER	(Intercept)	0.01536	0.2443			
Residual		0.05969	0.2443			
Fixed effects						
	Estimate	Std. Error	df	t value	Pr(>|t|)	
(Intercept)	-1,47E+03	3,40E+02	8,41E+04	-4.331	4.08e-05	***
MORPHEMETYPE plural	9,93E+02	3,66E+02	9,05E+04	2.717	0.00789	**
WORDFORMFREQ	2,25E+01	2,64E+01	8,38E+04	0.852	0.39646	
POSITION beginning	7,05E+01	3,61E+01	1,83E+06	1.952	0.05104	.
POSITION cutoff	-4,78E+02	1,06E+02	1,80E+06	-4.511	6.87e-06	***
POSITION disrupted	1,62E+02	2,80E+01	1,82E+06	5.787	8.44e-09	***
POSITION error	-2,84E+02	1,14E+02	1,77E+06	-2.495	0.01268	*
POSITION extension	1,66E+02	1,31E+02	1,84E+06	1.273	0.20325	
POSITION final	1,84E+02	3,69E+01	1,83E+06	4.994	6.49e-07	***
POSITION hesitation	-2,19E+02	2,58E+02	1,81E+06	-0.849	0.39596	
POSITION isolated	2,37E+02	9,86E+01	1,81E+06	2.404	0.01633	*
POSITION laugh	2,04E+02	8,05E+01	1,83E+06	2.535	0.01133	*
NUMPHON 3	-1,42E+02	1,88E+02	7,73E+04	-0.754	0.45318	
NUMPHON 4	7,48E+00	1,86E+02	7,76E+04	0.040	0.96808	
NUMPHON 5	1,98E+02	1,94E+02	8,02E+04	1.023	0.30951	
FINALSOUND z	1,44E+02	4,90E+01	1,01E+05	2.944	0.00402	**
SPEECHRATE	-7,54E+01	1,31E+01	1,83E+06	-5.765	9.59e-09	***
RIGHTBIGRAMPROB	-5,07E+00	2,14E+00	1,80E+06	-2.376	0.01759	*
MORPHEMETYPE plural: WORDFORMFREQ	-9,99E+01	3,43E+01	8,75E+04	-2.909	0.00460	**

The significant difference between monomorphemic and plural words ($p = 0.0041257$) indicates a categorical paradigm uniformity effect in the final model. While MORPHEMETYPE shows a significant effect on the stem duration, there is also a significant interaction between MORPHEMETYPE and WORDFORMFREQ, which illustrates that monomorphemic and plural words behave differently depending on their word form frequency, as illustrated in Figure 4.7.

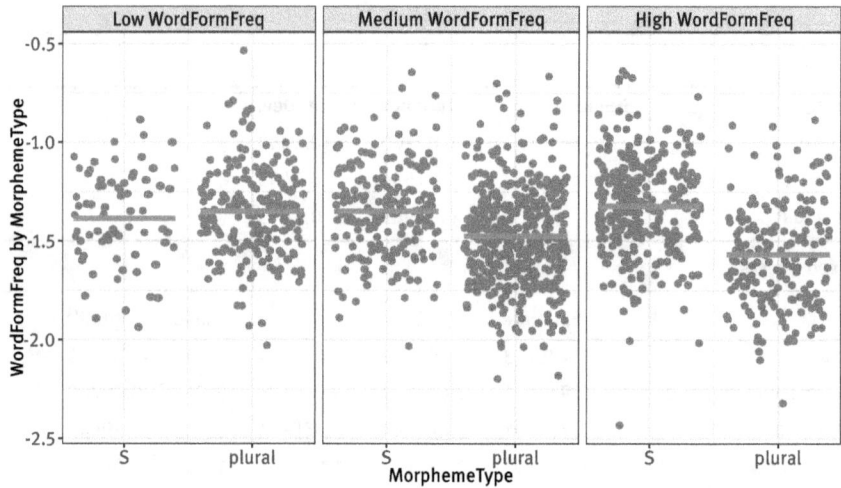

Fig. 4.7: Interaction between MORPHEMETYPE and WORDFORMFREQ in the final model for cpu_pl. In the low frequency quantile, monomorphemic and complex words behave similarly. In the medium and high frequency quantiles, it becomes apparent that the higher the frequency of the plural, the shorter the duration of the plural stem. All frequencies are log-transformed.

Figure 4.7 shows that the higher the word form frequency, the longer the duration of the monomorphemic pseudo-stem, whereas the higher the word form frequency, the shorter the duration of the plural stem. The latter is to be expected, as higher word form frequency goes hand in hand with shorter durations all over. However, it is not obvious as to why the durations of the monomorphemic pseudo-stems would become longer with higher word frequency, as here, also, we should expect a shortening effect instead.

It is possible that a frequency effect arises due to the specific items in this dataset – the dataset contains two very high frequent items, *place* (n= 324) and *house* (n = 134). These generally occur more often in final word position or before pauses, which may explain this trend. However, when removing these words from the dataset, the effect remains, therefore despite the uneven type-token ratio, these do not skew the results. Generally, the type-token ratio in this dataset is far from optimal, even despite attempts at controlling for this (e.g. by including only items that have at least 3 observations). This is one of the issues that often arise when using corpus data.

Third person singular
The model investigating stem duration for third person singular did neither show a significant effect of MORPHEMETYPE, nor an interaction between MorphemeType and WORDFORMFREQ, as both terms were eliminated by the step() function. In the final model for stem duration, only POSITION, speech rate and both bigram frequencies remained. Word position and speech rate were the strongest predictors in all models, so it is not surprising that these show the most significant effect on the stem duration.

The absence of MORPHEMETYPE indicates that there is no categorical paradigm uniformity effect for third person singular, as the type of morpheme does not have an influence on the stem duration - the model does not predict any significant durational differences between third person singular or monomorphemic stems.

A possible problem with this model is that the predictive power of the model is questionable. The residuals of the models are not optimal, even when trimmed to be between -2 and 2 standard deviations. This applies to almost all models for third person singular, and thus indicates a general problem with the dataset. A dataset that is very skewed due to a non-optimal type token ratio, a very small number of types, and overrepresentation of certain items or categories in covariates simply cannot produce reliable results. Pruning the dataset to be more balanced would remove too many items, thus the dataset would lose even more statistical power.

4.3.1.4.2 Gradient paradigm uniformity
I expect a gradient paradigm uniformity effect with higher frequency of the bare stem, and shorter duration of its related inflected stem. For example, the frequency of *day* should affect its related plural form *days*, if it has a very high frequent bare stem and is thus subject to phonetic reduction. On the other hand, if a word has a very low frequency bare stem, this should cause longer durations on its paradigm members. These differences should be significant even when taking into account general frequency effects (i.e. word form frequency) of the plural form itself, for example if *days* is already a high frequent word, it should be even shorter if *day* is also very high frequent, or vice versa.

The process for testing for such a gradient paradigm uniformity effect was very similar to that described for categorical paradigm uniformity. Using the datasets gpu_pl (for plural) and gpu_3sg (for third person singular), I created initial models including all pertinent covariates, such as STEMFREQ, POSITION, NUMPHON, FINALSOUND, SPEECHRATE, RIGHTBIGRAMPROB, LEFTBIGRAMPROB, PHONNEIGHBORDENSITY, GENDER, as well as SPEAKER and WORD as random effects. Furthermore, I created separate models using WORDFORMFREQ and RELATIVEFREQ as predictors. Using the step() function for these models, the majority of covariates were deemed insignificant by the function and were eliminated. The final models only included covariates that are highlighted in Table 4.13 under the columns which names begin with gpu_.

In addition to these models, I also created models using the datasets gpu_pl_freqband and gpu_3sg_freqband. These subsets only include a narrow frequency band in which the stem frequency and the word form frequency do not correlate. This allowed me to include both STEMFREQ and WORDFORMFREQ in the same model, thus testing for a gradient paradigm uniformity effect.

Plural

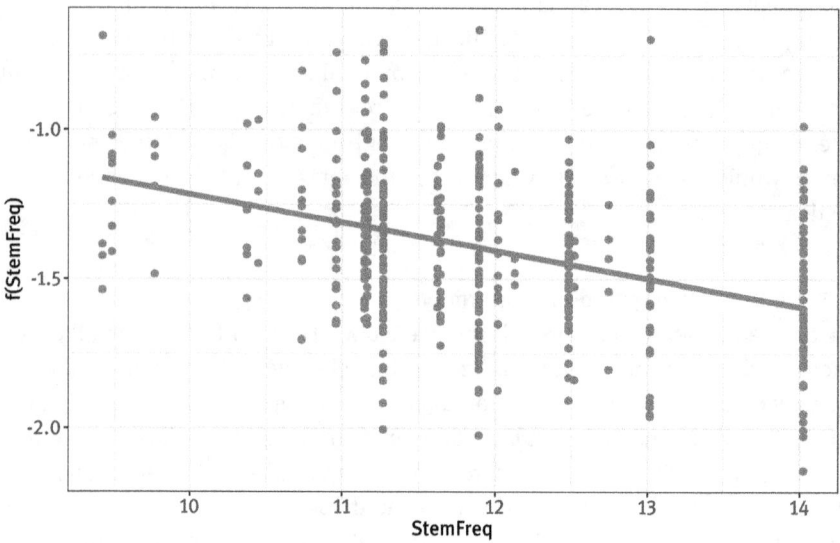

Fig. 4.8: Effect of STEMFREQ on the duration of the plural stem in the dataset gpu_pl_freqband. The higher the frequency of the stem (e.g. *day*), the shorter the duration of the stem of a plural form (e.g. *days*).

Stem frequency has a significant effect on stem duration ($p > 0.01$) in the model using stem frequency as the main predictor; plural stems are shorter if bare stem frequency is higher, as shown in Figure 4.8. Similarly, word form frequency also has a significant effect on stem duration ($p < 0.0001$) in the expected direction in the model using word form frequency as the main predictor. This provides solid evidence for a gradient paradigm uniformity effect for plural. The model using the decorrelated frequency is very similar, though here the effect of bare stem frequency is not as strong, and the word form frequency was eliminated by the step() function. Other remaining covariates behave as expected, and the models for vowel duration are very similar.

Altogether, these models provide solid evidence for a gradient paradigm uniformity effect for plural nouns, as the models have shown that the higher the frequency of a stem, the shorter the duration of the plural form.

Third person singular

Similar to categorical paradigm uniformity, the models for gradient paradigm uniformity for third person singular are not as straightforward to interpret as those for plural. The models using stem frequency and word form frequency as predictors are nearly identical to those for plural. Also, in the frequency band analysis, the stem frequency was eliminated. While are some indications for a gradient paradigm uniformity effect here, these do not hold up in the frequency band analysis, and thus is can be concluded that the effect found here is likely a masked word form frequency effect. Further doubt is cast by the varying nature of the other models using gpu_ datasets (see also the overview in Table 4.13). The datasets are relatively small (477 items in gpu_3sg and 365 items in gpu_3sg_freqband). In addition, similar to the models for third person singular categorical paradigm uniformity, the models for gradient paradigm also suffer from suboptimal residuals. This may indicate that the predictive power of the models is not strong enough, and thus one cannot trust the results generally.

To address the problem of the residuals, I rebalanced the dataset by creating a third person singular subset that only included representations of four vowels; ey, ih, iy, and ow. The distribution of vowels among morpheme types was very unbalanced in the third person singular datasets, thus making it akin to comparing apples with oranges (see Table 4.15).

Table 4.15: Distribution of stem vowels in the dataset cpu_3sg.

	ah	ay	eh	er	ey	ih	iy	ow	uh	uw
monomorphemic	0	0	0	0	75	22	19	16	0	163
3sg	10	31	16	71	122	12	43	120	54	0

Using this new subset containing only the four vowels that are represented for both monomorphemic and third person singular, I ran the step() function on the initial models again. The results were fairly similar to the models for the parent dataset, and the residuals did not improve significantly in this rebalanced dataset. The problem causing the skewed residuals may lie elsewhere, and as elaborated at the beginning of this chapter, using corpus data is always risky and bears a multitude of problems. To summarize, I did not find evidence for a gradient paradigm uniformity effect for third person singular items in either dataset.

4.3.2 Investigation of [t] and [d]

Previous studies on words ending in [t] and [d] have found very mixed results for the existence of a paradigm uniformity effect, as was also the case in Seyfarth et al. (2017), who found a null result. Based on such previous findings, it is unlikely that paradigm uniformity appears in words ending in [t] and [d]. An additional complication is the fact that there is a much smaller amount of suitable words for [t] and [d] in the English lexicon, raising concerns about statistical power. For comparison, my Buckeye dataset for categorical paradigm uniformity in [s] and [z] had 2076 tokens, while the dataset for [t] and [d] had only 776 tokens. Subsets for gradient paradigm uniformity were even smaller. However, as part of my replication of Seyfarth et al. (2017), I also included [t] and [d] in my Buckeye corpus study[15], and will compare my results to theirs.

My analysis of [t] and [d] was created and performed according to the same procedures as the analysis of [s] and [z], thus only the notable differences will be described in this subsection. To investigate paradigm uniformity in words ending in [t] and [d], I exported a dataset from the Buckeye corpus using the corpus query tool Coquery (Kunter 2017b), similar to how I exported the dataset of words ending in [s] and [z] (see 4.3.1 for details). The dataset was processed and cleaned to

---

[15] All files and analyses relating to this subchapter are available in the pertinent subfolder at https://osf.io/npvx8/?view_only=a1300aa10e0b42aea89557ffeb8bf105

contain only monosyllabic verbs that are either past tense or monomorphemic ending in [t] or [d]. Other parts of speech (such as ornative or adjectives) did not appear in usable amounts as there were only about 20 adjective tokens in the dataset before the cleaning process, which is not enough for a statistical analysis.

4.3.2.1 Data

Similar to the process in the analysis of [s] and [z], I also created several datasets for [t] and [d], an overview of which is given in Table 4.16. These datasets had a considerably smaller number of types and tokens than those for [s] and [z].

Table 4.16: Overview of the subsets of data used for the [t] and [d] investigation.

Datasets	Descriptions	Types	Tokens
cpu_past	monosyllabic, monomorphemic verbs and past tense words ending in [t] or [d]	60	776
↳ gpu_past	↳ subset of cpu_past with only past tense words	36	414
↳ gpu_past_freqband	↳ subset of gpu_past with word form and stem frequency values that do not correlate	18	215

4.3.2.2 Variables

The variables used in the dataset are identical to those in the [s] and [z] analysis and are described in detail in subchapter 4.1.3 in detail. Table 4.17 gives an overview of the descriptive statistics of the variables that are used in cpu_past.

Table 4.17: Variable information for dataset cpu_past in the Buckeye corpus, which was used for the analysis of categorical paradigm uniformity in past tense forms. Durations, speech rate and frequencies are log-transformed. The gradient paradigm uniformity datasets are a subset of this.

Variable	N	Mean	St. Dev.	Min	Max
Dependent variable					
STEMDURATION	742	-1.484	0.350	-2.411	-0.673
Numerical variables					
WORDFORMFREQ	60	11.141	1.193	7.639	13.223
STEMFREQ	60	11.644	1.266	7.883	13.667
SPEECHRATE	775	1.301	0.506	-1.230	2.198

Variable	N	Mean	St. Dev.	Min	Max
ExpWordDur	2072	-1.150	0.223	-1.573	0.036
LeftBigramProb	276	4.210	4.638	-2.303	12.172
RightBigramProb	302	5.391	4.273	-2.303	12.301
PhonNeighborDensity	27	18.581	10.092	3.00	49.00

Categorical variables		
Word	60 levels	
NumPhon	3 levels	3: 214; 4: 461; 5: 101
Speaker	40 levels	
Age	2 levels	old: 466; young: 310
Gender	2 levels	f: 385; m: 391
Position	9 levels	middle: 650; beginning: 21; cutoff: 2; disrupted: 30; error: 1; final: 61; isolated: 2; laugh: 5
FinalSound	2 levels	t: 469; d: 307
MorphemeType	2 levels	monomorphemic: 362; plural: 414

4.3.2.3 Correlations

Correlations are comparable to the correlations in the [s] and [z] datasets. Word form frequency and stem frequency are highly correlated. As elaborated in section 4.3.1.3, it is ill-advised to create statistical models in which correlated variables appear together. However, in order to investigate my research questions, both the effects of word form and stem frequency are important, and to allow using both in the same dataset, I also created a frequency band dataset that does not correlate for the analysis of [t] and [d], similar to that for [s] and [z].

Establishing a frequency band that does not correlate

The frequency band was selected by visual inspection of the data, as seen in Figure 4.9. Larger dots correspond to a higher number of observations. I selected a band between the horizontal and the vertical lines in which there are a high amount of observations, and created a subset gpu_past_freqband from these. Inspection of the resulting subset showed lower values for Pearson and Spearman correlations, as can be seen in Figure 4.10, which allow both frequencies to be used in the same model without risk of collinearity.

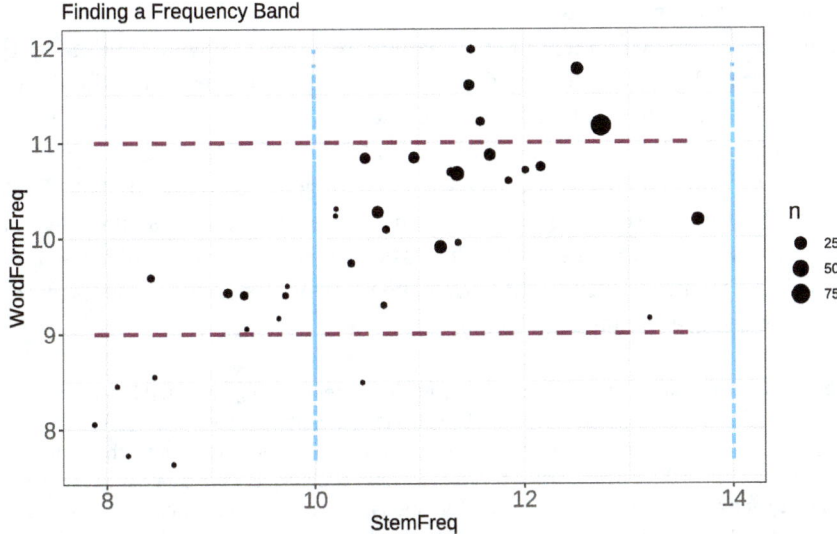

Fig. 4.9: Frequency band without correlation selected from gpu_past (this selection would become gpu_past_freqband). Larger size of the dots corresponds to a higher amount of observations in this range within the dataset.

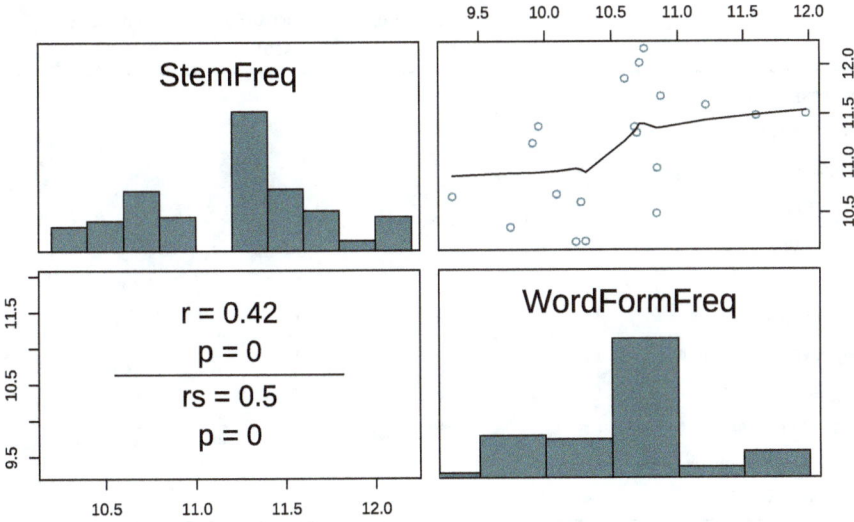

Fig. 4.10: Correlation between stem and word form frequency in the subset gpu_past_freqband.

4.3.2.4 Results and discussion

To analyze categorical and gradient paradigm uniformity in words ending in [t] or [d], I created four statistical models. Table 4.18 gives an overview of the significant variables in the final model for each dataset. From these overviews, it becomes immediately apparent that RIGHTBIGRAMPROB is the strongest predictor in all models, while for most models also LEFTBIGRAMPROB, POSITION and SPEECHRATE are significant to various degrees. Other covariates have varying significance in the different models. Similar to the discussion of [s] and [z], I will discuss categorical and gradient paradigm uniformity using examples of these models rather than discussing every model in detail.

Table 4.18: Significant variables for past tense models after applying the step() functions. These models predict STEMDURATION using the subsets cpu_past, gpu_past and gpu_past_freqband. Covariates are given in the rows, while the datasets used for the final models are given in the columns. Note that for gpu_past two models were created, one for stem frequency and one for word form frequency. Durations, speech rate and frequencies were log-transformed. Number of asterisks correspond to significance as reported by the model output (p-value 0 '***'; 0.001 '**'; 0.01 '*'; 0.05 '.': 0.1 ' ' 1). 'NA' means that this variable was not included or eliminated during the step-analysis, while '*ns*' means that this variable was not eliminated, but is not significant by itself.

	cpu_past	gpu_past (STEMFREQ)	gpu_past (WORDFORM FREQ)	gpu_past_ freqband
MORPHEMETYPE	**	NA	NA	NA
WORDFORMFREQ	**	NA	NA	NA
STEMFREQ	NA	*	NA	NA
POSITION	***	*	*	NA
NUMPHON	***	NA	NA	NA
FINALSOUND	.	NA	NA	NA
SPEECHRATE	***	**	**	NA
PHONNEIGHBORDENSITY	NA	NA	NA	NA
LEFTBIGRAMPROB	***	**	**	NA
RIGHTBIGRAMPROB	*	***	***	***
Interaction: MORPHEMETYPE * WORDFORMFREQ	*	NA	NA	NA

Detailed model outputs for all models are given in the online repository, which is linked in the appendix.

4.3.2.4.1 Categorical paradigm uniformity

In this analysis, I tested for a categorical paradigm uniformity effect using the dataset cpu_past. The initial model included all pertinent covariates (MorphemeType, WordFormFreq, Position, NumPhon, FinalSound, SpeechRate, RightBigramFreq, LeftBigramProb, PhonNeighborDensity, Gender, as well as Speaker and Word as random effects). Additionally, interactions were included between MorphemeType and WordFormFreq, as well as between MorphemeType and FinalSound. Using the step() function, the majority of covariates were deemed insignificant by the function and were eliminated. The final model only included the covariates that are highlighted in Table 4.18. As the residuals of the final model were not within expected boundaries, the residuals were trimmed to include only data points with a standard deviation of no higher than 2. All values given are for the trimmed model.

In the final, trimmed model, there are significant effects of MorphemeType, WordFormFreq, Position, NumPhon, SpeechRate, LeftBigramProb and RightBigramProb on the StemDuration, as well as a near-significant effect of FinalSound. However, MorphemeType only became significant (from near-significant) after trimming the residuals.

Most of these effects are to be expected and are well established effects within the literature (cf. 4.1.3). The significant difference between monomorphemic and plural words ($p > 0.01$) indicates a categorical paradigm uniformity effect. However, there is also a significant interaction between MorphemeType and WordFormFreq, which illustrates that monomorphemic and past words behave slightly differently depending on their word form frequency, as illustrated in Figure 4.11. When looking at the figure, the reason for this interaction becomes apparent – there are no high frequency past tense words in this dataset. This explains the seemingly strange effect, and highlights that this dataset is not particularly balanced and does not have sufficient statistical power. From the figure, it can be generally concluded that low word form frequency goes together with longer durations.

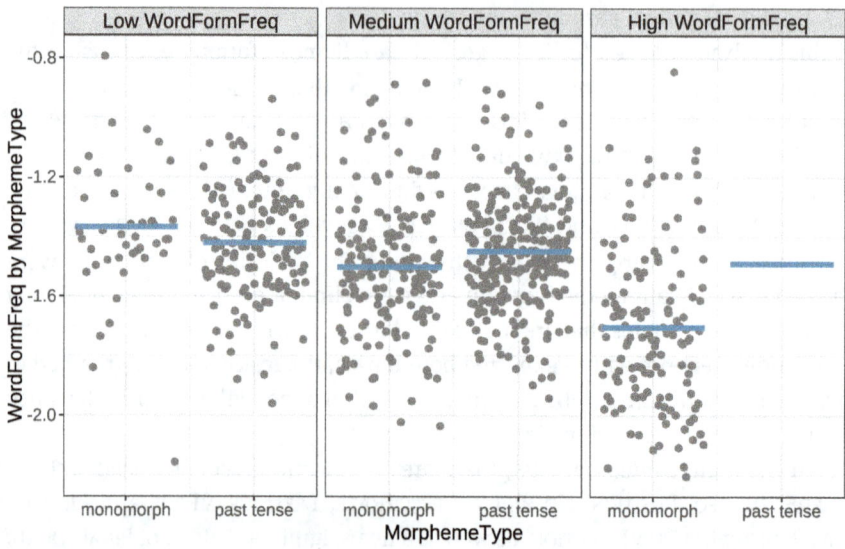

Fig. 4.11: Interaction between MORPHEMETYPE and WORDFORMFREQ in the model for cpu_past. In the low frequency quantile, monomorphemic and complex words behave similarly, but there are only few datapoint for monomorphemic words. In the mid-frequency quantile, past tense words are longer than monomorphemic words. The high frequency quantile does not have data points for past tense words, so no comparison is possible. All frequencies are log-transformed.

To summarize, the model predicts a significant difference between STEMDURATION and MORPHEMETYPE, and thus would indicate that there appears to be a categorical paradigm uniformity effect for past tense words. However, the dataset is skewed and does not contain high frequency past tense words, making the interpretation of an effect of word form frequency problematic. To address this issue, I created an additional dataset without high frequency monomorphemic words ($n = 538$). In this model, MORPHEMETYPE was not significant, indicating that a categorical paradigm uniformity effect for past tense items does not exist in this dataset.

4.3.2.4.2 Gradient paradigm uniformity

In gradient paradigm uniformity, I expect that the stem of a complex word is shorter the higher the frequency of the bare stem. In my model examining gradient paradigm uniformity using stem frequency as main predictor, this is the case; stems are significantly shorter the higher the stem frequency ($p > 0.05$). However, unlike in the models for [s] and [z], here in the model using word form frequency as the main predictor (the model testing a general frequency effect), word form frequency was eliminated in the step-process. This appears to be consistent with the results for categorical paradigm uniformity, where we saw in the interaction between word form frequency and morpheme type that the past tense words do not show a paradigm uniformity effect – however, as Figure 4.11 showed, the dataset is unbalanced. This could be a possible explanation for the null result of any kind of frequency in the model using gpu_past_freqband (model using a frequency band that does not correlate). In this model, both frequencies were eliminated in the step process, and RIGHTBIGRAMPROB remained as the only significant predictor.

Altogether, these models do not provide any solid or reliable evidence for a gradient paradigm uniformity effect. While the model using the dataset gpu_past with stem frequency as the main predictor shows a significant effect of stem frequency on the duration of the stem, there are problems with the frequencies being unbalanced in this dataset, and this effect does also not persist in the model using an uncorrelated frequency band. Therefore, I conclude that the status of paradigm uniformity in words ending in [t] or [d] is unclear and while further research might provide clearer results, past research has already shown that words ending in [t] and [d] generally do not seem to show the same kind of effects that can be seen on words ending in [s] and [z] (see chapter 2.3 for an overview of past studies).

4.3.3 Summary

The Buckeye corpus study provides some evidence for both a categorical and a gradient paradigm uniformity effect in plural words. However, no conclusive evidence was found for third person singular words or past tense words. This may be due to the comparatively small datasets (the plural dataset had 2072 items, while the third person singular dataset had 795 items and the past tense dataset 776 items, or 538 after removing high frequency monomorphemic words). It is possible that datasets on the smaller side simply do not have enough statistical power and are too unbalanced to reliably investigate an effect of paradigm uniformity. Therefore, further research using different corpora and using experimental data, as showcased in the upcoming chapters, might provide more clarity.

4.4 Summary and comparison of QuakeBox and Buckeye results

Both corpus studies have delivered somewhat similar results, however there are also notable differences. Some inconclusive evidence for a categorical paradigm uniformity effects was found only in the Buckeye corpus study for plural and for past tense, but not for third person singular, and not at all in the QuakeBox data. A gradient paradigm uniformity effect was present for plural in both corpora, but not for third person singular or past tense, which were only investigated using Buckeye data. An overview of the presence or absence of paradigm uniformity effects is given in Table 4.19.

Table 4.19: Overview of the presence or absence of paradigm uniformity in the different corpora and different datasets, with number of items in the final statistical model given. For gradient paradigm uniformity, models with stem frequency, word form frequency (general frequency effect) and both (with a non-correlating frequency band) were created, therefore all three are listed in separate columns for each.

	Categorical Paradigm Uniformity Effect	Gradient Paradigm Uniformity Effect		General frequency effect (WORDFORMFREQ)
		STEMFREQ	Freq. band	
QuakeBox: plural [z]	absent (n=422)	present (n=287)	present (n=159)	absent (n=287)
Buckeye: plural [s] and [z]	unclear (n=1894)	present (n=949)	present (n=503)	present (n=949)
Buckeye: 3sg [s] and [z]	absent (n=742)	present (n=452)	absent (n=348)	present (n=452)
Buckeye: past tense [t] and [d]	absent (n=729)	present (n=414)	absent (n=215)	absent (n=414)

A comparison between the QuakeBox and Buckeye study has to be done with caution, as there are a number of differences between the two datasets. As an example, a notable difference is in the structure of the variable for speaker age, which in the Buckeye corpus is simply listed as a binary variable (young or old), but in the QuakeBox consists of several continuous numerical values corresponding to age brackets. Additionally, the QuakeBox dataset contained a variable for voicing ratio, which the Buckeye dataset did not contain. It is uncertain to what degree these covariates might have influenced the presence or absence of paradigm uniformity in the final models.

While plural words seem to be the most promising environment to enable phonetic paradigm uniformity, the corpus studies have found incongruent evidence for categorical as well as gradient paradigm uniformity effects within my datasets. These unclear results are possibly due to the unreliable and unbalanced nature of corpus data. An example of this can be seen in the dataset for past tense items, which does not contain high frequency past tense items. Balance can only be brought into data that was tailored to a specific research question – which is why the production experiment described in the next chapter is an ideal complement to the corpus studies.

5 Production experiment

A major factor of the ongoing replication crisis (see 2.1) is that most research focuses on only one type of method. Most published papers deal with either experimental data (33% of papers in a survey from 2020) or corpus data (18%), while only 5% of journal articles used multi-method approaches (Martínez 2020)[16]. Single-method approaches are often subject to the 'from-corpus-to-cognition fallacy' (Kortmann 2021), meaning that linguists generally do not put significant effort into testing the cognitive reality of corpora. Therefore, it is generally recommended to confirm corpus findings with experimental data. Both corpora and experiments come with numerous advantages and disadvantages that pose some risks to drawing definite conclusions from research performed using theses approaches, which is why it is recommended to use a multi-method approach in research.

As such, the purpose of performing the production experiment was to further investigate the phonetics of inflectional stems in a carefully controlled environment. The previously performed corpus studies delivered some promising results for my hypotheses, but are prone to a number of problems due to the noisy nature of corpus data. Experiments, on the other hand, allow for a much cleaner and more streamlined dataset that is tailored to my purposes. Since the corpus studies have proven that there are indeed differences in the duration of inflectional vs. pseudo-stems, my intent with the production experiment was to confirm these effects with experimental data.

Similar to how there are advantages and disadvantages to using corpus data, there are a certain number of advantages and disadvantages to working with experimental data. In the case of production experiments, the most notable disadvantage is the time required for annotation and segmentation. While there are scripts that can be used to make the process easier, those usually caused some errors in my attempts of using them. Ideally, experimental data should be annotated and segmented manually, as this is the method guaranteeing the best possible outcome with the least amount of errors, but it is also a very time-consuming method.

Another disadvantage of performing experiments goes directly hand in hand with their biggest advantage: since experiments are tailored to a specific research question, they always also have a risk of not reflecting natural speech due to the

---

16 Other methods listed by Martínez (2020) included questionnaires, observations, or ethnographic data collection. See also Tables 3-6 in Martínez (2020).

constructed nature of carrier sentences. Simple carrier sentences such as "John said X again" (where X is the target word) do not occur often in natural speech, and reading out these sentences also turns the experiments into a monotonous task for participants. To avoid the monotony and the unnaturalness of this, I decided to use a more creative approach, a cloze task, in my production experiment, as described in chapter 5.1.

Experiments also come with a number of advantages, most importantly that they can be specifically tailored to investigate a particular research question. In the case of the investigation of the phonetics of inflectional stems, this can be accomplished by embedding the target word into a carrier sentence and then recording a native speaker reading or reciting this sentence. This ensures that the target word is always in the same position, and that there is no unusual intonation by the speaker.

Another advantage, especially for production experiments in which speech is recorded at a phonetics lab, is that the sound quality can be controlled and optimized. If participants were to record their tasks at home, for example, they could at any time be disrupted by family members, pets, doorbells or phones, etc., and the sound quality is likely to be less than ideal.

Experiments allow for a certain degree of flexibility in their methodological design, which can be advantageous to investigate the same hypothesis from a different angle. For example, while in the corpus studies I compared words of type A (monomorphemic) to words of type B (morphologically complex words), in the experiment I used homophone word pairs. Homophones are well suited to investigate paradigm uniformity, as they allow for a direct comparison of phonetically identical words, such as for example *days* vs. *daze*. Furthermore, to investigate gradient paradigm uniformity, I also decided to include the bare stem into my selection of items. This allowed me to compare not only the stem of the complex word to a phonetically identical monomorphemic word, but also to a paradigm member. Since one of my hypotheses states that paradigm members influence other members of a paradigm, this direct comparison of durations of triplets such as *day-days-daze* will allow me to investigate the two different types of paradigm uniformity (categorical and gradient) – with *days* and *daze* concerning categorical paradigm uniformity, and *day* and *days* concerning gradient paradigm uniformity.

To summarize, the production experiment was designed to replicate and expand upon the corpus studies that I performed while also addressing the numerous problems that I encountered while working with corpus data. Experiments can address some of the problems that arise when working with corpus data by establishing carefully controlled circumstances and item choices. My primary aim in the selection of items for my production experiment was to find homophonous words that are spread over a number of different frequency constellations, as explained in 4.1.1. These allow me to investigate categorical and gradient paradigm uniformity conveniently and simultaneously, as the homophones can be used to directly compare monomorphemic to morphologically complex words, and the different frequency constellations allow me to see how, for example, a low frequency bare stem affects a high frequency complex stem. For convenience, the research questions are repeated here:

Research questions
I. Categorical paradigm uniformity
   a) Are morphologically complex words like *days* longer or shorter in duration than monomorphemic homophones like *daze*?
II. Gradient paradigm uniformity
   a) How does the frequency of a bare stem affect its paradigm members (e.g. how does the frequency of *day* affect *days*)?
   b) Do low frequency bare stems cause longer durations of paradigm members? Vice versa, do high frequency bare stems cause shorter durations?

To investigate these research questions, I developed a production experiment that elicits speech data through a cloze task emulating natural speech. The design process of this experiment will be described in detail in the following methodology subsections.

5.1 Methodology

5.1.1 Experimental design for elicitation of speech data

After evaluating a number of different methods for the elicitation of speech data (such as for example the often-used simple carrier sentence "John said ___ again"), I decided to use a cloze task in which the beginning and ending of a sentence are given to the participants, but they have to fill in the gap with the two to five provided words in the correct order. While this task still bears some minor risks, such as the possibility that participants will change the form (tense, number) of the target item despite being instructed to not do so, it has the advantages that it attempts to emulate natural speech as much as possible while also keeping the participants engaged in the task. This type of task creates a controlled environment, in which the target item will ideally always be uttered as intended, while not creating an extensive amount of hypercorrection, as might be the case in simple carrier sentences.

"The mailman_____into the postbox."

Fig. 5.1: Example for a cloze task from the production experiment. This item is an example used for demonstration purposes that does not include any of the target items.

The task was embedded into a narrative "The jumbled suitcase" acting as instructions. In this narrative, the participant has lost their suitcase, and when it is returned to them, the words are all jumbled up and they are asked to put them into the correct order. An example of this can be seen in Figure 5.1.

5.1.2 Selection of items

For the experiments, I needed simplex-complex homophonous words pairs plus the bare stem of the complex words, resulting in triplets such as for example *day-days-daze*. These allowed me to investigate both categorical and gradient paradigm uniformity while also addressing the numerous problems that I encountered in my corpus studies. To find such triplets, I established a number of strict criteria for the selection of my target items. The first three of these criteria are identical to those used for the corpus studies, and are explained in detail in section 4.1.1. For the experiments, I added another three criteria, the purpose of which is to balance the unevenness that I encountered in the corpus data. I am summarizing all six criteria here, and will then explain criteria 4, 5 and 6 in detail.

Criteria for selection of target items
Criterion 1: they are either monomorphemic or morphologically complex (plural, third person singular or past tense)
Criterion 2: they end in /s/, /z/, or /t/, /d/17
Criterion 3: they are monosyllabic
Criterion 4: words have homophones in the other category (i.e. a simplex word has a complex homophone)
Criterion 5: words are not multiple homophones and have transparent word form frequency
Criterion 6: bare stems/complex/monomorphemic words fall into specific frequency constellations

Criterion 4: Words are homophones
Seyfarth et al. (2017) used homophone simplex-complex word pairs. For the corpus studies, this was not viable, as it was not possible to find many of these types of word pairs in the corpora I used. However, in my experiments, I based my choice of items on Seyfarth's by using simplex-complex homophone word pairs, as they allow a direct comparison of monomorphemic and complex words. Homophones have the advantage that they have the exact same phonological form, therefore it is very easy to establish whether morphologically complex homophones differ from their monomorphemic counterparts – for example whether *days* differs phonetically from *daze*.

Criterion 5: No multiple homophones
A problem with some of the homophone word pairs was that these were actually multiple homophones. One such example is *rows* and *rose*. In the case of *rows*, this word can either be a third person singular form of the verb *row*, or a plural form of the noun *row*. To further complicate matters, in the case of *rose*, this can either be the noun *rose* (flower), or the irregular past tense form of *rise*. Similarly, some words related to these homophones also occur as proper nouns, such as for example the base of *rays*, which may occur as the male name *Ray*. Such cases of multiple homophony were omitted, and only homophones that do not have any further homophones were kept in the dataset. Seyfarth et al. (2017)'s study did not include any words that were subject to ambiguous homophony, therefore it is sensible to also exclude these in my replication.

---
17 I investigated [t] and [d] only in the Buckeye corpus study.

To eliminate multiple homophones, I extracted frequency values from the web interface of the Corpus of Contemporary American English (COCA) (Davies 2008), for the grammatically tagged word form (e.g. *rows* as 3sg), as well as the frequencies for all pertinent strings, irrespective of their grammatical status as reflected by the syntactic tagging. I will call this frequency 'raw frequency'. I then calculated a ratio of word form and raw frequency, and log-transformed the result. I excluded all homophones from my list that had a ratio of lower than 0.9. The closer this frequency value was to 1.0, the better suited the item, as it is not subject to multiple homophony. On the other hand, the closer it is to zero, the more unreliable this item is, as this is evidence that this word is subject to conversion or can have multiple meanings across different parts of speech. Two examples of this are given in Table 5.1:

Table 5.1: Example frequencies and frequency ratios for potential target items

Word	POS	Triplet	Word Form Freq	Raw Freq	Freq Ratio
days	NNS	day-days-daze	209879	209941	0.9997
rose	NN	row-rows-rose	19538	69707	0.2802

In these examples we can see that *days* has a frequency ratio of almost 1, therefore it is an ideal candidate indicating that *days* occurs in its plural form most frequently. On the other hand, *rose* as a singular noun has a frequency ratio of 0.28, indicating that this word is used in some cases in a form that is not singular (but rather, its homophone, the irregular past tense of *rise*), making it a potentially problematic target item.

This process ensured that the frequency values for the word forms are more reliable, and that forms with multiple homophony or conversion pairs do not cause significant problems. By excluding words that have a low frequency ratio, I ensured that the selected items are optimally suitable for the investigation of gradient paradigm uniformity.

Criterion 6: Frequency constellations
Choosing suitable homophones came with a number of challenges, one of which was finding triplets (e.g. *day-days-daze*) that fit into certain frequency constellations that allow me to investigate gradient paradigm uniformity (see the hypotheses and research questions in 2.6). In order to find these constellations, I created a list of homophone word pairs that have a monomorphemic (e.g. *daze*) and morphologically complex (e.g. *days*) member, and looked up frequencies for these,

plus frequencies for their bare stem (*day*) in the COCA. I transformed these frequencies using logarithm and grouped them into high and low frequency according to the median of the word form frequency. Any item that had a log-transformed frequency of lower than 3.48 (the median) was categorized as low frequency, and any item with a higher log-transformed frequency as high frequency. Using these cut-off points was necessary in order to be able to categorize the items into constellations of 'high' and 'low' frequencies, which later allowed for the analysis of gradient paradigm uniformity in the production experiment.

The final list of items contains 16 triplets of items that are listed in Table 5.2[18]. As can be seen in the table, it was not possible to find triplets for all possible frequency constellations. However, this distribution covers almost all of them and thus is a good basis for the investigation of my hypotheses.

Table 5.2: List of items used for the production experiment and the comprehension task and their frequency constellations. The column 'Frequency' lists the categorization of the frequencies of the word triplets in the order bare stem – complex word – monomorphemic word, the same order in which these words are also displayed in the column 'Word triplets'. The column 'Triplets' merely gives a count of the number of triplets that fall into this frequency constellation.

Frequency	Word triplets	n
high-high-high	gene, genes, jeans; know, knows, nose;	2
high-high-low	day, days, daze; guy, guys, guise; hurt, hurts, hertz; link, links, lynx;	4
high-low-high	sigh, sighs, size;	1
high-low-low	bay, bays, baize; coke, cokes, coax; tea, teas, tease;	3
low-high-high	NA	0
low-high-low	NA	0
low-low-high	chew, chews, choose; paw, paws, pause; yew, yews, use;	3
low-low-low	brew, brews, bruise; brow, brows, browse; tuck, tucks, tux	3

Filler items

In addition to the target items, I also included a number of filler items. The purpose of filler items was to prevent participants from adjusting their behavior in case they were able to determine the subject of interest. Fillers were selected to match the target items in regards of frequency and part of speech, and they also

---

18 These items were later also used in the comprehension task (see 6.2)

had to meet the six criteria mentioned above. With 48 target items (from the 16 triplets), I decided to add 30 filler items as follows:
- 5 high frequency plural words
- 5 high frequency 3sg words
- 5 low frequency plural words
- 5 low frequency 3sg words
- 5 plural base words selected randomly from the previously chosen high and low frequent plural words
- 5 3sg base words selected randomly from the previously chosen high and low frequent 3sg words

In order to find these words, I searched COCA for plural or third person singular words and selected five suitable words from the most and least frequent words. I selected only regularly inflected words and words that do not undergo sound change in the transformation from bare form to inflected form (as for example *do* [du] and *does* [dʌz]). From the resulting list of high and low frequency words, I randomly selected five words from the plural and five words from the third person singular words according to the criteria named above. I added these as 'bare stem' filler items, imitating the bare stems among the target items (e.g. *day*).

Contexts
Target sentences that act as contexts for the cloze task needed to conform to a certain structure in order to allow for an acceptable amount of control over the prosody of the sentence. Target sentences start with a noun phrase that has between three and five syllables, and ideally end with a prepositional phrase that has around five syllables. Due to the tense structure of English (present tense is used for habits, and present progressive is used for the actual present), there is some variation regarding tense in the structure of the target sentences in this experiment. A list of target sentences can be found in the online repository which is listed in the appendix.

Performing the experiment
The experiment was run in OpenSesame (Mathôt, Schreij & Theeuwes 2012). Participants are introduced to the narrative of having lost their suitcase and having to reorder and read out the words that got jumbled up in their suitcase as part of in the task. This narrative is graphically illustrated throughout the experiment. After the instructions, there were four practice items, followed by a short pause

with the opportunity to ask questions. Afterwards, participants were presented with the 78 target and filler items.

To avoid priming, a randomization was implemented, which states that items from the same triplet are separated by at least five cycles (e.g. *bay, bays, baize*), and items of the same stimulus type (monomorphemic, base or complex), are separated by a distance of at least one, meaning that two items of the same type will never appear after one another. As OpenSesame's sound recording capabilities are immensely outdated (last update 2012), a recording software was run in the background.

The experiment was run at the University of Canterbury in Christchurch, New Zealand and grouped together with an experiment by Dominic Schmitz (Schmitz 2022; Schmitz et al. 2021b; Schmitz et al. 2021a; Schmitz et al. 2022). After both experiments were run, participants had to fill out the anonymous Statistical Information Sheet, and then were handed a gift voucher in the value of 20 NZD for their participation.

5.1.3 Participants

45 participants were recruited for this experiment group, containing my production experiment and one of Schmitz's experiments. Out of these participants, five were excluded because they indicated that they spent most of their life outside of New Zealand, thus I assumed that they cannot be classified as native speakers of New Zealand English.

After concluding the experiment, participants were asked to fill in an extensive statistical information sheet, in which they were asked to provide sociodemographic information about themselves, as well as information that could play a role in their performance in a production experiment. Among this information were gender, age, bilingualism, education, as well as a number of a number of hobbies/activities such as playing instruments, role-playing games and acting. The statistical information collected about the participants was included in the exploratory analysis of the experimental data. None of the variables showed any interesting results in the final analysis, and most were distributed in such as way that they did not have notable statistical power.

5.1.4 Processing audio recordings

The audio files were delivered as one long file containing all sentences read by one participant. Due to the automatic randomization of OpenSesame, it was necessary to annotate and segment these recordings, which was done manually by four student assistants using the acoustic analysis software Praat (Boersma & Weenink 2015).

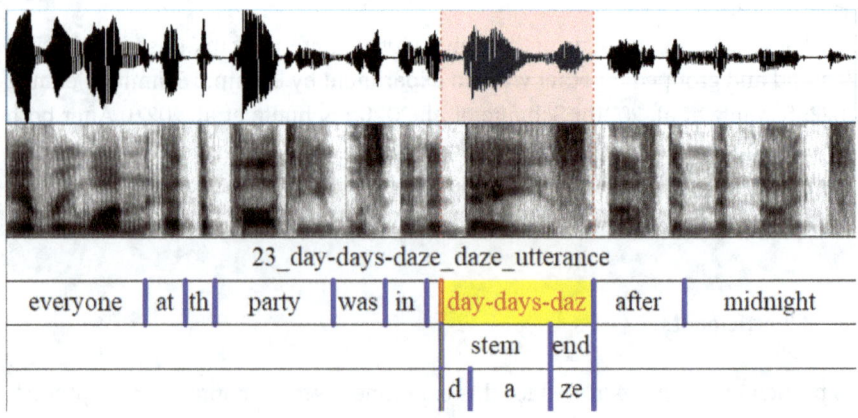

Fig. 5.2: Example of annotation of production items in Praat.

Files for the production experiment were annotated on four different tiers, which can be seen in Figure 5.2: the first tier included only the item number and file name, which was used for automatic processing using Praat scripts. In the second tier, each word was annotated. This tier was later used to calculate speech rate. In the third tier, the morphemes for the target items were annotated (simply by separating (pseudo-)stem and ending), which were used to extract (pseudo-)stem duration. Finally, on tier four, the different segments of the target word were annotated.

Student assistants were given very detailed instructions for the annotation process. In a first step, they had to identify the items (all sound files were randomized) and instructed to not annotate any filler items. Then they were instructed to add the 4 tiers explained above, and annotate the file accordingly. For segmentations, they were instructed to determine boundaries both by visual inspection of the waveform and the spectrogram, and by auditory inspection. As a last step, they were asked to move the boundary to the nearest zero crossing.

5.1.5 Variables

A number of the variables used in the production experiment are identical to those used in the corpus studies and are explained in detail in 4.1.3. However, there are additional variables that were included due to the nature of the experiment.

FREQCONST: lists the frequency constellation between the base, complex and monomorphemic word (see Criterion 6 in section 5.1.2 for explanation).

FREQCONST2: is similar to FREQCONST, but contains only the constellation between the types of morphemes that were present in that particular subset (e.g. in the subset containing only complex and monomorphemic words, only the constellation for these two was included).

FREQRATIO controls for words that are subject to conversion (e.g. *brews*, which is used as noun in the experiment, but also occurs as a verb). This variable calculated a ratio of the word form frequency (e.g. *brews* as noun) and the raw frequency (*brews* without restrictions to word form). Though stimuli were selected to not be affected by multiple homophony, some items were still subject to conversion, as it was required to find low frequency items matching a particular part of speech, as is the case with *brews*.

CLOZEPOSITION: Due to the nature of the cloze task, it was necessary to control for the position of the item within the cloze with the variable CLOZEPOSITION, which was either front, middle or back. This strongly correlated with PARTOFSPEECH (verbs are generally at the front of the cloze, nouns at the back), therefore only CLOZEPOSITION was included in the analysis, as it is the more suitable variable for this analysis.

NUMPAUSES, PRECPAUSEDUR & FOLLPAUSEDUR concern the number of pauses (NUMPAUSES) and the duration of pauses preceding (PRECPAUSEDUR) and following (FOLLPAUSEDUR) the target item. These variables were extracted from the TextGrid with the help of WebMAUS (Kisler, Reichel & Schiel 2017).

ANNOTATOR: Contains the initials of the student assistant who segmented the audio recordings. Four different student assistants worked on the segmentations.

UTTERANCEORDER: Contains the order in which sentences were read during the experiment. The order was randomized by OpenSesame to ensure that targets and fillers occur in a balanced manner.

PHONNEIGHBORDENSITY: This variable is identical to that used in the corpus studies. However, not all items used in the experiment had a value for phonological neighborhood density in CLEARPOND. As these are homophones, they would have identical phonological neighborhood density values as their homophone partners, therefore the value of their homophones was manually assigned to these items.

Descriptive statistics of variables

Table 5.3 gives an overview of the descriptive statistics of the variables that are used in the main dataset of interest for categorical paradigm uniformity alongside their summaries and distributions.

Table 5.3: Descriptive statistics of the variables in dataset d_h1, which was used for the analysis of categorical paradigm uniformity. All durations, speech rates and frequencies are log-transformed. The analysis of gradient paradigm uniformity was conducted with a subset of this data.

Variable	N	Mean	St. Dev.	Min	Max
Dependent variable					
STEMDURATION	1080	-1.120	0.294	-2.272	-0.440
Numerical variables					
WORDFORMFREQ	32	8.046	2.202	4.248	12.254
STEMFREQ	17	9.316	2.125	5.991	13.749
SPEECHRATE	306	1.282	0.204	0.519	1.859
PRECPAUSEDUR	42	-2.290	0.232	-2.996	-0.329
FOLLPAUSEDUR	109	-2.277	0.341	-4.605	0.637
PHONNEIGHBORDENSITY	14	20.957	9.327	9	39
UTTERANCEORDER	52	24.198	13.973	1	54
NUMPAUSES	8	1.049	1.275	0	7
NUMPHON	3	3.536	0.616	3	5
AGE	10	22.419	4.552	18	37
Categorical variables					
WORD	32 levels	...			
PARTICIPANT	40 levels	...			
GENDER	3 levels	female: 923; male: 198; other: 33			
CLOZEPOSITION	3 levels	back: 722; front: 322; middle: 110			
MORPHEMETYPE	2 levels	complex: 589; monomorphemic: 565			
FREQCONST	6 levels	1: High-High-High: 135; 2: High-High-Low: 279; 3: High-Low-High: 71; 4: High-Low-Low: 214; 7: Low-Low-High: 254; 8: Low-Low-Low: 201			
FREQCONST2	4 levels	High-High: 135; High-Low: 279; Low-High: 325; Low-Low: 415			

5.2 Analysis

To investigate the different hypotheses concerning categorical and gradient paradigm uniformity (see chapter 2.6), I created different subsets of the data. To investigate categorical paradigm uniformity, I created a subset including complex and monomorphemic words, as the main research question here is whether there is a durational difference between these two types of words.

To investigate gradient paradigm uniformity, several different subsets were created. To check whether higher frequency of a bare stem causes shorter durations of the inflected stems, I created a subset with only the bare stems and complex words, as well as a subset with only the complex words in which I predicted the stem duration using the stem frequency. Vice versa, I also created a subset with only the bare stems and predicted their durations using the inflected frequency. An overview of the subsets, their contents and their purposes is listed in Table 5.4.

Table 5.4: Overview of subsets, which types of words these contain, and their purpose

Subset	Content	Used for
d	all items	Exploratory analysis
d_h1	complex & monomorphemic words	Categorical Paradigm Uniformity
d_h2a	bare stems & complex words	
d_h2b	only complex words	Gradient Paradigm Uniformity
d_h2c	only bare stems	

The datasets were analyzed using the modelling procedure described in 4.1.2, using mixed-effects regression modelling (lmer() from the R package lme4 (Bates et al. 2017)) and a step-wise elimination process. The STEMDURATION was the response variable, with a number of pertinent variables having been included as covariates. Several variables were considered as covariates, but were not included due to collinearity issues, low statistical prediction power, or problematic variable generation.

As predictor variable, the variable of interest for categorical paradigm uniformity was MORPHEMETYPE, which was either complex or monomorphemic, and for gradient paradigm uniformity it was STEMFREQ. Additional analyses were performed with WORDFORMFREQ, FREQCONST or FREQCONST2 as variables of interest. As fixed effects, variables included were FREQRATIO, NUMPAUSES, PRECPAUSEDUR, FOLLPAUSEDUR, the log-transformed SPEECHRATE, the type of the sound preceding the word-final /s, z/ PRECSOUNDTYPE, the phonological neighborhood density PHONNEIGHBORDENSITY, the number of phonemes NUMPHON, the annotator of the audio file ANNOTATOR, as well as the AGE and GENDER of the participant. Most of these covariates were eliminated during the modelling process as they did not show significant effects. As random effect, the PARTICIPANT, the WORD, as well as the UTTERANCEORDER were included.

5.3 Results

Before investigating the subsets aimed at investigating categorical and gradient paradigm uniformity, I ran an explorative model using the entire dataset (dataset **d**). In this model, neither the type of word (bare stem, complex word or monomorphemic word) were significant in predicting stem duration, nor the word form frequency. The effect of word form frequency goes in the expected direction, with stems becoming shorter the higher the frequency, but this effect is not statistically significant. In the variable MORPHEMETYPE, it can be observed that bare stems have the longest stem duration, followed by monomorphemic pseudo-stems, and complex stems.

An identical model with FREQCONST instead of the frequency was fitted, which also didn't show a significance for FREQCONST and no interactions with MORPHEMETYPE. The only variables that are significant in both models are the AGE of the participant (older participants speak slower), as well as the SPEECHRATE. The majority of these results are reflected in the models for the subsets.

5.3.1 Categorical paradigm uniformity

Using the subset **d_h1**, I investigated whether stems of inflected words have longer durations than the pseudo-stems of monomorphemic words, and in what ways the frequencies of the bare stem or complex word might affect these durations. I created three different models for this purpose. The models were identical except for the covariates WORDFORMFREQ, FREQCONST and FREQCONST2. I created different models for these because these variables predict very similar things, and including all of them in the same model might cause collinearity issues. In the models containing FREQCONST and FREQCONST2, these were eliminated during the step-wise elimination process. In the model containing WORDFORMFREQ (see Table 5.5), this variable survived the elimination process, indicating that the word form frequency has an influence on the duration of the stem. However, and crucially, in all three models, the main variable of interest, the MORPHEMETYPE, was eliminated.

Table 5.5: Fixed effects and random effects in the model d_h1_lmerstep1_trimmed, which uses subset d_h1 for the analysis of categorical paradigm uniformity. Durations and frequencies are log-transformed.

Random effects

Groups	Name	Variance	St. Dev.
PARTICIPANTID	(Intercept)	0.010	0.103
ITEM	(Intercept)	0.022	0.150
Residual		0.016	0.128

Fixed effects

	Estimate	Std. Error	df	t value	Pr(>|t|)	
(Intercept)	-0.486	0.155	95.831	-3.131	0.002	**
WORDFORMFREQ	-0.027	0.013	28.144	-2.100	0.044	*
SPEECHRATE	-0.175	0.027	1055.465	-6.395	< 0.001	***
PRECPAUSEDUR	0.119	0.024	1022.296	4.890	< 0.001	***
FOLLPAUSEDUR	0.025	0.013	1038.562	1.917	0.055	.
CLOZEPOSITION: front	-0.135	-0.135	28.167	-2.198	0.036	*
CLOZEPOSITION: middle	-0.242	0.095	28.024	-2.534	0.017	*
NUMPAUSES	0.025	0.004	1056.691	5.595	< 0.001	***
AGE	0.008	0.003	34.091	2.159	0.038	*

It can be concluded that stems of inflected words do not have longer durations than the pseudo-stems of monomorphemic words, as the type of morpheme does not affect the duration of the stem. This means that there is no evidence for a categorical paradigm uniformity effect, contrary to the findings of Seyfarth et al. (2017). This null result was further validated by a Bayes factor analysis, which showed a very strong favor for the null hypothesis with a factor of 179.33 (cf. Raftery 1995, Table 6) indicating that type of word is not significant in predicting the duration of the (pseudo-)stem.

5.3.2 Gradient paradigm uniformity

The higher the frequency of the bare stem, the shorter the duration of the inflected stem – this is what I aimed to find out using the subset **d_h2b**, which contains only complex words. I created a number of different models to investigate this hypothesis. The models were identical except for the variables of interest, which (similar to the investigation of categorical paradigm uniformity as explained in 5.3.1) were not all included in the same model because of possible collinearity issues.

In a dataset containing only complex words, I used STEMFREQ as the main variable of interest in order to test a gradient paradigm uniformity effect. This model has shown that higher bare stem frequency can cause shorter stem duration of the complex stem. The output for this model is listed in Table 5.6.

Table 5.6: Fixed effects and random effects in the model d_h2b_lmerstep_2b_trimmed, which uses subset d_h2b (complex words only) for the analysis of gradient paradigm uniformity. Durations, speech rate and frequencies are log-transformed.

Random effects			
Groups	Name	Variance	St. Dev.
PARTICIPANTID	(Intercept)	0.011	0.108
ITEM	(Intercept)	0.016	0.129
Residual		0.015	0.123

Fixed effects					
	Estimate	Std. Error	df	t value	Pr(>|t|)
(Intercept)	-0.636	0.189	27.216	-1.354	0.186
STEMFREQ	-0.077	0.021	12.001	-3.618	0.003 **
LEFTBIGRAMPROB	0.038	0.011	2.040	3.374	0.005 **
PRECPAUSEDUR	0.096	0.033	503.615	2.917	0.003 **
FOLLPAUSEDUR	0.030	0.022	522.455	1.349	0.177
NUMPAUSES	0.028	0.006	533.224	4.524	<0.001 ***
SPEECHRATE	-0.190	0.036	524.350	-5.181	<0.001 ***
PHONNEIGHBORFREQ	0.013	0.004	12.085	2.737	0.017 *

How does the frequency of the bare stem and the frequency of the complex stem affect the duration of the complex stem? It is possible that a higher frequency of a complex word may mitigate a paradigm uniformity effect or vice versa. To investigate this, I examined which frequency constellations have which effect on the duration of the stem. In the model including FreqConst2 as variable of interest, I found that if both stem and complex word are low frequent (case 1) the stem of the complex word is longer, and if both are high frequent (case 2), the stem is shorter. However, if the stem is high frequent and the complex word is low frequent (case 3), the stem of the complex word is very long, even longer than in case 1 (the output for this model is given in Table 5.7).

Table 5.7: Fixed effects and random effects in the model d_h2b_lmerstep_2c_trimmed, which uses subset d_h2b (complex words only) for the analysis of gradient paradigm uniformity. The baseline for FREQCONST2 is Low–Low. Durations and speech rate are log-transformed.

Random effects						
Groups	Name	Variance	St. Dev.			
PARTICIPANTID	(Intercept)	0.011	0.108			
ITEM	(Intercept)	0.012	0.109			
Residual		0.015	0.123			
Fixed effects						
	Estimate	Std. Error	df	t value	Pr(>|t|)	
(Intercept)	-0.672	0.120	282.490	-5.572	< 0.001	***
FREQCONST2: High–High	-0.200	0.068	12.178	-2.925	0.012	*
FREQCONST2: High–Low	0.198	0.074	12.050	2.643	0.021	*
LEFTBIGRAMPROB	0.037	0.009	12.119	4.209	0.001	**
PRECPAUSEDUR	0.031	0.022	522.580	1.394	0.163	
FOLLPAUSEDUR	0.098	0.033	503.000	2.971	0.003	**
NUMPAUSES	0.029	0.006	533.532	4.677	< 0.001	***
SPEECHRATE	-0.190	0.036	526.747	-5.181	< 0.001	***

This output for FREQCONST2 is somewhat confounding and may be caused by means of a masked word form frequency effect, which might also be the case with the previously reported model from Table 5.6 – while the model in Table 5.6 appears to provide evidence for a gradient paradigm uniformity effect, a Bayes factor analysis showed a strong favor for the null hypothesis with a factor of 3.6, indicating that the statistical evidence for an effect of bare stem frequency on inflected words is not robust. To further investigate this, I created another subset of the data which is suited to include both word form frequency and bare stem frequency in the statistical model, which should make clearer whether we are dealing with a masked word form frequency effect.

5.3.2.1 Frequency band analysis

As the aforementioned results might occur due to a masked word from frequency effect, I created a frequency band analysis using a subset of the dataset in which the word form and bare stem frequencies do not correlate, similar to the QuakeBox corpus study (see 4.1). Using this subset for the analysis has shown that the effect found in the previous models (Table 5.6 and Table 5.7) is not robust, as both frequencies were eliminated from the model in the step-wise elimination process (see Table 5.8).

Table 5.8: Fixed and random effects in the final model d_h2b_lmer_3, which uses a subset frequency band in which the bare stem and word form frequency do not correlate.

Random effects			
Groups	Name	Variance	St. Dev.
PARTICIPANTID	(Intercept)	0.006	0.081
ITEM	(Intercept)	0.004	0.070
Residual		0.028	0.169

Fixed effects						
	Estimate	Std. Error	df	t value	Pr(>|t|)	
(Intercept)	-1.093	0.138	84.718	-7.907	<0.001	***
NUMPAUSES	0.031	0.011	275.846	2.747	0.006	**
SPEECHRATE	-0.294	0.068	243.206	-4.320	<0.001	***
PRECSOUNDTYPE: diphthong	0.275	0.069	5.087	3.962	0.010	*
PRECSOUNDTYPE: vowel	0.252	0.069	5.162	3.613	0.014	*
AGE	0.009	0.003	35.261	2.546	0.015	*

The final model with this subset only contains NUMPAUSES, SPEECHRATE, PRECSOUNDTYPE and AGE as covariates. This is further evidence that the results found in the model in Table 5.6 might indeed be due to a masked word form frequency effect, rather than due to a gradient paradigm uniformity effect. Altogether, the statistical evidence for gradient paradigm uniformity is inconclusive.

These results contradict the results found in the QuakeBox corpus study, where a frequency band analysis confirmed a gradient paradigm uniformity effect. Possible reasons for this discrepancy will be addressed in the discussion (chapter 7).

5.3.2.2 General frequency effect

Using the dataset containing only complex words, I was able to confirm a general frequency effect. In a model containing word form frequency as the main predictor, I found that the higher the word form frequency of the inflected word form, the shorter the duration of the stem of the inflected word form, as seen in Table 5.9.

Table 5.9: Fixed and random effects in the model d_h2b_lmerstep_2d, which tests a general frequency effect.

Random effects

Groups	Name	Variance	St. Dev.			
PARTICIPANTID	(Intercept)	0.009454	0.09723			
ITEM	(Intercept)	0.012588	0.11220			
Residual		0.032504	0.18029			

Fixed effects

	Estimate	Std. Error	df	t value	Pr(>|t|)	
(Intercept)	-0.769	0.137	21.952	-5.615	< 0.001	***
WORDFORMFREQ	-0.182	0.044	11.912	-4.076	0.001	**
LEFTBIGRAMPROB	0.049	0.011	11.981	4.304	0.001	**
FOLLPAUSEDUR	0.340	0.148	563.585	2.284	0.022	*
PRECPAUSEDUR	0.963	0.207	549.238	4.644	< 0.001	***
NUMPAUSES	0.037	0.008	574.882	4.549	< 0.001	***
SPEECHRATE	-0.225	0.051	578.892	-4.358	< 0.001	***
PHONNEIGHBORDENSITY	0.013	0.004	12.097	3.203	0.007	**

This is a general phonetic reduction effect as established in the literature, and this word form frequency effect is likely the cause of the confusing results of the aforementioned models examining gradient paradigm uniformity, which then also disappeared upon using a frequency band analysis including both frequencies.

5.4 Summary

The production experiment has not delivered any solid evidence, neither for a categorical paradigm uniformity effect, nor for a gradient paradigm uniformity effect. These results are contrary to previous findings. Based on the findings by Seyfarth et al. (2017), I would have expected to be able to replicate a categorical paradigm uniformity effect. However, in my models, this is not the case, as the type of morpheme does not seem to play a role in the duration of the stem.

Similarly, based on my own previous findings in the QuakeBox and Buckeye corpora (chapter 4), I would have expected to also find a gradient paradigm uniformity effect. However, this is not the case, as the paradigm member's frequency is almost always excluded from the final model, and the findings do not hold up in the frequency band analysis. Rather, the most likely explanation for my findings is a masked word form frequency effect, further proof for which is evident in the model testing a general frequency effect.

6 Perception experiments

The previously presented production experiment expands my research on paradigm uniformity by collecting and analyzing speech data to investigate research questions analogous to the previously performed corpus studies. By also including perception into my research, I want to investigate whether durational differences, such as those that are theorized to occur in paradigm uniformity, can also be perceived by native speakers of English, and whether this information is used in comprehension.

The perception experiment was divided into two different but related tasks which were combined into one single experiment – a same different task, and a comprehension task. Combining these into one experiment has a number of advantages, both from a theoretical and practical point of view. Running both tasks as one experiment allowed me to use the same participants for both tasks. This is not only convenient, as I needed to recruit fewer participants in total, but also opens up the possibility to compare the participants' performances across the two tasks. From a theoretical point of view, this means that if a participant can for example not hear any durational differences at all in the same-different task, it means that they are very unlikely to also perceive the differences in the spliced forms in the comprehension task. This kind of coupling of different observations from the same participants was successfully used by Kunter (2017a).

In my experiment, participants first did the comprehension task, followed by the same-different task. This order was chosen so that participants will not be 'trained' during the same-different task, as the comprehension task is the task primarily designed to provide evidence for my research questions, while the same-different task is primarily designed to find more concrete evidence on which participants are sensitive to phonetic detail.

My research questions regarding the perception experiments are as follows:

a) Can listeners perceive possible durational differences between the same strings in complex and simplex words? More specifically, can listeners perceive differences between a word and an artificially lengthened version of the same word (lengthened by [10, 25, 50, 75] milliseconds)? Which of these durational differences can they perceive?

b) Are listeners slowed down in their lexical processing when they are exposed to a form with a mismatched stem, e.g. when they expect to hear *days*, but they hear the pseudo-stem of *daze* with an added plural *s*?

These were investigated using a two-in-one experiment, which was presented to participants embedded into the narrative "The nose knows but does the ear hear?", in which they were encouraged to find out whether they can hear the difference between homophones such as *nose* and *knows*.

To run the perception experiment, I used the free software OpenSesame 3.2 (Mathôt, Schreij & Theeuwes 2012) with the Mousetrap plug-in (Kieslich & Henninger 2017). It is a software developed for the creation of experiments in behavioral science and offers a variety of features including measuring reaction times. It has a graphical user interface that makes creating experiments relatively convenient, while also allowing advanced configuration using Python scripting.

I used OpenSesame for my perception experiment by creating several sequences for the two different tasks, preceded and followed by instructions and divided into two larger units. The trials for the comprehension task lasted for about 10 minutes. After this task, participants see a screen indicating that they may pause for as long as needed before continuing to the next task. Then this procedure is repeated in a similar manner for the same-different task, which in total also lasted about 10 minutes.

Despite the tasks being run in the order comprehension and then same-different task (to avoid priming), they were analyzed in the reverse order. This allowed me to see which participants in the same-different task were sensitive to the phonetic differences, and to use this sensitivity as an additional variable in the analysis of the same-different task. Therefore, the tasks will also be presented here in the reverse order of how they were run, starting with the same-different task.

6.1 Same-different task

The same-different task tests whether listeners are sensitive to durational differences in words, similar to the durational differences that I found for production in my corpus studies. In previous research, it was found that listeners are able to distinguish durational differences (e.g. Klatt 1975; Shatzman & McQueen 2006). In the same-different task, I tested this ability by using artificially lengthened stimuli to investigate at which durational increases participants will be able to perceive a difference. They listened to two sound files that are played one after the other, and were then asked whether the two files they heard were the same or different by pressing a corresponding key on the keyboard. Their answer (correct or incorrect) was recorded, and in addition their reaction time was measured. I intended to find out which durational differences they can perceive and whether they have slower or faster reaction times to certain combinations of durational differences.

As I am merely interested in whether listeners can perceive certain durational differences of the same word, it was not necessary to use homophones in this task. Therefore, I chose six monomorphemic and six plural words as stimuli. These were recorded and then the stems of these words were manipulated into five different durations, which were labelled with identifying letters from A-E:

A unmanipulated, original length
B increased stem duration by 10 milliseconds
C increased stem duration by 25 milliseconds
D increased stem duration by 50 milliseconds
E increased stem duration by 75 milliseconds

In the same-different task, listeners were exposed to two of these sound files in nine possible combinations, which include either twice the same duration, or two different durations, one of which was always the original length. The possible combinations of stimuli durations are listed in Table 6.1.

Table 6.1: Stimuli combinations of same and different durations in the same-different task.

Pair	Same or different	Durational difference
A + B	Different	10ms
A + C	Different	25ms
A + D	Different	50ms
A + E	Different	75ms
A + A	Same	none
B + B	Same	none
C + C	Same	none
D + D	Same	none
E + E	Same	none

The perceptual threshold for durational differences in fricatives has been estimated at about 25 to 30 milliseconds (Klatt & Cooper 1975; Shatzman & McQueen 2006) and based on this, I chose these durational differences to investigate whether this also applies to the stems preceding fricatives. I added a shorter distinction of 10 milliseconds to confirm this, with the expectation that listeners will not be able to perceive this difference. Additionally, I added longer durations of

50 milliseconds and 75 milliseconds, with the expectation that listeners will definitely be able to perceive these. In short, I am primarily interested in confirming whether listeners will be able to perceive the 25 millisecond difference.

6.1.1 Methodology

6.1.1.1 Selection of items

The target items were chosen for this task in accordance to Criterion 1 and 3 as established for the corpus studies in 4.1.1. The targets were twelve monosyllabic words ending in voiced [s] or voiceless [z] preceded by a vowel or diphthong. Out of these twelve, six items were monomorphemic, and six were plural words. The twelve items were chosen to have an equal distribution of the final voicing, as well as of the type of vowel before the final sound (short, long, diphthong), as far as this was possible. The monomorphemic target items were *chess, buzz, ace, house, goose, clause*, and the plural target items were *boys, foes, ways, bees, blues, flaws*. Item candidates were selected by querying the ELP (Balota et al. 2007) using the corpus query tool Coquery (Kunter 2017b) and restricting the results to monosyllabic words ending in [s] or [z] respectively, that were either morphologically complex or plural words. The candidates were then evaluated based on the vowel preceding the final [z], [s], and were deemed suitable if they were relatively frequent in COCA.

A similar procedure was used to acquire the filler items. However, for the filler items I decided to use words ending in [f], [v], [θ] or [ð]. Reasons to include these are similar to the reasons fillers were included in the other experiments; to distract participants from the final [z], [s] items in the experiment, as they might adjust their behavior if they discover a focus on these types of words in the experiment. Fillers were also selected to have an even distribution of voicing among the final sounds and of the different types of preceding vowels, as far as possible[19]. The six fillers ending in [f] or [v] are *riff, wife, grief, love, wave,* and *grieve*, while the six fillers ending in [θ] and [ð] are *death, myth, growth, path, bathe,* and *soothe*. A complete list of target and filler items is given in the appendix.

---

[19] It was, for example, not possible to find words ending in voiced [ð] that are preceded by a short vowel, as no such words exist in English.

Recording and processing

The stimuli for both tasks were recorded in the phonetics laboratory of the Department of General Linguistics[20] at Heinrich-Heine-University Düsseldorf. All stimuli were embedded into the carrier sentence "John said ____ to me", with each carrier sentence being recorded three times in three different randomized orders. The sentences were spoken by a female native speaker of New Zealand English who had been living near Düsseldorf for about six months at the time of the recording. For each stimulus, three recordings were made and the most fluent recording was used to create the new files with manipulated durations.

The stimuli were recorded as one large audio file, which was chopped into files containing only the carrier sentences. The newly chopped and renamed audio files were then opened in Praat and the carrier sentence and the target word were manually segmented. This was done by identifying the onset / word boundary of the target word, the morpheme boundary (if present, i.e. only for words in which the complex stem and pseudo-stem were investigated), and the word boundary at the end of the word, with a similar process applying to the beginning and end of the carrier sentences (see Figure 6.1 for an example).

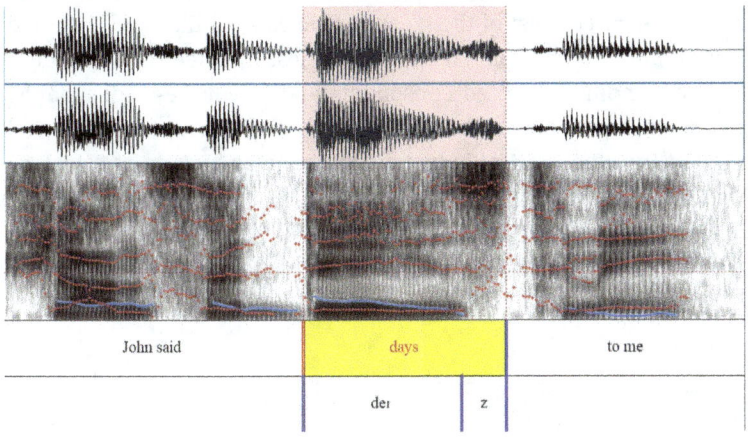

Fig. 6.1: Example for the segmentation of a carrier sentence into target, and of a target word into stem and suffix in the acoustic analysis software Praat.

---

20 Many thanks to Prof. Dr. Ruben van de Vijver for giving me the opportunity to use the phonetics lab of the Institute of Language and Information at the University of Düsseldorf.

Identification of these boundaries was done by visual inspection of the waveform and the spectrogram, as well as by auditory inspection of the audio file. Once a satisfactory decision was reached about the placement of the boundaries, the boundaries were moved to the nearest zero crossing. This also helped to ensure inter-annotator reliability, as the audio files were processed by four different student assistants.

Once the audio files were segmented and the corresponding TextGrids contained all the necessary boundaries, a Praat script was used to extract the necessary information. The newly generated audio files were then further processed for the purposes of the experiment by manipulating the duration.

6.1.1.2 Durational manipulation

The durational manipulation was done separately for words ending in voiced consonants and for words ending in voiceless consonants. The reason for this is that voicing has an effect on the duration of the preceding vowel, an effect that is well-researched and established in the literature (House 1961; House & Fairbanks 1953; Raphael 1972; Klatt & Cooper 1975; Giegerich 1992: 235). I confirmed this allophonic vowel lengthening rule by investigating the durations of my stimuli in R. Using Praat, I generated a list of the stem durations of all files and imported this into R. Then, after adding some helpful variables, I plotted the stem durations for the items ending in voiced consonants and in voiceless consonants, which can be seen in Figure 6.2. As the curves in this plot have notable bumps, I further split apart the words not only by voicing, but also by type of vowel, as plotted in Figure 6.3.

Same-different task — 129

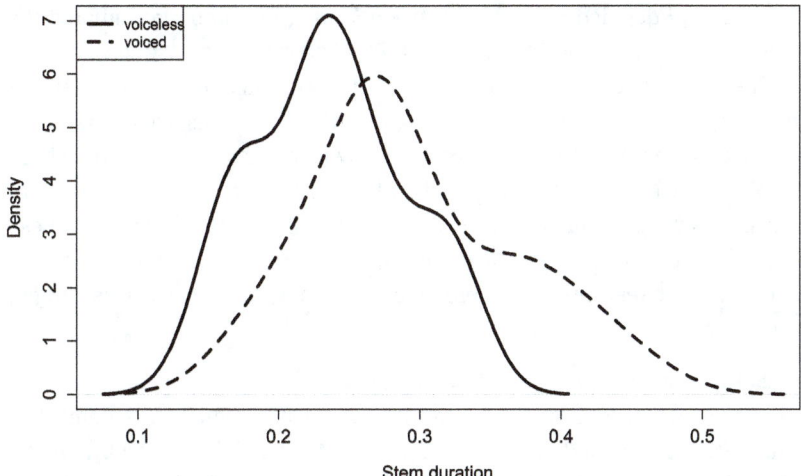

Fig. 6.2: Distribution of stem durations in all items by voicing of the word-final consonant. Words ending in a voiced consonant have longer stems than words ending in a voiceless consonant. The lines have bumps because of the distribution of the vowels (see Figure 6.3).

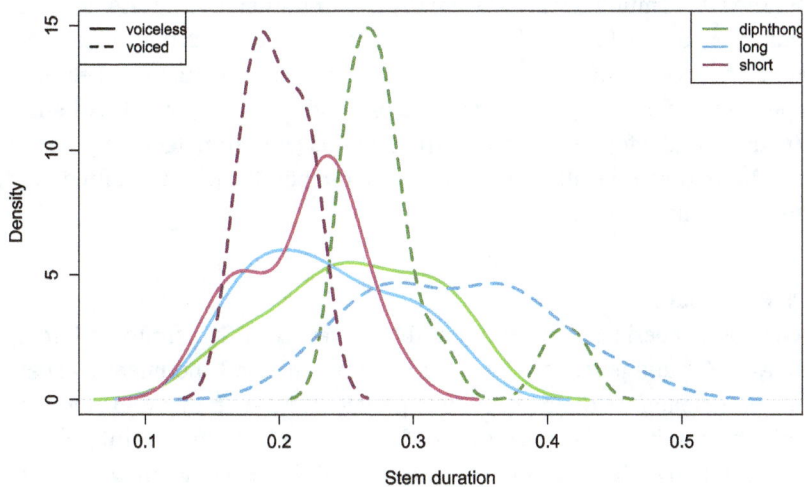

Fig. 6.3: Distribution of stem durations in all items by voicing of the word-final consonant and vowel type before final consonant. Words ending in a voiceless consonant generally have shorter stems than words ending in a voiced consonant (solid vs. dashed lines), while the different types of vowels have different lengths (colored lines).

As there is a lot of variation between the different types of vowels and their respective voicing, I decided to work with these 6 categories and manipulated the durations of the stems accordingly. I used a Praat script to increase the stem durations. The script takes a fixed baseline duration and increases it by a defined amount, therefore it was necessary to categorize the audio files according to the type of final consonant voicing and preceding vowel length, to ensure a matching durational increase. Baselines were defined according to this categorization. These baselines were the means of the durations of all words that fall into these 6 categories[21], and were then increased by 10, 25, 50 or 75 milliseconds using the Praat script and the resulting files were labelled with A, B, C, D or E accordingly.

6.1.1.3 Setup and performance in OpenSesame

There are 24 items in total in the same-different task; twelve target items and twelve filler items. Each of these can occur paired in nine different combinations. These were implemented into OpenSesame using a randomization algorithm to avoid priming. After seeing a fixation cross for 450 milliseconds followed by a short silence of 500 milliseconds, participants were then presented with two auditory stimuli (as per the pair described in Table 6.1), played one after another, with the shorter stimuli preceding either an identical one or a longer one. After this, they had 2000 milliseconds to react. They were then asked to respond whether the two stimuli they heard were the same or different by pressing a corresponding key on the keyboard. For "same", they had to press the "A" key, for "different" they had to press the "K" key. Participants were instructed to keep one finger per hand on each key at all times and respond as fast as possible (whether participants actually followed these instructions was unfortunately not possible to control). After the time allocated for reacting ran out, the process started over and the next items were presented.

6.1.1.4 Participants

The perception experiments were run at the University of Canterbury in Christchurch, New Zealand (simultaneously with the production experiment). 42 participants participated in the perception experiment. After an initial exploratory check of the data, it was revealed that 2 of these were ineligible for this experiment, as their native language background was not New Zealand English. These

---

[21] The categories were: long vowel + voiceless final sound, short vowel + voiceless final sound, diphthong + voiceless final sound, long vowel + voiced final sound, short vowel + voiced final sound, diphthong + voiced final sound.

had to be removed, leaving a total of 40 participants for the final analysis of the data.

Similar to the production experiments, participants were asked to fill in an extensive statistical information sheet after concluding the experiment. In this sheet, they were asked to provide sociodemographic information about themselves, as well as information that could play a role in their performance in a production experiment. Among this information were gender, age, handedness, eyesight, speech impediments, bilingualism, education, as well as a number of hobbies/activities such as playing instruments, role-playing games and acting. The statistical information collected about the participants was included in the exploratory analysis of the experimental data. None of the variables showed any interesting results in the final analysis.

6.1.1.5 Variables

The same-different task includes a number of variables unique to this task. These will be explained here. Other variables are identical to those used in the corpus studies and production experiment; these were explained in 4.1.3.

RESPONSE is the response participants gave while doing the task, which is either same or different. Participants had to respond using the keyboard and pressing either the A key for same, or the K key for different.

DURDIFF is the durational difference in milliseconds of the two stimuli (see 6.1 for the possible durational differences of stimuli combinations), as a categorical variable with the values 10, 20, 50 and 75.

VOICING indicates whether the stimulus ends in a voiced or voiceless consonant.

HANDEDNESS indicates whether the participant was right-handed, left-handed or ambidextrous.

VISION indicates whether the participant was near-sighted, far-sighted or had normal vision.

6.1.2 Data and analysis

The data was analyzed using R. The primary variable of interest in this task was the response to the posed question (RESPONSE), but reaction times were also automatically recorded by OpenSesame. Reaction times were used to filter items where it took participants an abnormally long time to respond (more than the 2000ms allocated in the OpenSesame setup), indicating that participants did not perform the task for the corresponding item correctly. Furthermore, all instances of participants not responding at all (not pressing a key as instructed but letting the timer run out), were removed from the dataset. For the analysis, only target items (items ending in [s] or [z]) were included. The final cleaned and filtered dataset included 4313 data points produced by 40 participants.

Preliminary data inspection was performed by generating a number of plots showing the results by participant, delivering first indications that some participants performed the task less reliably than others, as illustrated in Figure 6.4.

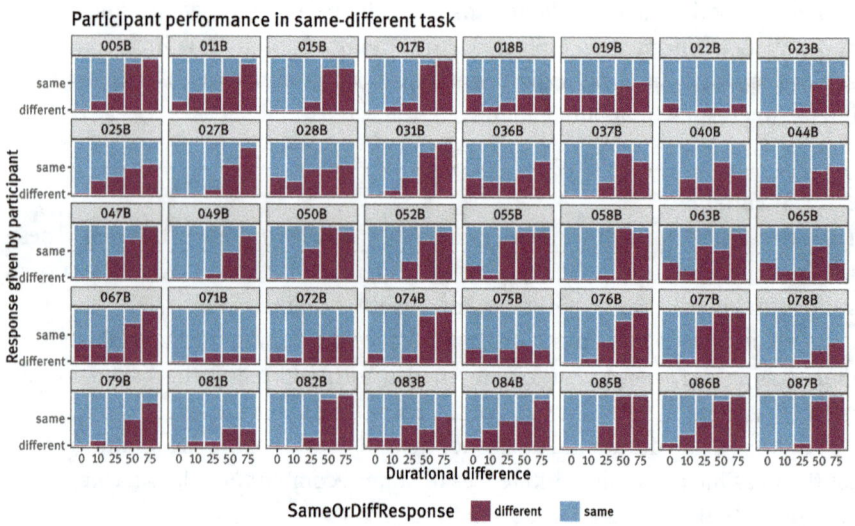

Fig. 6.4: Participant performance in the same-different task. The x-axis shows the durational difference of the given item pair (same for zero, or the difference in duration), while the y-axis shows the responses given by participants, which is also color-coded.

6.1.3 Signal Detection Theory

The same-different task was analyzed using Signal Detection Theory, which provides reliable and established measurements of participant sensitivity and bias. Signal Detection Theory (SDT) (see for example Macmillan & Creelman 2004; Stanislaw & Todorov 1999; Henry & McAuley 2013) attributes participant responses to a combination of sensitivity and bias and can be applied whenever two possible stimulus types need to be discriminated. It is a well-established measure in psychological and psycholinguistic literature.

In the case of the same-different task, I am particularly interested in how well a participant can detect differences between signals, thus how sensitive a participant is to these. High sensitivity indicates that the participant has a good ability to discriminate between stimuli, while low sensitivity indicates a poor ability to discriminate. However, when detecting sensitivity, it is important to also take into account participant bias. Participants may behave conservatively during an experiment, meaning that they provide fewer 'different' responses overall. A participant may, for example, have an overall tendency to respond 'same' rather than 'different' in a same-different task, or vice versa, as illustrated in Figure 6.5.

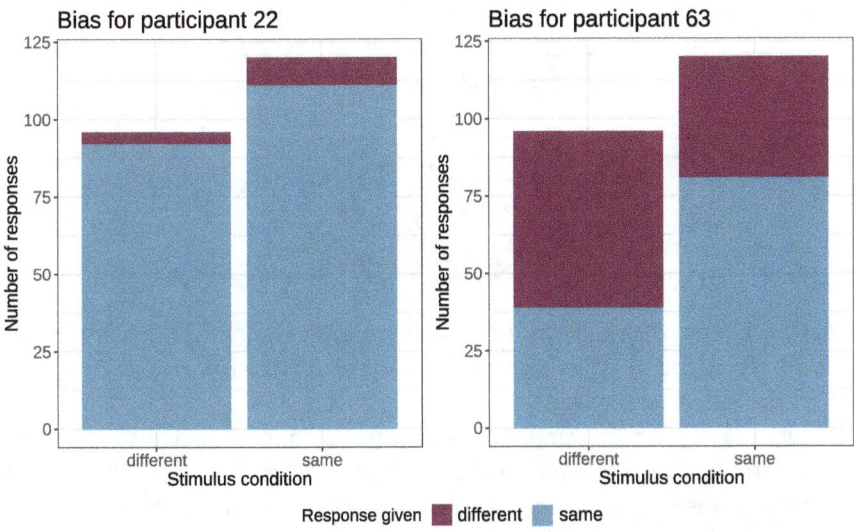

Fig. 6.5: Visualization of possible participant bias in the same-different task. On the left, participant 22 is shown to have a strong bias towards answering 'same' (blue/light shaded responses) also for items which have the condition 'different' (leftmost column), whereas on the right, participant 63 is shown to respond more nuanced with more 'different' responses (red/dark shaded areas), even for about a third of items that have the condition 'same' (rightmost column). Signal Detection Theory helps to transform these observations into quantifiable measurements.

Signal Detection Theory can detect sensitivity while accounting for participant bias. It comes with a number of different measures. The measure that I focused on is a' (a prime), which is the non-parametric estimate of sensitivity. In order to understand the motivation behind this value and its application, I will give a brief overview of Signal Detection Theory. For a more detailed explanation, see Macmillan & Creelman (2004).

SDT is applied whenever two possible stimulus types need to be discriminated, such a for example 'same' and 'different in the case of a same-different task. Responses to these types of stimuli can be described using the terms *hit*, *miss*, *false alarm* or *correct rejection*. These are visualized in Table 6.2. If a participant responds 'same' to a combination of stimuli that are the same, this is considered a *hit*. If they respond 'different' to stimuli that are different, this is considered a *correct rejection*. On the other hand, if they respond 'different' to stimuli that are the same, this is a *miss*, while a 'same' response to different stimuli is a *false alarm*.

Table 6.2: Signal Detection Theory: Stimulus classes (column 1) vs. responses (row 1)

		Participant responds 'same'	Participant responds 'different'
S_2	Stimuli are same (AA, BB, CC, DD, EE)	Hit	Miss
S_1	Stimuli are different (AB, AC, AD, AE)	False alarm	Correct rejection

From these responses, a *hit rate* (H), as well as a *false-alarm rate* (F) may be calculated, which can be written as conditional probabilities $H = P(\text{"same"}| S_2)$ and $F = P(\text{"same"}| S_1)$, respectively.

The values H and F attempt to capture a participant's sensitivity. A perfectly sensitive participant would have a hit rate of 1 and a false alarm rate of 0, whereas a completely insensitive participant would be unable to distinguish the stimuli at all. There are several ways of establishing a sensitivity measure, such as for example simply subtracting H and F, or calculating a proportion of correct responses. A commonly used measure is d' (d prime), which defined as $d' = z(H) - z(F)$, where z is the inverse of the normal distribution which converts a hit or false-alarm rate to a z score. A d' value at 0 corresponds to a participant being completely unable to distinguish stimuli, hence the performance is at chance level.

A problem with d' is that it assumes a normal distribution of the data. An alternative measurement is a', which is better suited because it is the non-parametric counterpart to d' and is an average between minimum and maximum performance of the participant. The formula to calculate a' is given in the following; for a more detailed and precise explanation, see also Macmillan & Creelman (2004: 101):

$$\text{if } H \geq F: \quad a' = \frac{1}{2} + \frac{(H-F)(1+H-F)}{4H(1-F)}$$

$$\text{if } H \leq F: \quad a' = \frac{(F-H)(1+F-H)}{4F(1-H)}$$

The a' values were calculated using an R function from the psycho package (Makowski et al. 2021). Resulting values for a' range from 0 to 1. A value near 1 indicates perfect participant performance, whereas a value near 0.5 is suggested to indicate chance level. Values smaller than 0.5 may be due to sampling errors or participants not being particularly sensitive.

I used a' in the analysis of the same-different task in order to establish participant sensitivity. In a preliminary step, I plotted the raw a' values. Afterwards, I used the a' value as a main predictor to analyze participant sensitivity in beta regression.

6.1.3.1 Visualization of a'

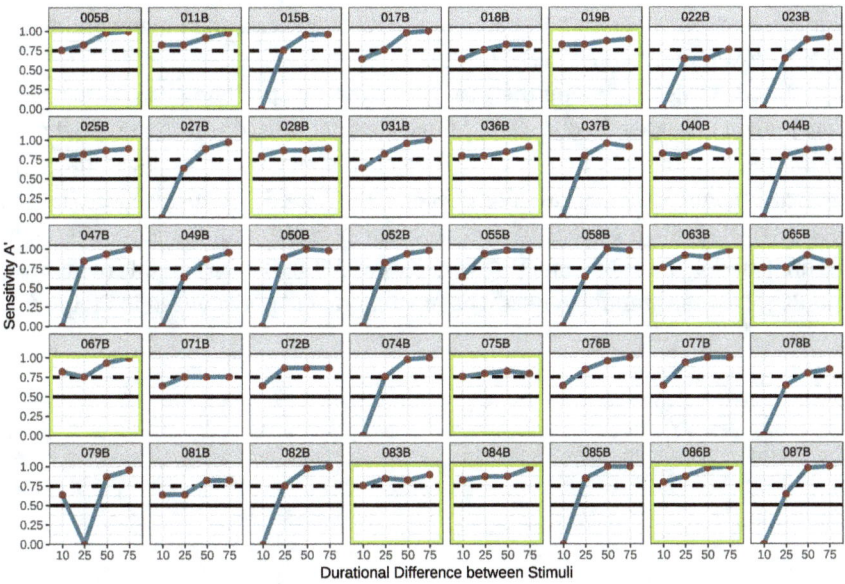

Fig. 6.6: Visualization of a' for all participants. Values below .5 indicate less sensitivity (below solid line). Values near 1 indicate near perfect participant sensitivity (above dotted line). Highlighted in green are participants that are able to perceive all differences based on visual inspection. Some of these did not have statistically significant results in the preliminary data analysis using linear mixed-effects regression (compare to Figure 6.4).

In Figure 6.6 we can see a visualization of participant sensitivity in the same-different task. In this graph, the participants that appear to be sensitive to durational differences starting at 10ms are highlighted with a green border, as their *a'* value for this durational difference is above 0.75 (dashed line), indicating sensitivity. Those whose *a'* value is below 0.5 (solid line) are likely not sensitive, as anything below 0.5 indicates chance level. In order to further investigate this, I also modelled the *a'* values using beta regression.

6.1.3.2 Beta regression with *a'*

Statistical analysis of the Signal Detection Theory data was performed using beta regression with generalized additive models (GAMs). GAMs are a regression tool suitable for analyzing data that is unevenly spread over areas, over time, and for non-linear data, such as for example reaction time in lexical decision tasks or mousetracking data. This type of data tends to have wiggly curves, which would lead to errors in linear mixed effects regression models; therefore this method is unsuitable for such data. For such data, GAMs are more suitable, as well as for data that is distributed between a value of 0 and 1, as is the case in *a'* value in Signal Detection Theory. An in-depth overview of the uses and inner workings of GAMs is given in Baayen & Linke (2020).

I fitted GAMs in R using the `gam()` function by specifying `family=betareg` from the `mgcv` package (Wood 2021). I fitted a model with *a'* as the main predictor, DurDiff as variable of interest, Age, Handedness and Vision as covariates, and Participant and Word as random effects. I then used a step-wise elimination process to evaluate the predictive power of the covariates and random effects. In the final model, the only remaining variables were DurDiff as variable of interest, and Participant as random effect. The prediction of *a'* is visualized in Figure 6.7.

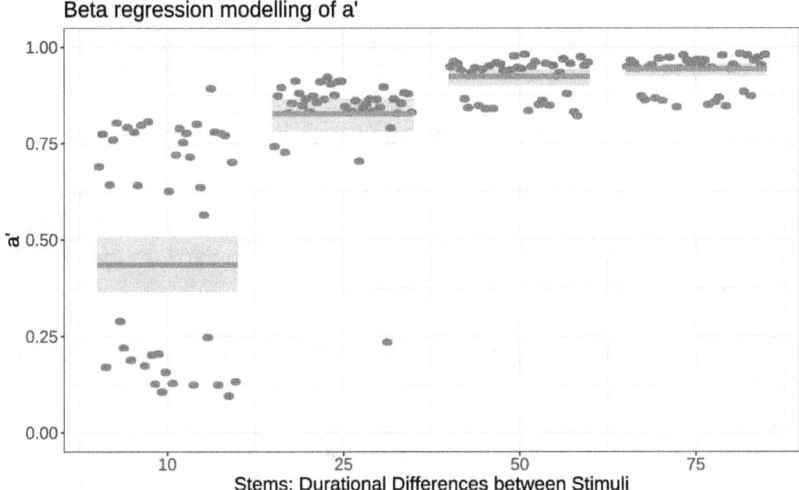

Fig. 6.7: Visualization of *a'* in the beta regression model.

In the chart, we can see that about half of participants are insensitive to the durational differences of up to 10 milliseconds (dots at 10ms in the lower part of the chart), as an *a'* value below 0.5 indicates chance level. The 25, 50 and 75 millisecond differences, are however, close to a value of 1, indicating that participants are generally sensitive to these durational differences (with one notable outlier at 25ms). Table 6.3 lists the model output of the beta regression model, which indicates that there are statistically highly significant differences between the 10 millisecond condition (the baseline) and all other, larger durational differences. The model output also indicates that participant as a random effect is highly significant.

Table 6.3: Parametric coefficients and significance of smooth terms in the beta regression model of *a'*. Signif. codes: 0 '***' 0.001 '**' 0.01 '*' 0.05 '.' 0.1 ' ' 1

Parametric coefficients:					
	Estimate	Std. Error	z value	Pr(>|t|)	
(Intercept)	-1.02549	0.11018	-9.307	<2e-16	***
DurDiff: 25	1.82626	0.06529	27.971	<2e-16	***
DurDiff: 50	2.74798	0.06600	41.636	<2e-16	***
DurDiff: 75	3.05100	0.06611	46.149	<2e-16	***

Approximate significance of smooth terms:

	edf	Ref.df	Chi.sq	p-value
S(PARTICIPANT)	36.99	39	711.8	<2e-16 ***

The model output shows only the comparisons as used within the experiment (AB (10ms), AC (25ms), AD (50ms), AE (75ms)). Using additional models with different baselines, it is also possible to estimate other possible comparisons, as listed in Table 6.4. All comparisons reach significance.

Table 6.4: Least Squares Means table, estimating sensitivity between comparisons other than those used in the experiment.

	Estimate	Std. Error	z value	Pr(>|t|)
DURDIFF 25 - DURDIFF 50	0.921	0.065	13.994	< 0.001 ***
DURDIFF 25 - DURDIFF 75	1.224	0.065	18.561	< 0.001 ***
DURDIFF 50 - DURDIFF 75	0.303	0.066	4.544	< 0.001 ***

6.1.4 Summary of the same-different task

To summarize, the analysis of the same-different task using Signal Detection Theory and beta regression modelling has shown that participants can perceive possible durational differences between different types of stems in complex and simplex words.

Furthermore, the analysis has shown that listeners show a variable pattern in that some listeners are more sensitive to perceiving the differences, while others are not. Taking into account participant bias, the calculation of a' indicates that some listeners are more sensitive to the durational differences than others. Some perceive 25 and 50 millisecond differences, while almost all participants can perceive 75 millisecond differences reliably, as can be seen in Figure 6.6.

As the same-different task has shown that some listeners are able to perceive durational differences, a logical next step would be to investigate whether these listeners also make use of this information in comprehension. This is precisely what I aimed to do in the comprehension task, which is presented in the following subchapter.

6.2 Comprehension task

The comprehension task addresses the question of whether listeners make use of durational differences, such as those found in the same-different task, in comprehension. More precisely, it aims to find out whether listeners are affected in their lexical processing when they are exposed to a form with a stem-suffix mismatch. To investigate this, items were created in which the stem and suffix were spliced together from recordings of monomorphemic and/or complex words. Participants listened to an audio stimulus and were shown two options on the screen. This was either a monomorphemic word such as *daze*, or a complex word such as *days*. They were then asked to click on the option that they think they heard using the mouse. Their behaviour in answering was recorded in the form of mouse tracks, with the expectation that mouse tracks should differ according to condition.

The experiment was modelled after the studies performed by Kemps, Wurm, et al. (2005) and Kemps, Ernestus, et al. (2005). An important methodological precaution from their studies was that in order to reliably investigate spliced forms, all forms should be spliced. In their early experiments, they presented participants with normal and constructed forms, in which only the constructed forms were spliced. This led to a participant bias, and to solve this issue all forms were spliced in subsequent experiments, including those that act as 'normal' forms (cf. Kemps, Wurm, et al. 2005). I used a similar methodology for creating my stimuli. I created four different types of stimuli; two mismatched forms and two matched forms, all of which were spliced, as described in detail in the following sections.

The goal of this task was to find out if listeners show different response patterns when they are exposed to a form with a mismatched stem and ending, for example when they expect to hear *days*, but they actually hear the pseudo-stem of *daze* with a spliced plural *s*.

6.2.1 Methodology

To perform the experiment, recordings of the different types of words that I am investigating had to be made – the complex word and the monomorphemic homophonous words. These were labeled with **B** and **C**[22]; these letters correspond to the type of word/stem in the recording;

---

[22] In the development of this task, there was also the condition **A** present, corresponding to the bare stem. This was disregarded later to simplify the analysis, but the labels **B** and **C** were kept for consistency with the data files.

B = complex e.g. *days*
C = monomorphemic e.g. *daze*

To test my hypothesis, I spliced these recordings into the matched and mismatched combinations of stems and endings that are displayed in Table 6.5.

Table 6.5: Combinations of matched and mismatched spliced forms that were created for the comprehension task. Examples highlight the parts of the recordings that were used to splice together the final form.

Splice	Part 1	Part 2	Example	
BB	complex stem	complex ending	*day*s [deɪ]	+ *day*s [z]
BC	complex stem	monomorphemic ending	*day*s [deɪ]	+ *daze* [z]
CB	pseudo-stem	complex ending	*daze* [deɪ]	+ *day*s [z]
CC	pseudo-stem	monomorphemic ending	*daze* [deɪ]	+ *daze* [z]

As mentioned previously, I also spliced the matched forms **BB** and **CC** from two separate recordings of these target words alongside the mismatched forms in order to prevent participant bias based on splicing as such (cf. Kemps, Wurm, et al. 2005). I expected listeners to show different behavior in their mouse tracks when exposed to a mismatched spliced form (**BC** or **CB**), but not when exposed to a matched spliced form (**BB** or **CC**).

The recordings for the stimuli were spoken by a native speaker of New Zealand English who had been living in Germany for about six months, and were recorded in the phonetics lab of Heinrich Heine Universität Düsseldorf. For each stimulus, three recordings were made and the most fluent two of these were used for the splicing process. For details on the recording process, also see section 6.1.1.1.

6.2.1.1 Target and filler items

The stimuli for the comprehension task are the 16 homophone word pairs plus the bare stem (i.e. 16 triplets) that I used as target items in the production experiment. These already went through a thorough selection process (see 5.1.2) and are ideally suited to investigate my research questions (see 2.6).

In addition to the target items, I also added another 16 items of similar nature. These 16 items were selected from the homophone word pairs used by Seyfarth et al. (2017). The difference to the target items here was that the filler items also include words that were deemed too problematic for the production task (see 5.1.2), as well as words ending in [t] and [d]. A complete list of target and filler items is given in the appendix.

Only the target items were spliced. Filler items were not spliced as these act as a distraction to the target items. A further advantage of unspliced filler items is that they should be easier to be responded to in that they will provide a baseline reaction time, and thus can be compared to the reaction times for the spliced items in a final analysis.

Each target item was recorded three times using three different lists read by the speaker. Out of these three recordings, two were used to create the spliced forms. For the mismatched forms **BC**, **CB**, recordings from the same list were used. For the matched forms **BB** and **CC**, recordings from two different lists were combined. The recordings were spliced using Praat. The resulting files for the target items numbered four different spliced forms (matched as well as mismatched; **BB**, **BC**, **CC**, **CB**). For the filler items, there were always two different unmanipulated files (e.g. *bored* and *board*).

6.2.1.2 Setup in OpenSesame

Altogether, there were 16 target stimuli pairs and 15 filler stimuli pairs in the experiment. The target items appeared in four different matched or mismatched combinations. The filler items were not spliced and there were only two files for each filler item. However, for equal balancing, each filler was also included four times in the experiment (two times as complex and two times as monomorphemic word).

To create this task in OpenSesame, an excel sheet was populated with the filenames and additional information that will help in the subsequent analysis, such as the selectable option (randomized), which type of splicing occurred (if available), and what type of item is being investigated. This excel sheet was copied into OpenSesame's trial list. To avoid priming, a randomization was implemented, which ensured that items from the same block were separated by at least three cycles, and items of the same stimulus type (target or filler), were separated by a distance of at least two cycles.

OpenSesame by default records a vast array of measurements that can later be analyzed, such as reaction times. Since I was particularly interested in whether listeners show different response patterns, I also implemented mouse-tracking into this task using the OpenSesame plugin mousetrap (Kieslich & Henninger 2017), which is also accompanied by an R package to analyze this data.

6.2.2 Analysis using QGAMs

Preliminary analysis of the data from the comprehension task was done by investigating and modelling the reaction times collected by OpenSesame, and visual inspection of the mousetracking data. An investigation of the reaction times did not provide any notable results and was merely used to filter out trials in which the participants did not provide a response within the given time limit.

Mousetracking data consists of a timeseries of changing spatial coordinates, which are characterized by strong correlations between the position at time t and that at t-1. This autocorrelation is not fixable in most statistical methods, such as for example in Generalized Additive Models (GAMs). A subtype of GAMs are Quantile Generalized Additive Mixed Models (QGAMs) introduced by Fasiolo et al. (2021), which offer a distribution-free method for estimating the predicted values for any given quantile of the response distribution. They are essentially the same as GAMs, except that they look only at one particular part of the curve. QGAMs are modelled separately for the x and y coordinates. It is up to the researcher to decide on which and how many quantiles they would like to investigate. For the analysis of my comprehension task, I looked at quantiles 0.1, 0.3, 0.5, 0.7, and 0.9 for the x and y coordinates of the mousetracking curves separately, so I ended up with ten different models per analyzed dataset. I used QGAMs also because GAMs had issues with autocorrelation in my data, as the data points are not independent and part of a mousetracking trajectory. QGAMs, on the other hand, offer much more accurate predictions even with autocorrelated data. For further reading on autocorrelation, GAMs, and QGAMs, I recommend Tomaschek et al. (2021:182).

For the interpretation of QGAMs, it is important to understand that each subsequent quantile contains also the previous quantile, i.e. QGAMs deal with conditional quantiles. To visualize this, Figure 6.8 shows a mousetracking curve next to the means of the fitted values of the five different quantiles that were calculated by the QGAMs for my data set containing the complex items (BB and CB).

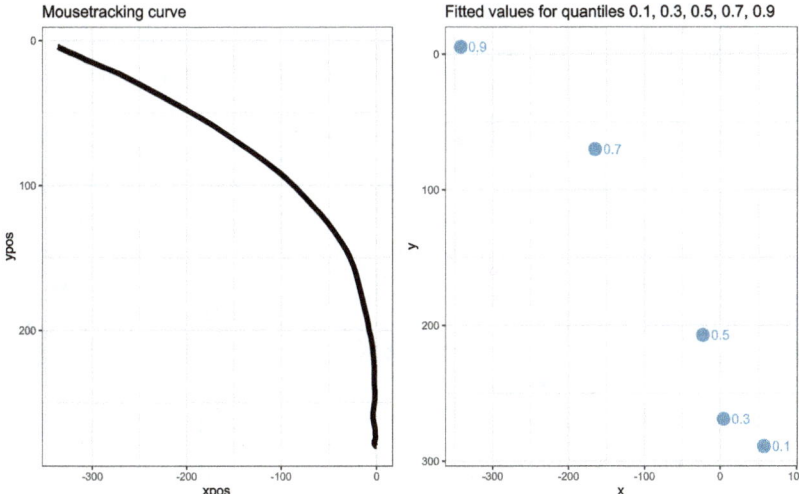

Fig. 6.8: Comparison of mousetracking curve and fitted values of quantiles. The left plot shows the mousetracking curve aggregated from all data in the dataset for complex items, while the left plot shows the means of the fitted values in the QGAM for complex items for each of the five quantiles.

It is not possible to determine the true locations of quantiles within a curve due to the method of calculation of individual quantiles, which is why the mean locations of these quantiles are slightly off if they would be overlayed on the curve. Each quantile is calculated individually anew, taking into account all independent variables. Furthermore, a direct overlay is not possible because the curve displays the raw data, while the QGAM fitted values are calculated by the model.

Figure 6.8 also shows that the majority of data points are located in the first and third quantiles, as these points are very close to the starting point to which the mouse was reset after each trial. This cluster represents the start of the trial during which participants are listening and comprehending, while not moving the mouse as much yet. In quantiles 0.5 and 0.7, there are less data points, but towards quantile 0.9, as participants make a decision, more mouse movement is recorded again. To better understand this density of data points, it is visualized in Figure 6.9. This figure shows an aggregated mouse tracking curve alongside the density of x data points (top plot) and y data points (right-hand plot).

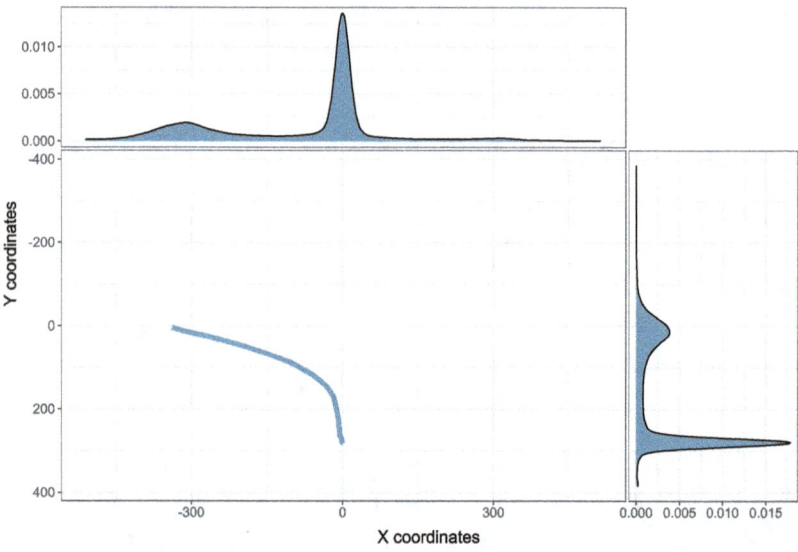

Fig. 6.9: Density of mouse movements in relation to the mousetracking curve. The curve is aggregated from all mouse movements in all datasets. The right-hand plot shows the density of datapoints for the y-axis, and the top plot shows the density of datapoints for the x-axis.

How exactly can QGAMs model the x and y coordinates of a mouse track? To illustrate how this is accomplished, compare the plots in Figure 6.10. The right-hand plot depicts the mouse tracks for the complex data set, with the blue curve representing matched items (BB), and the green curve representing mismatched items (CB). Using the mousetrap R package (Kieslich & Henninger 2017), these were spatially transformed in that the mouse tracks towards the right option shown to the participants on the screen were vertically mirrored onto the other side – this makes it easier to compare the two curves. Additionally, the mouse tracks were time-normalized, which makes them comparable without the influence of time as a third dimension.

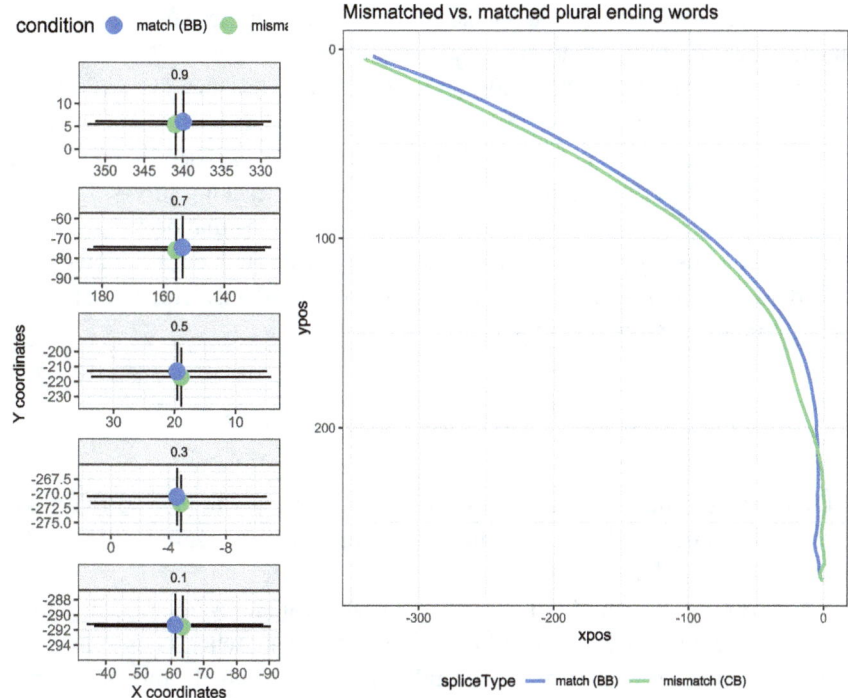

Fig. 6.10: Comparison of QGAM xy plots (left) and a mousetracking plot (right). The position of the dots in the xy plot corresponds to the curve in the mousetracking plot. Note that the mousetracking curve represents raw data and the xy plot predicted values. Matched condition equals BB, and mismatched condition equals CB. Scales are reversed in the mouse tracking plot.

Depicted in the left-hand plot are the x and y positions of the curves relative to each other as in the mousetracking plot[23]. This becomes apparent when taking a closer look at a particular quantile. Looking at, for example, the x 0.1 quantile, we can see that the blue dot is towards the left of the green dot. These positions correspond to the location of the blue (matched) and green (mismatched) lines in the mousetracking plot that is depicted on the right. Recall that the majority of datapoints are located in the first 3 quantiles, and that the location of the mean values of these are all relatively close the beginning of the curve (see Figure 6.8). This explains why the blue dot is still left of the green dot in quantile 0.5, and

---

23 QGAM xy plots were generated using the mtqgam package for R (Schmitz 2021).

only in quantile 0.7 they switch positions. A closer look at these positions will be taken in the upcoming results section.

Regarding participant behavior, it was technically possible for participants to click on an item before the entire stem of the word has been heard. As I am interested in whether or not their behavior differs when exposed to matched or mismatched stems, this could lead to confusing mouse tracking curves. To avoid this problem, all timestamps for the mousetracking curves that occur before the stem has been heard (i.e., timestamps smaller than the stem duration), were removed from the dataset and then analysis was conducted only with data after the point in time when the stem was heard.

6.2.3 Variables

The comprehension task includes a number of variables unique to this task. These will be explained in this section. Other variables are identical to those described in 4.1.3 and 6.1.1.5.

CONDITION is the condition according to which items were spliced, as explained in detail in 6.1.1. Values for this were either matched or mismatched. These were labelled as BB (matched plural splice), CC (matched monomorphemic splice), BC (mismatched monomorphemic ending splice with a false stem), and CB (mismatched plural ending splice with a false stem) in the specific subsets.

RESPONSE indicates what the participants clicked on in the experiments, which was either the complex option (e.g *days*) or the monomorphemic option (e.g. *daze*).

SENSITIVITY is a measure determined during the same-different task using the product of the *a'* values from Signal Detection Theory. This value is an indicator of whether the participant was more sensitive to the durational differences in the same-different task. A higher value indicates better sensitivity to durational differences, whereas a lower value indicates less sensitivity. Using the product of the *a'* values (as opposed to the sum or mean) has the advantage that differences between high and low values are more extreme, which better display the individual differences between participants. See also 6.1.1.5 and 6.1.2 for details on Signal Detection Theory.

ORDER is the order in which items were presented to participants in the task. This order was randomized in such a way that presentation of spliced items and filler items was balanced.

CUMULATIVEFREQ is the cumulative frequency of the complex and the monomorphemic word. Since the items were spliced together from complex and monomorphemic words, the frequencies of for example *days* and *daze* were added to create a cumulative frequency value. This frequency value was log-transformed.

PHONNEIGHBORDENSITY is equivalent to the phonological neighborhood density as used in the other studies. However, here it should be noted that the value for the complex word was used. Neighborhood density values are generally identical for homophones (e.g. *days* and *daze* have the same density value).

REACTIONTIME was automatically recorded during the experiment by OpenSesame. These were investigated in the preliminary analyses, but as there were not significant effects of REACTIONTIME, is was disregarded during the pro-cess of the analyzing the data.

6.2.4 Results

An analysis of reaction times using GAMs showed that there was no significant effect of CONDITION on the REACTIONTIME (see 6.2.2). This indicates that listeners are not slowed in their reaction time when exposed to a form with a mismatched stem, and thus, reaction time was not considered in any of the succeeding analyses

However, visual inspection of the mousetracking data indicates that participants behave differently when exposed to a form with a mismatched stem, as shown in Figure 6.11 for the two different types of words. The curves in the respective graphs show that participants behave differently when exposed to matched or mismatched items, particularly in the lower sections of the curve.

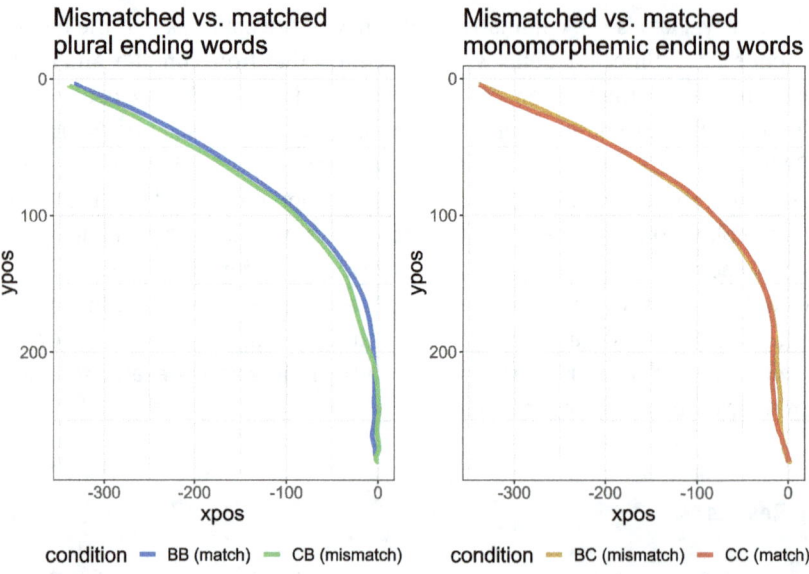

Fig. 6.11: Comparison of mouse tracks for plural (left) and monomorphemic (right) items. The differently colored lines show whether the condition was matched or mismatched.

However, these curves represent the raw data. In order to draw conclusions from these, I modelled them using quantile generalized additive mixed models (QGAMs), which provide a distribution-free method for estimating the predicted values for any given quantile of the response distribution, and allow stable prediction for data showing high levels of autocorrelation, as is the case in mouse-tracking curves.

6.2.4.1 QGAMs

QGAMs have to be fitted for the x and y coordinates of the mouse tracks separately, and may be fitted for any number of quantiles. I chose to generate QGAMs for five quantiles per coordinate; for 0.1, 0.3, 0.5, 0.7 and 0.9. Thus, modelling QGAMs for my data consisted of ten separate models; five for the x quantiles and five for y quantiles.

I modelled several different sets of QGAMs containing different sets of covariates. The QGAMs presented here are those which were deemed to have the best predictive power after comparing AIC scores of different models. Furthermore, I modelled the two types of matched and mismatched word endings separately, meaning that I created a set of QGAMs for the condition comparison between **BB** and **CB** (items with plural endings, matched or mismatched), and another set of

QGAMs for the condition comparison between **CC** and **BC** (items with monomorphemic endings, matched or mismatched).

In order to be able to get an overview of this large number of models at a glance, I created tables indicating the significance levels of each variable in each model[24]. These are Table 6.6 and Table 6.7, which will be discussed in their respective subsections below, one for each comparison (complex items with matched and mismatched stems, as well as monomorphemic items with matched and mismatched stems).

6.2.4.1.1 Complex items with matched and mismatched stems

Table 6.6 shows that for some quantiles, there is a significant difference between the matched (**BB**) and mismatched (**CB**) condition for both the x and y quantiles. This can be seen in the row of interest, which is CONDITION: mismatched, which lists the significance of the mismatched stem when compared to the matched stem (which is the baseline).

Here it can be seen that the difference in splicing condition is significant for the x 0.1, x 0.7, x 0.9 and for the y 0.1, y 0.3, y 0.5 and y 0.9 quantiles. As discussed in chapter 6.2.2, it is to be expected that the middle quantiles show less activity, as the vast majority of data points for the mouse movements occur in the lowest and highest quantiles (see also Figure 6.9). This can especially be observed in the x quantiles in this model, as only the first and the ninth quantile are highly significant.

Regarding participant behaviour, the significance of the first and ninth x quantiles would indicate that participants show uncertainty at the beginning of the task, and once they make a decision, they move their mouse either to the left or to the right (which is captured and represented here by the x-axis).

For the y axis, in this model all quantiles except quantile 0.7 are highly significant. Similar to the values for x, this indicates that participants show some uncertainty before making a final decision and moving their mouse upwards to the answer option (captured and represented here by the values for y axis).

Additionally, there are two other covariates and one interaction in this model. The covariate SENSITIVITY is a variable indicating how this participant performed during the same-different task. Participants who were sensitive had a higher values here, and participants who were less sensitive had a lower value.

---

[24] Detailed model outputs for each quantile can be found in the online repository.

Table 6.6: Significance of variables in the set of QGAMs comparing complex items with matched and mismatched stems are listed in the columns corresponding to a particular quantile of x (left) and y (right) coordinates. The variable of interest is CONDITION. Signif. codes: 0 '***' 0.001 '**' 0.01 '*' 0.05 '.' 0.1 'ns' = not significant.

Var Type	Variable	X 0.1	X 0.3	X 0.5	X 0.7	X 0.9	Y 0.1	Y 0.3	Y 0.5	Y 0.7	Y 0.9
	Intercept	***	ns	***	***	***	***	***	***	*	**
Parametric coefficients	baseline: CONDITION: matched (BB)										
	CONDITION: mismatched (CB)	***	ns	ns	*	***	***	**	***	ns	***
	baseline: RESPONSE: complex										
	RESPONSE: monomorphemic	***	*	ns	ns	***	***	ns	ns	**	***
	CONDITION mismatched (CB) * RESPONSE monomorphemic	***	.	ns	*	***	***	ns	ns	ns	***
Smooth terms	ORDER	ns	***	***	***	***	***	***	***	***	***
	CumulativeFreq	ns	ns	ns	ns	ns	ns	***	***	*	*
	PhonNeighborDensity	*	ns	ns	ns	ns	ns	ns	ns	**	ns
	Sensitivity	ns	ns	.	*	ns	ns	ns	ns	ns	ns
	Item	***	***	**	***	***	***	**	.	ns	***
	ParticipantID	***	***	***	***	***	***	***	***	***	***

The covariate RESPONSE lists what participants clicked on – the monomorphemic answer option (e.g. *daze*), or the complex answer option (e.g. *days*). Due to the nature of this experiment, the location of these answer options was randomized in the task, therefore this was added as a covariate as it could affect the mouse tracks.

Finally, there was also an interaction between CONDITION and RESPONSE. This is significant for some quantiles. This interaction delivers insight into what participants clicked on based on which condition they were exposed to, which is visualized in Figure 6.12. The interaction arises because for some quantiles, the curves flip position when responding complex or monomorphemic, especially in quantile 0.9 and 0.1 (which are also the quantiles which contain the most data points).

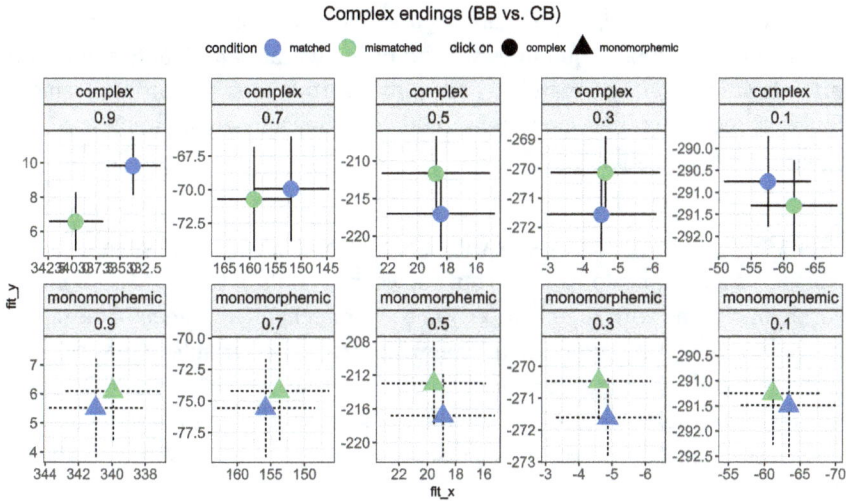

Fig. 6.12: Interaction for complex items between condition and participant response in the QGAM models. Colors refer to the matched or mismatched CONDITION. Dots (top row) indicate that participants clicked on the complex answer option on the screen, while triangles (bottom row) indicate they clicked on the monomorphemic option on the screen. Lines display ¼ of the calculated confidence intervals. Quantile 0.9 (left) is closest to the response given.

The dots in Figure 6.12 show the location of the mouse track in the corresponding quantile for cases in which participants clicked on the complex answer option on the screen (e.g. *days*). Locations further to the left (x axis) and locations higher (y axis) indicate that participants made faster decisions, and thus it can be assumed that they answered with more certainty. Locations lower and more to the right would therefore indicate that participants were less decisive in performing the task.

In Figure 6.12 we can see a general trend that on the x-axis, there is an advantage for matched items in the later quantiles (0.7, 0.9) when monomorphemic was responded, but not when complex was responded). On the y-axis, there is an advantage for matched items in the early quantiles (0.1) when complex was answered, and an advantage for matched items when monomorphemic was answered in the later quantiles (0.7, 0.9).

All of the items in this dataset are complex items, either with a spliced matched stem, or with a false monomorphemic stem. With this in mind, participants would be expected to always choose the complex answer with most certainty when listening to the matched item. As the model output for this model indicates that there is a significant interaction between condition and response for quantile 0.1 and 0.9, these quantiles are where we would most likely be able to see an effect. In both quantiles we can observe that participants show more certainty when hearing a matched item with regard to their upwards movement. However, regarding their movement to the left, they appear slightly less certain towards the end in quantile 0.9.

6.2.4.1.2 Monomorphemic items with matched and mismatched stems

Table 6.7 is analogous to Table 6.6 but shows the results of the QGAMs for monomorphemic items with matched (**CC**) and mismatched (**BC**) stems. The results show more variation than those for complex items. The variable of interest, CONDITION, is significant for a number of quantiles, especially 0.7 and 0.9. Other covariates behave similarly to the complex models, and also the interaction between CONDITION and RESPONSE is present in some quantiles, most notably in almost all x quantiles.

Table 6.7: Significance of variables in the set of QGAMs for monomorphemic items, comparing these with matched and mismatched stems are listed in the columns corresponding to a particular quantile of x (left) and y (right) coordinates. The variable of interest is CONDITION. Signif. codes: 0 '***' 0.001 '**' 0.01 '*' 0.05 '.' 0.1 'ns' = not significant.

Var Type	Variable	X 0.1	X 0.3	X 0.5	X 0.7	X 0.9	Y 0.1	Y 0.3	Y 0.5	Y 0.7	Y 0.9
Parametric coefficients	Intercept	***	***	***	***	***	***	***	***	***	ns
	baseline: CONDITION: matched (CC)										
	CONDITION: mismatched (BC)	.	***	**	***	***	.	*	**	***	***
	baseline: RESPONSE: complex										
	RESPONSE: monomorphemic	*	***	ns	ns	*	*	**	**	***	ns
	CONDITION mismatched * RESPONSE monomorphemic	.	***	**	***	***	*	**	**	***	ns
Smooth terms	ORDER	*	***	***	***	***	***	***	***	***	***
	CumulativeFreq	ns	ns	.	ns	ns	***	ns	ns	ns	ns
	PhonNeighborDensity	ns	ns	ns	ns	ns	ns	ns	ns	ns	.
	Sensitivity	ns	**	*	.	.	ns	ns	ns	ns	ns
	Item	***	***	***	***	***	***	***	***	***	***
	ParticipantID	***	***	***	***	***	***	***	***	***	***

As in the model for complex items, this model also shows an interaction between CONDITION and RESPONSE. This interaction is visualized in Figure 6.13. In this dataset, one would expect an advantage for matched items for the RESPONSE monomorphemic, which can, to some extent, be seen in the lower half of Figure 6.13. For the y axis, matched items indeed show an advantage, for the x axis this is only strongly visible in quantile 0.9, which is however, the important quantile as it represents the participant's decision. This quantile is also highly significant for both x and y by itself, as well as in the interaction between CONDITION and RESPONSE.

What Figure 6.13 shows fairly clearly though, is that mismatched items are at a more obvious disadvantage, regardless of which response participants clicked on. In all quantiles, participants were slower to answer with the upward mouse movement (y axis), and in a number of quantiles they were also slower to answer in their horizontal movements (x axis). With a focus on quantile 0.9, which represents the final decision, contains a large amount of datapoints, and is statistically highly significant for both x and y, it can be concluded from this data that participants do behave differently, i.e. respond slower and with more uncertainty, when exposed to a mismatched stem.

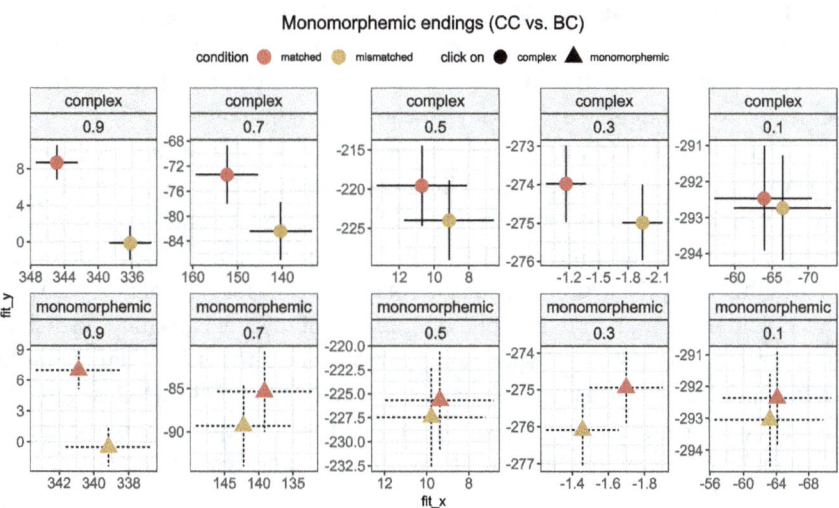

Fig. 6.13: Interaction for monomorphemic items between condition and participant response in the QGAM models. Colors refer to the matched or mismatched condition. Dots (top row) indicate that participants clicked on the complex answer option on the screen, while triangles (bottom row) indicate they clicked on the monomorphemic option on the screen. Lines display ¼ of the calculated confidence intervals. Quantile 0.9 (left) is closest to the response given.

6.2.5 Summary of comprehension task

Comparing the results of the QGAMs for complex items and of the QGAMs for monomorphemic items, the monomorphemic QGAMs appear to be more straightforward and interpretable. A possible cause for this discrepancy is that monomorphemic words are simpler in their nature – listeners do not expect any complexity in monomorphemic words. In complex words, on the other hand, listeners would expect complexity, thus listeners overall responded less confidently.

There are a number of other possible explanations for the difference in behavior between monomorphemic and complex words. Another example would be possible durational differences between the stems of monomorphemic and complex words. Seyfarth et al. (2017) found that stems of monomorphemic words are shorter than stems of complex words. Shorter monomorphemic stems, could then represent the quicker and more confident responses that I observed in the QGAMs. However, since I found contrary results concerning durational differences of monomorphemic and complex stems in my own studies, drawing conclusions from the influence of durations does not seem plausible at this point.

Finally, there are a number of other factors that could have affected the mouse movements of participants. An obvious factor would be left- or right-handedness of the participant. HANDEDNESS was included in early stages of the analysis, however, due to the distribution of the data, there was not enough predictive power for this variable - there was one participant who was left-handed, one participant who was ambidextrous, and 38 who were right-handed.

To summarize, the analysis of the mousetracking data using QGAMs has shown that CONDITION significantly influences mouse tracks in some models, particularly in those for monomorphemic ending items, and to some extent those for complex ending items. Participants show different response patterns based on the whether the spliced form was matched or mismatched for most of the quantiles. This is evidence for an influence of the phonetics of the stem on comprehension. Furthermore, the RESPONSE (what participants clicked on) is also significant in some quantiles. These results would suggest that fine phonetic detail is stored in the mental lexicon to some degree, and influences participants during comprehension. I will discuss the theoretical implications of my results in section 7.3.

7 Discussion

The results of my studies have shown that there does not appear to be such a thing as a 'well-established' phonetic paradigm uniformity effect. I attempted to replicate and evolve research on paradigm uniformity by Seyfarth et al. (2017), and largely did not succeed. I performed two corpus studies and a production experiment, which all provided mixed results with regards to possible paradigm uniformity effects. Additionally, I performed two exploratory perception experiments, which have shown that listeners are sensitive to durational differences. However, the interpretation of these in regards to paradigm uniformity provides to be somewhat challenging, as they do not directly investigate the perception of paradigm uniformity, but rather more generally the perception of phonetic properties similar to it.

In this chapter, I will discuss my findings within the larger context of research and the replication crisis, compare my results to findings from other publications, and attempt to explain possible implications for theory resulting from my findings. I will discuss categorical paradigm uniformity, gradient paradigm uniformity, and perception in their own respective subchapters.

7.1 Categorical paradigm uniformity

My concept of categorical paradigm uniformity originates from Seyfarth et al. (2017)'s prediction that stems of morphologically complex words should be longer due to gestural scores. Recall that Seyfarth's conceptualization of paradigm uniformity is based on the idea that the articulatory plan of freestanding stems is co-activated when producing related complex forms, e.g. when producing *days*, the articulatory plan of *day* is co-activated. Seyfarth et al. (2017) predicted that the stem of *days* would be pronounced longer than the pseudo-stem of monomorphemic homophones such as *daze*. This occurs because of the related form *day* being elongated as it ends in an open syllable and the articulatory plan of *day* is transferred to *days*.

In their experiment, Seyfarth et al. (2017) found that stems of complex words ending in [s, z] are longer than pseudo-stems of monomorphemic words ending in [s, z]. For words ending in [t, d], they found a null result. My studies delivered mixed results contrary to Seyfarth's findings, an overview of which is given in Table 7.1. In the QuakeBox corpus, there was no evidence for a categorical paradigm uniformity effect. In the Buckeye corpus, I did not find a categorical paradigm uniformity effect for third person singular words, but I did find an effect with an interaction of word form frequency for plural and past tense words, rendering these results unclear. The effect that I found was in the opposite direction of what Seyfarth and colleagues predicted: stems of complex words were shorter than stems of monomorphemic words. Finally, in my production experiment I did not find conclusive evidence for a categorical paradigm uniformity effect, as the type of morpheme did not have an effect on the stem duration at all.

Table 7.1: Summary of the results for categorical paradigm uniformity in all of my studies, as well as number of types and tokens in each dataset used. Column 1 show the dataset, column 2 the presence of absence of a categorical paradigm uniformity effect (i.e. a significant difference between the stem duration of monomorphemic and complex words).

Study	Categorical Paradigm Uniformity	Tokens/Types
QuakeBox: plural [z]	absent	422 tokens, 38 types
Buckeye: plural [s] and [z]	unclear	1894 tokens, 95 types
Buckeye: 3sg [s] and [z]	absent	742 tokens, 32 types
Buckeye: past tense [t] and [d]	absent	729 tokens, 60 types
Production Experiment: [s] and [z]	absent	1154 tokens, 32 types

To sum up, the paradigm uniformity effect as established by Seyfarth et al. (2017) could not be replicated, as I found different results in corpora and in my own experimental setup. One can only speculate for possible causes of this irreplicability. A likely confounding factor is homophones. Seyfarth's experiment used frequency-matched homophone word pairs, and it is probable that it is the homophones that influence each other in production, rather than the suggested influence of paradigm members. Any analysis of homophones comes with certain challenges, as explained in detail in chapter 3.2.2.

Frequency-matched homophone pairs are especially complicated, and in the case of Seyfarth's study they present a rather exceptional sample drawn from a much larger population of forms that are subject to many different influences in production. In my studies, I did not use frequency-matched homophones. Rather, in the corpus studies I used non-matched non-homophones, whereas in the production experiment I used homophones that represented different frequency constellations (e.g. high frequency monomorphemic words compared to low frequency complex words or vice versa).

The lack of categorical paradigm uniformity due to the role of homophones in these experiments raises the question of how homophones influence each other in the mental lexicon. Do they have a shared phonological representation, as suggested in the Two-Stage Model by Levelt, Roelofs & Mayer (1999), or do they have independent lexical representations, as suggested in the Independent Network model by Caramazza (1997)? As mentioned in chapter 3.2.2, there does not appear to be a consensus on the lexical processing of homophones; some researchers have found evidence for a shared phonological representation, while others argue for independent phonological representations. Additional complications are the frequency of occurrence, the orthographic status (heterographic or homographic), and the morphological structure of homophones.

Based on my lack of findings for a categorical paradigm uniformity effect, one could argue for a shared representation, as the type of morpheme did not play a role in the prediction of the stem duration. This would suggest that homophones such as *days* and *daze* would be accessed from the same source node within the mental lexicon, whereas the contrary findings of Seyfarth at el. would argue for independent representations. My findings would also be in line with Biedermann & Nickels (2008), who assume that homophones have a shared representation – regardless of whether they are homographic or heterographic.

The homophones used in my experiment add another level of complication to this discussion – many of them are not only homophonous, they are also often subject to conversion. I selected items to avoid this problem as best as possible, but most verbs and nouns in English can still be subject to conversion. Additionally, I used a variable specifically to control for conversion pairs (such as for example *brews*, which is used as a noun in my experiment, but which also occurs as a verb). Despite these efforts, it is plausible that there is some sort of residual effect of noun-verb homophones on each other (see Lohmann (2018b) on the effect of lemma frequency on noun-verb homophones), in addition to these words also having monomorphemic homophones (in this case, *bruise*).

To summarize, homophones are accompanied by serious problems, and as of now, it is quite unclear how to make reliable predictions based on experimental designs that use homophones. There is already an established body of research on the representation of homophones in the mental lexicon, with some arguing for separate representation, and others arguing for shared representations. One might conclude that homophones are not a good means to investigate phonetic effects, as the problems that they bring with them seem to outweigh the benefits. Generally, it appears that they seem to behave differently from non-homophones in their properties.

Aside from the homophone problem, there are a number of other possible causes for the lack of a solid categorical paradigm uniformity effect. For instance, there may be a lack of statistical power in some of my studies. The QuakeBox dataset was comparatively small with only 431 tokens and 38 types, and the selection of items was highly restrictive (only monosyllabic words ending in a vowel plus /z/ sequence were used). The Buckeye datasets were bigger and less restrictive (which, however, can cause new problems). The plural dataset had 1894 items ending in [s] or [z], the third person singular dataset had 742 items ending in [s] or [z], and the past tense dataset had 729 items ending in [t] or [d]. My production experiment data had a larger number of items with 1154, but only had 16 different homophone pairs (i.e. 32 lexemes). For all corpora, the number of types was usually sampled with fewer restrictions and larger compared to those in mine and Seyfarth's experiment. To compare, Seyfarth et al. (2017), who found a categorical paradigm uniformity effect, had 16 plural forms and 16 homophones, but a larger amount of tokens.

Finally, the methodological differences are a likely contribution to the inconclusive results of my studies. Seyfarth et al. (2017) observed categorical paradigm uniformity under laboratory conditions. It is advisable to test such effects also under the conditions of everyday language use, such as in a corpus – which I did using two different corpora. There are certainly discrepancies between the findings of these, as well as between my own corpus studies and production experiment. Not only that, but also other studies, such as Frazier (2006) or Seyfarth, Vander Klok & Garellek (2019), produced inconclusive or null results. Herein lies a challenge for future studies on categorical paradigm uniformity; find a solid methodology that addresses all the problems of mine and other previous studies in order to find evidence for or against the existence of a categorical paradigm effect, and possibly lead us a step further away from the current replication crisis.

7.2 Gradient paradigm uniformity

To discuss gradient paradigm uniformity, it is important to recall the two different predictions that I made. The first prediction is based on Seyfarth et al. (2017)'s idea that greater activation strength of the bare stem leads to a stronger influence on the duration of the morphologically related form. In my studies, I found no evidence of such an effect. In fact, the QuakeBox study shows the opposite direction of the effect predicted by that approach.

The absence of the alleged effect is, however, expected, when taking well-known frequency-related phonetic reduction effects into account. A higher frequency of the bare stem goes together with shorter duration of the bare stem. Likewise, a higher frequency of the plural word goes together with shorter duration of the plural stem (general frequency effect). And if the influence on the duration of related forms is exerted via the articulatory plans, it can be expected that shorter duration of the high-frequency bare stem will lead to a shorter duration of the plural stem.

In other words, one would not only expect a general frequency effect, but also a gradient paradigm uniformity effect in which high bare stem frequency shortens the duration of its related plural form. This raises the problem of collinearity. Bare stem frequency and word form frequency (e.g. frequencies of *day* and *days*) have been shown to be highly correlated in most of my datasets, raising the concern that what I hypothesized to be a gradient paradigm uniformity effect might actually be a masked word form frequency effect. In my studies, I have certainly found some indications for such a masked word form frequency effect, but all over, my results are rather contradictory at a glance. Table 7.2 lists the studies that I performed alongside their results. The three rightmost columns show the presence or absence of an effect of bare stem frequency on the stem duration as well as of word form frequency (with only one of these being present in the respective model), and the results of a frequency band analysis. In the latter, I reduced the dataset to items in which stem frequency and word form frequency do not correlate, and then included both bare stem frequency and word form frequency in the model.

Table 7.2: Summary of the results for gradient paradigm uniformity in all of my studies, as well as number of types and tokens in each dataset used. Column 1 shows the dataset, column 2 the presence or absence of an effect of bare stem frequency on the stem duration of the complex word, column 3 the presence or absence of an effect of bare stem frequency in a sub-dataset which also includes the word form frequency, and column 4 shows a general frequency effect (with the same dataset as that used for bare stem frequency).

Study	Gradient Paradigm Uniformity		General Freq. Effect
	Stem Freq	Freq. band	Word Form Freq
QuakeBox: plural [z]	present (287 tokens, 20 types)	present (159 tokens, 10 types)	absent (287 tokens, 20 types)
Buckeye: plural [s] and [z]	present (949 tokens, 60 types)	present (503 tokens, 20 types)	present (949 tokens, 60 types)
Buckeye: 3sg [s] and [z]	present (452 tokens, 20 types)	absent (348 tokens, 14 types)	present (452 tokens, 20 types)
Buckeye: past tense [t] and [d]	present (414 tokens, 36 types)	absent (217 tokens, 19 types)	absent (414 tokens, 36 types)
Production experiment: [s] and [z]	present (556 tokens, 16 types)	absent (287 tokens, 8 types)	present (589 tokens, 16 types)

As listed in the table, an effect of gradient paradigm uniformity (i.e. bare stem frequency influences the stem duration of the complex form) was present in all my studies. The general frequency effect (using word form frequency to predict the stem duration of the complex word) was not present in the QuakeBox corpus dataset, and also not in the Buckeye dataset for past tense, but it was present in all other datasets. This is a somewhat confusing, as this is an effect that I would expect in any dataset – a general phonetic reduction effect due to high frequency has been very well established in the literature (Bell et al. 2003; Pluymaekers, Ernestus & Baayen 2005b; Aylett & Turk 2006; Gahl 2008; Bell et al. 2009; Gahl, Yao & Johnson 2012). It is possible that the lack of an effect is due to a lack in statistical power, as the QuakeBox dataset and the Buckeye past tense datasets are both rather small.

This lack of statistical power is likely also a cause for the somewhat contradictory results that I found for the frequency band analysis in most of my studies. As listed in Table 7.2 a gradient uniformity effect was still present in the QuakeBox and Buckeye plural datasets when simultaneously also controlling for an effect of word form frequency. In these datasets, stems in plural words that are based on low frequency bare stems show longer durations, while plurals based on high frequency bare stems show shorter durations. This is fully in line with the idea that higher frequency of occurrence of a form leads to shorter durations. Following up on the idea that the stored articulatory gestures of a bare stem may influence the gestures used to produce morphologically related forms, these related forms show traces of the stem pronunciation, in this case its duration.

However, such an effect was not found for any of the other datasets, and also not in the production experiment (which as an additional complication used homophones). Also, recall that Seyfarth et al. (2017) found that neither the absolute frequency of the stem nor relative frequency had any effect on the duration of the inflected stems. How can the discrepancy between their results for gradient paradigm uniformity and my results for some of my datasets be explained? Seyfarth et al. do not discuss their null result concerning gradient paradigm uniformity, but concede from the beginning that their "analyses should be interpreted with caution, in particular because the stimuli were not selected to include a broad range of either frequency measure" (2017:9). This begs to wonder whether the items in the QuakeBox dataset represent a broad range of frequency that allowed this effect to surface. However, the dataset is very small with only 159 items, and thus the statistical power is likely not sufficient to draw solid conclusions from this data. It is entirely possible that the effect in the frequency band analysis surfaced in this dataset by chance. The results from most of the other datasets also most likely indicate that there is no solid evidence for a gradient uniformity effect.

The effects of word form frequency found in the QuakeBox dataset are in line with those for lemma frequency (Jurafsky et al. 2001; Bell et al. 2009; Gahl 2008; Lohmann 2018b) and those for word form frequency elsewhere (Caselli, Caselli & Cohen-Goldberg 2016; Lõo et al. 2018). Particularly pertinent are the findings in Caselli, Caselli & Cohen-Goldberg (2016). These authors demonstrated that the bare stem frequency of words inflected with *-ed* and *-ing* negatively correlates with the duration of these words in speech. Although Caselli, Caselli & Cohen-Goldberg (2016) did not measure the stem duration of the inflected words (but the duration of the whole word instead), it can be safely assumed that not only the whole word, but also the stem showed this negative correlation between bare stem frequency and duration of the plural stem (see Plag, Homann & Kunter (2017) and Plag et al. (2020) for evidence and discussion of the general relation between word duration and stem duration).

However, the lack of results in some of my other datasets begs the question of how useful bare stem duration truly is. In a paper focusing on the processing and storage of words, Baayen, Wurm & Aycock (2007) concluded that both root frequency (bare stem frequency) and surface frequency (word form frequency) can show an effect on processing, but they conclude that word form frequency is more useful and more prominent, whereas bare stem frequency is not so well suited.

So what does bare stem frequency as a measure for the processing of complex words tell us? Does a gradient paradigm uniformity effect exist? There does not appear to be a consensus on this, neither in previous research, nor in my own studies. Due to the different results from different datasets, it is presently impossible to make generalizations on the existence of a gradient paradigm uniformity effect and the possible processing of such effects in the mental lexicon. The present studies were unable to replicate not only the predictions by Seyfarth et al. (2017), but also my own findings from the QuakeBox corpus study by using the Buckeye corpus. More research would be needed to make reliable claims on the existence of gradient paradigm uniformity.

7.3 Perception

Previous research has shown that there are differences in the phonetic realization of English morphologically complex words – such as for example in some, but not all of my studies. Other researchers have found systematic differences between different types of word-final /s/ depending on the morphological context (Plag, Homann & Kunter 2017b; Schmitz, Baer-Henney & Plag 2020). However, findings such as these beg the question of what purpose these differences serve in perception. Is it possible that listeners actually make use of these differences in perception and comprehension?

Questions such as those motivated the addition of two perception studies to my research. I conducted two experiments – a same-different task to determine whether durational differences of 10, 25, 50 or 75 milliseconds are perceivable, and a comprehension task following up on that to investigate whether durational differences affect the comprehension of listeners.

The analysis of the same-different task has shown that participants can perceive possible durational differences between different types of stems in complex and simplex words. There is a variable pattern in that some listeners perceive 25 and 50 millisecond differences, while almost all participants can perceive 75 millisecond differences reliably.

Similarly, the analysis of the mouse tracking data in the comprehension task has shown that the matched or mismatched splicing condition significantly influences mouse tracks in all models, those for monomorphemic items, and those for complex items. The results indicate that listeners perceive and are affected by the subtle differences in the stimuli, and that the comprehension system makes use of such information. These results are consistent with a large body of research providing evidence that listeners perceive fine phonetic detail, and morphological and boundary-related information in particular (Blazej & Cohen-Goldberg 2015; Shatzman & McQueen 2006; Schmitz et al. 2021b; Davis, Marslen-Wilson & Gaskell 2002; Kemps, Wurm, et al. 2005; Kemps, Ernestus, et al. 2005; Lee, Kaiser & Goldstein 2020; Salverda, Dahan & McQueen 2003).

My research, as well as previous research, has shown that participants evaluate durational differences. There are different types of models of speech perception that could be used to explain my results, which were introduced in chapter 3.3. Abstractionist models do not assume that subphonemic detail such as duration plays a role in the disambiguation of speech signals. Therefore, these models do not seem suitable to explain my findings. Similarly, feature-based models also do not account for fine phonetic detail, as they assume that only marked (irregular or unusual) information is useful in comprehension.

Exemplar-based models, such as those introduced by Goldinger (1998) would be more suitable to explain the results of both the same different task and the comprehension task, as these models assume that perceptual details of speech are stored in the mental lexicon and are important factors in speech perception. In Goldinger (1998)'s approach, spoken words were represented by vectors of simple elements, which allow for storage of segment durations and voice characteristics – the latter of which could explain the ability of speakers to determine matched and mismatched items as in the comprehension task.

Another exemplar-based model that allows such features to be stored in the mental lexicon is the model by Johnson (1997). In this model, prosodic and durational information specific to the word can be stored in the mental lexicon. Johnson (1997)'s model was trained on vector-quantized speech data, and was able to correctly anticipate whether an incoming syllable was followed by another syllable or not. This suggests that in this model, a constructed (matched or mismatched) stem with short segment durations would less effectively activate the 'normal' stem node than the actual stem. The model suggested by Pierrehumbert (2001; 2003) makes similar predictions.

While useful to a certain degree, neither of these models makes any clear predictions about the perception of matched and mismatched phonetic details such as those I used in my comprehension task. There has been no research on words constructed from simplex-complex homophones, and no speech perception models presently exist to explain the emergence of the fine phonetic detail that sets apart simplex-complex homophones. To conclude, there are certain models on perception that could be applied to explain my findings, but they are not ideally suited and my findings call for more adequate and more elaborate models of speech perception and comprehension.

7.4 Summary and outlook

My studies have shown that the existence of paradigm uniformity effects as conceived by Seyfarth et al. (2017) is nowhere near confirmed. Though a large body of research has shown that phonetic effects on morphology exist, the question of the phonetic consequences of the possible existence of paradigm uniformity may be seen as part of a much larger set of questions concerned with the mutual influence of lexically related forms in speech production. Consulting recent literature that focuses on acoustic properties, there is one study in particular that has looked at the effects of frequency on how similar words influence each other's pronunciation: Goldrick et al. (2011). That study, like my studies, tested conflicting predictions across pairs of forms of varying frequency. These authors investigated how in speech errors (like in the outcome *path* for intended target *bath*) the frequency of the target and of the erroneous outcome influence the phonetic properties of the outcome. They find that low frequency targets produce larger phonetic traces in the outcomes than high frequency targets, and that low frequency outcomes are less influenced by phonetic traces of the target. These phonetic traces include vowel duration as a secondary cue to voicing. These results are in line with other studies that have shown that low frequency words exhibit enhanced phonetic processing, resulting in, among other things, longer durations (see 3.2.1).

Other researchers have proposed that morphologically conditioned phonetic effects may arise from competition between language-specific general phonological patterns and word-specific structures, leading to intermediate forms or greater variability (e.g. Gafos (2006); Van Oostendorp (2008); Winter & Roettger (2011)). Consider the velarization of /l/ in English. The /l/ in suffixed forms like *knee.l#ing* is considerably darker than the /l/ in the same syllabic position of mono-morphemic words (Sproat & Fujimura 1993; Lee-Kim, Davidson & Hwang 2013). This may be explained as an effect of paradigmatic uniformity, such that the velarized coda-/l/ of the stem influences the pronunciation of the onset-/l/ in the morphologically related suffixed form. Alternatively, the phonetic traces of the stem may arise through the competition between the general preference for clear [l] in onset position in English on the one hand, and the word-specific expectation for [ɫ] (cf. *kneel, kneels, knelt,* all featuring [ɫ]). However, the variability in the duration of stems does not involve a tension between general versus word-specific phonological patterns. This is therefore not a valid explanation for some of my findings, such as those from the QuakeBox corpus.

The results of my studies are inconclusive at best, therefore it is questionable as to in how far one should try to find possible explanations for my findings (or lack thereof). If there was such a thing as paradigm uniformity effects after Seyfarth, this would be a challenge for modular phonological theories (such as Lexical Phonology (Kiparsky 2015)), and for modular, strictly feed-forward models of speech production (such as the Levelt model in Levelt, Roelofs & Mayer (1999)). In these models morphological information is no longer available at post-lexical stages. Paradigm uniformity effects thus would seem to provide prima facie evidence for interactive models of speech production, in which spreading activation of morphologically related words plays a prominent role (e.g. Ernestus & Baayen 2006; Ernestus & Baayen 2007; Baayen et al. 2007; Roettger et al. 2014; Dell 1986; Goldrick 2006; Goldrick 2014).

Paradigm uniformity and the replication crisis
Quite obviously, with its failure of successful replication, my project adds to the ongoing replication crisis in quantitative linguistics. I set out to replicate findings by Seyfarth et al. (2017), and not only did I find contrary findings to their study, but I was also unable to replicate those findings again in my own follow-up studies. With this, I am further demonstrating that many "well-established" effects in linguistics are not reproducible in follow-up studies.

It is quite possible that in my own studies I fell into some of the methodological fallacies that were mentioned by Sönning & Werner (2021), and that some of my studies suffer from methodological shortcomings for which solutions have yet to be discovered as part of the cyclical evolution of scientific theory. Returning to the topic of the special issue on the replication crisis by Sönning & Werner (2021a), some contributors argue that it is not surprising at all that empirical research will often fail to replicate. Grieve (2021: 1344) argues that "even when best and consistent research practices are followed, [...] language is an inextricably social phenomenon, making it impossible for linguists to fully control social context across independent replications". Language is indeed vastly different in its characteristics, and unlike in physical sciences, the parameters of an experiments are impossible to keep stable across replications when dealing with language. A linguistic experiment is by necessity always a unique social event and exact replication is impossible – point in case are my two corpora, one of which uses emotional monologues of speakers of New Zealand English, while the other uses conversational speech of American English. Though in my experiment I also used New Zealand English, here the methodology was entirely different again, as rather than monologues, participants were asked to read out a cloze task. But even in an exact replication with the exact same speakers, there will always be variation when dealing with language, as the setting, time of day or the social context may be different and it is a known fact that nobody pronounces the same word twice in exactly the same way – this is physically impossible (see also Grieve 2021: 1352).

Methodology and sample size also play a significant role in the context of the replication crisis, as Vasishth & Gelman (2021: 1320) discuss; "conclusions based on data are almost always uncertain, and this is regardless of whether the outcome of the statistical test is statistically significant or not". Furthermore, they argue that "[w]hen power is low, any significant effect that is found in a particular experiment will tend not to replicate. In other words, in larger-sample direct replication attempts, the effect size will tend to be smaller and a statistically significant effect will tend to be found to be non-significant" (2021: 1317). My replication attempts had varying, mostly small sample sizes and numbers of types and tokens, which could indicate a lack of statistical power. The datasets were also restricted to certain morphological and phonetic criteria, making generalizations difficult to establish.

Finally, as Sönning & Werner (2021c) encourage, I will not draw strong conclusions from my data – not only because that seems presently impossible, but also to encourage other researchers to follow up on my research. My data is freely available online[25], and anyone who is interested in advancing research on paradigm uniformity effects is most welcome to re-analyze my data.

---

[25] The link to the online repository is available in the appendix.

8 Conclusion

What exactly happens phonetically in the production of stems? Do inflectional stems indeed differ phonetically from monomorphemic words? Can these differences be perceived? Inspired by the study by Seyfarth et al. (2017), I aimed to answer these questions in a replication project by investigating data from two corpora and a production experiment, as well as by extending my research with two perception experiments. I investigated what happens phonetically in the stems of words that end in homophonous suffixes, and whether listeners can perceive these subtle phonetic differences.

To investigate paradigm uniformity effects in production, I have performed three studies involving speech production: two corpus studies and an experiment. With these studies, I aimed to replicate the findings by Seyfarth et al. (2017) that stems of words ending in [s, z] have longer durations if these words are inflected words, whereas the pseudo-stems in monomorphemic words ending in [s, z] have shorter durations. This potential effect I termed 'categorical paradigm uniformity'. I was not able to replicate the results by Seyfarth et al. (2017) conclusively with either of my production studies. Rather, I developed further hypotheses from Seyfarth's idea taking into account the effect of frequency, which I termed 'gradient paradigm uniformity'. I found such an effect in 2 out of the 5 different datasets I used in the corpus studies and in the production experiment, but for most datasets, this effect did not hold up in the subsets of the data in which stem frequency and word from frequency do not correlate (the frequency band analyses). Therefore, the effect that I found in some of the datasets before establishing a frequency band is likely a masked word form frequency effect.

In addition to the investigation of effects in production, I also looked at the perception of phonetic detail based on the question whether listeners can perceive fine phonetic detail such as that theorized to be present in paradigm uniformity effects. I found that indeed, listeners are sensitive to durational differences between the stems of different words, and that they make use of the phonetic information within stems in comprehension to some extent. To conclude, I have found that listeners can perceive subtle phonetic differences and that they use phonetic detail in comprehension, but the theoretical implications regarding the processing of matched and mismatched information, such as that used in the comprehension task, remain unclear.

But more research is needed to draw conclusions from what has been observed in this dissertation – as far as that is even possible. As suggested by Sönning & Werner (2021c) in light of the replication crisis in quantitative linguistics, drawing strong conclusions from data is not recommended, as many effects have not been replicable in follow-up studies – including those that I attempted to replicate by Seyfarth et al. (2017), as well as my own findings from the QuakeBox study. However, I still encourage future research on this topic using different methodologies which may be more suitable to investigate paradigm uniformity effects.

Appendix

Terminology

Table 9.1: Terms used to refer to the different types of "stems" in this dissertation, and examples for the phonetic material they correspond to in a given example word.

Term used	Example phonetic material	Example word
"bare stem"	[deɪ]	day
"complex stem"	[deɪ] in [deɪz]	days
"pseudo-stem"	[deɪ] in [deɪz]	daze

Link to online repository

The online repository can be found at
https://osf.io/npvx8/?view_only=372e209f39fe4edaa19c7304e515fdea

Appendix to 6.1 (Same-different task)

Table 9.2: List of target and filler items used in same-different task with additional morphological and phonetic information for each item.

ITEM	TYPE	TARGET	POS	PRECSOUNDTYPE	VOICING
ace	monomorphemic	target	NN1	diphthong	voiceless
chess	monomorphemic	target	NN1	short	voiceless
goose	monomorphemic	target	NN1	long	voiceless
house	monomorphemic	target	NN1	diphthong	voiceless
buzz	monomorphemic	target	NN1	short	voiced
clause	monomorphemic	target	NN1	long	voiced
bees	plural	target	NN2	long	voiced
blues	plural	target	NN2	long	voiced
boys	plural	target	NN2	diphthong	voiced
flaws	plural	target	NN2	long	voiced
foes	plural	target	NN2	diphthong	voiced
ways	plural	target	NN2	diphthong	voiced
grief	filler f	filler	NN1	long	voiceless

Open Access. © 2023 the author(s), published by De Gruyter. This work is licensed under the Creative Commons Attribution-NonCommercial-NoDerivatives 4.0 International License.
https://doi.org/10.1515/9783111017754-009

Item	Type	Target	POS	PrecSoundType	Voicing
riff	filler f	filler	NN1	short	voiceless
wife	filler f	filler	NN1	diphthong	voiceless
grieve	filler f	filler	VVI	long	voiced
love	filler f	filler	NN1	short	voiced
wave	filler f	filler	NN1	diphthong	voiced
death	filler th	filler	NN1	short	voiceless
growth	filler th	filler	NN1	diphthong	voiceless
myth	filler th	filler	NN1	short	voiceless
path	filler th	filler	NN1	long	voiceless
bathe	filler th	filler	VVI	diphthong	voiced
soothe	filler th	filler	VVI	long	voiced

Appendix to 6.2 (Comprehension task)

Table 9.3: List of target and filler items used in comprehension task alongside morphological and phonetic information for each item.

Word	Triplet / Pair	Type	POS	PrecSoundType
baize	bay-bay-baize	target	NN1	diphthong
bay	bay-bay-baize	target	NN1	diphthong
bays	bay-bay-baize	target	NN2	diphthong
brew	brew-brews-bruise	target	NN1	vowel
brews	brew-brews-bruise	target	VVZ	vowel
bruise	brew-brews-bruise	target	NN1	vowel
brow	brow-brows-browse	target	NN1	diphthong
brows	brow-brows-browse	target	NN2	diphthong
browse	brow-brows-browse	target	VVI	diphthong
chew	chew-chews-choose	target	VVI	vowel
chews	chew-chews-choose	target	VVZ	vowel
choose	chew-chews-choose	target	VVI	vowel
coax	coke-cokes-coax	target	VVI	diphthong
coke	coke-cokes-coax	target	NN1	diphthong
cokes	coke-cokes-coax	target	NN2	diphthong
day	day-days-daze	target	NN1	diphthong
days	day-days-daze	target	NN2	diphthong

Word	Triplet / Pair	Type	POS	PrecSoundType
daze	day-days-daze	target	NN1	diphthong
gene	gene-genes-jeans	target	NN1	vowel
genes	gene-genes-jeans	target	NN2	vowel
jeans	gene-genes-jeans	target	NN2	vowel
guise	guy-guys-guise	target	NN1	diphthong
guy	guy-guys-guise	target	NN1	diphthong
guys	guy-guys-guise	target	NN2	diphthong
hertz	hurt-hurts-hertz	target	NN1	consonant
hurt	hurt-hurts-hertz	target	VVI	consonant
hurts	hurt-hurts-hertz	target	VVZ	consonant
know	know-knows-nose	target	VVI	diphthong
knows	know-knows-nose	target	VVZ	diphthong
nose	know-knows-nose	target	NN1	diphthong
link	link-links-lynx	target	NN1	consonant
links	link-links-lynx	target	NN2	consonant
lynx	link-links-lynx	target	NN1	consonant
pause	paw-paws-pause	target	NN1	vowel
paw	paw-paws-pause	target	NN1	vowel
paws	paw-paws-pause	target	NN2	vowel
sigh	sigh-sighs-size	target	NN1	diphthong
sighs	sigh-sighs-size	target	VVZ	diphthong
size	sigh-sighs-size	target	NN1	diphthong
tea	tea-teas-tease	target	NN1	vowel
teas	tea-teas-tease	target	NN2	vowel
tease	tea-teas-tease	target	VVI	vowel
tuck	tuck-tucks-tux	target	VVI	consonant
tucks	tuck-tucks-tux	target	VVZ	consonant
tux	tuck-tucks-tux	target	NN1	consonant
use	yew-yews-use	target	VVI	vowel
yew	yew-yews-use	target	NN1	vowel
yews	yew-yews-use	target	NN2	vowel
boos	boos-booze	filler	VVZ	-
booze	boos-booze	filler	NN1	-
board	bored-board	filler	NN1	-
bored	bored-board	filler	VBD	-
brewed	brewed-brood	filler	VBD	-

Word	Triplet / Pair	Type	POS	PrecSoundType
brood	brewed-brood	filler	NN1	-
ducked	ducked-duct	filler	VBD	-
duct	ducked-duct	filler	NN1	-
frees	frees-freeze	filler	VVZ	-
freeze	frees-freeze	filler	VVI	-
laps	laps-lapse	filler	NN2	-
lapse	laps-lapse	filler	NN1	-
paced	paced-paste	filler	VBD	-
paste	paced-paste	filler	VVI	-
packed	packed-pact	filler	VBD	-
pact	packed-pact	filler	NN1	-
passed	passed-past	filler	VBD	-
past	passed-past	filler	NN1	-
quarts	quarts-quartz	filler	NN2	-
quartz	quarts-quartz	filler	NN1	-
road	rowed-road	filler	NN1	-
rowed	rowed-road	filler	VBD	-
sacks	sacks-sax	filler	NN2	-
sax	sacks-sax	filler	NN1	-
suede	swayed-suede	filler	NN1	-
swayed	swayed-suede	filler	VBD	-
tide	tied-tide	filler	NN1	-
tied	tied-tide	filler	VBD	-
tracked	tracked-tract	filler	VBD	-
tract	tracked-tract	filler	NN1	-
rapt	wrapped-rapt	filler	AJ0	-
wrapped	wrapped-rapt	filler	VBD	-

References

Albright, Adam. 2004. The morphological basis of paradigm leveling. In *Paradigms in phonological theory*. Oxford University Press.

Antilla, Raimo. 1977. Analogy (Trends in Linguistics, State—of-the-Art Reports, 10). *Journal of Linguistics* 16(2). viii+ 152. https://doi.org/10.1017/S0022226700006630.

Aylett, Matthew & Alice Turk. 2006. Language redundancy predicts syllabic duration and the spectral characteristics of vocalic syllable nuclei. *The Journal of the Acoustical Society of America* 119(5). 3048–3058. https://doi.org/10.1121/1.2188331.

Baayen, R. Harald. 2008. *Analyzing linguistic data: a practical introduction to statistics using R*. Cambridge University Press. https://doi.org/10.1017/CBO9780511801686.

Baayen, R. Harald, W. Levelt, Robert Schreuder & Mirjam Ernestus. 2007. Paradigmatic structure in speech production. In *Proceedings from the annual meeting of the Chicago linguistic society*, vol. 43, 1–29. Chicago Linguistic Society.

Baayen, R Harald & Maja Linke. 2020. Generalized additive mixed models. In Magali Paquot & Stefan Th. Gries (eds.), A Practical Handbook of Corpus Linguistics, 563–591. Springer. https://doi.org/10.1007/978-3-030-46216-1_23.

Baayen, R. Harald & Robert Schreuder. 1999. War and peace: morphemes and full forms in a noninteractive activation parallel dual-route model. *Brain and language* 68(1–2). 27–32. https://doi.org/10.1006/brln.1999.2069.

Baayen, R. Harald & Elnaz Shafaei-Bajestan. 2019. languageR: Analyzing Linguistic Data: A Practical Introduction to Statistics. https://CRAN.R-project.org/package=languageR. (20 April, 2020).

Baayen, R. Harald, Lee H. Wurm & Joanna Aycock. 2007. Lexical dynamics for low-frequency complex words: A regression study across tasks and modalities. *The Mental Lexicon* 2(3). 419–463. https://doi.org/10.1075/ml.2.3.06baa.

Babyak, Michael A. 2004. What you see may not be what you get: a brief, nontechnical introduction to overfitting in regression-type models. *Psychosomatic medicine* 66(3). 411–421. https://doi.org/10.1097/01.psy.0000127692.23278.a9.

Balota, David A., Melvin J. Yap, Michael J. Cortese, Keith A. Hutchinson, Brett Kessler, B. Loftis, James H. Neely, Douglas L. Nelson, Greg B. Simpson & Rebecca Treiman. 2007. The English Lexicon Project. *Behavior Research Methods* 39. 445–459.

Bartoń, Kamil. 2009. MuMIn: multi-model inference. https://cran.r-project.org/web/packages/MuMIn/index.html. (29 April, 2022).

Bates, Douglas, Martin Maechler, Ben Bolker, Steven Walker, Rune Haubo Bojesen Christensen, Henrik Singmann, Bin Dai, Gabor Grothendieck & Peter Green. 2017. lme4: Linear Mixed-Effects Models using "Eigen" and S4. https://cran.r-project.org/web/packages/lme4/index.html. (24 October, 2017).

Bauer, Laurie, Rochelle Lieber & Ingo Plag. 2015. *The Oxford Reference Guide to English Morphology*. Oxford University Press. https://doi.org/10.1093/acprof:oso/9780198747062.001.0001.

Bell, Alan, Jason M. Brenier, Michelle Gregory, Cynthia Girand & Dan Jurafsky. 2009. Predictability effects on durations of content and function words in conversational English. *Journal of Memory and Language* 60(1). 92–111. https://doi.org/10.1016/j.jml.2008.06.003.

Bell, Alan, Daniel Jurafsky, Eric Fosler-Lussier, Cynthia Girand, Michelle Gregory & Daniel Gildea. 2003. Effects of disfluencies, predictability, and utterance position on word form variation in English conversation. *The Journal of the Acoustical Society of America* 113(2). 1001–1024. https://doi.org/10.1121/1.1534836.

Bell, Melanie J., Sonia Ben Hedia & Ingo Plag. 2021. How morphological structure affects phonetic realization in English compound nouns. *Morphology* 31. 87–120. https://doi.org/10.1007/s11525-020-09346-6.

Ben Hedia, Sonia. 2019. *Gemination and degemination in English affixation: Investigating the interplay between morphology, phonology and phonetics* (Studies in Laboratory Phonology). Vol. 8. Language Science Press. http://doi.org/10.5281/zenodo.3232849.

Ben Hedia, Sonia & Ingo Plag. 2017. Gemination and degemination in English prefixation: Phonetic evidence for morphological organization. *Journal of Phonetics* 62. 34–49. https://doi.org/10.1016/j.wocn.2017.02.002.

Bethin, Christina Y. 2012. On paradigm uniformity and contrast in Russian vowel reduction. *Natural Language & Linguistic Theory* 30(2). 425–463. https://doi.org/10.1007/s11049-012-9166-4.

Biedermann, Britta, Gerhard Blanken & Lyndsey Nickels. 2002. The representation of homophones: Evidence from remediation. *Aphasiology* 16(10–11). 1115–1136. https://doi.org/10.1016/j.cortex.2006.07.004.

Biedermann, Britta & Lyndsey Nickels. 2008. Homographic and heterographic homophones in speech production: does orthography matter? *Cortex; a Journal Devoted to the Study of the Nervous System and Behavior* 44(6). 683–697. https://doi.org/10.1016/j.cortex.2006.12.001.

Bies, Ann, Mark Ferguson, Karen Katz, Robert MacIntyre, Victoria Tredinnick, Grace Kim, Mary Ann Marcinkiewicz & Britta Schasberger. 1995. Bracketing guidelines for Treebank II style Penn Treebank project. *University of Pennsylvania* 97. 100.

Blazej, Laura J. & Ariel M. Cohen-Goldberg. 2015. Can We Hear Morphological Complexity Before Words Are Complex? *Journal of Experimental Psychology: Human Perception and Performance* 41(1). 50–68. https://doi.org/10.1037/a0038509.

Blevins, James P. 2003. Stems and paradigms. *Language* 79(4). 737–767. https://doi.org/10.1353/lan.2003.0206.

BNC Consortium. 2007. British National Corpus (BNC). University of Oxford: Distributed by Bodleian Libraries, University of Oxford, on behalf of the BNC Consortium. https://www.english-corpora.org/bnc/. (15 May, 2020).

Boersma, Paul & David Weenink. 2015. Praat: doing Phonetics by Computer. (Version 6.0.08). http://www.fon.hum.uva.nl/praat/.

Burzio, Luigi. 1998. Multiple correspondence. *Lingua* 104(1–2). 79–109. https://doi.org/10.1016/S0024-3841(97)00025-9.

Byrd, Dani. 1994. Relations of sex and dialect to reduction. *Speech Communication* 15(1–2). 39–54. https://doi.org/10.1016/0167-6393(94)90039-6.

Byrd, Dani, Jelena Krivokapić & Sungbok Lee. 2006. How far, how long: On the temporal scope of prosodic boundary effects. *Journal of the Acoustical Society of America* 120(3). 1589–1599. https://doi.org/10.1121/1.2217135.

Caramazza, Alfonso. 1997. How Many Levels of Processing Are There in Lexical Access? *Cognitive Neuropsychology* 14(1). 177–208. https://doi.org/10.1080/026432997381664.

Caramazza, Alfonso, Albert Costa, Michele Miozzo & Yanchao Bi. 2001. The specific-word frequency effect: Implications for the representation of homophones in speech production.

Journal of Experimental Psychology: Learning, Memory, and Cognition 27(6). 1430. https://doi.org/10.1037/0278-7393.27.6.1430.

Carroll, J. B., P. Davies & B. Richman. 1971. The American heritage intermediate corpus. In *Proceedings of the International Conference on Computational Linguistics*. New York: American Heritage Publishing Co, vol. 1, 281–285. https://doi.org/10.3115/992532.992559.

Caselli, Naomi K., Michael K. Caselli & Ariel M. Cohen-Goldberg. 2016. Inflected words in production: Evidence for a morphologically rich lexicon. *The Quarterly Journal of Experimental Psychology* 69(3). 432–454. https://doi.org/10.1080/17470218.2015.1054847.

ceismic.org.nz. UC CEISMIC Canterbury Earthquake Digital Archive. http://www.ceismic.org.nz/. (23 March, 2020).

Cho, Taehong. 2001. Effects of morpheme boundaries on intergestural timing: Evidence from Korean. *Phonetica* 58(3). 129–162. https://doi.org/10.1159/000056196.

Chomsky, Noam & Morris Halle. 1968. The sound pattern of English.

Christophe, Anne, Sharon Peperkamp, Christophe Pallier, Eliza Block & Jacques Mehler. 2004. Phonological phrase boundaries constrain lexical access I. Adult data. *Journal of Memory and Language* 51(4). 523–547. https://doi.org/10.1016/j.jml.2004.07.001.

Clahsen, Harald. 1999. Lexical entries and rules of language: A multidisciplinary study of German inflection. *Behavioral and brain sciences* 22(6). 991–1013. https://doi.org/10.1017/s0140525x99002228.

Cohen, Clara. 2014. Probabilistic reduction and probabilistic enhancement. *Morphology* 24(4). 291–323. https://doi.org/10.1007/s11525-014-9243-y.

Cohen-Goldberg, Ariel M. 2013. Towards a theory of multimorphemic word production: The heterogeneity of processing hypothesis. *Language and Cognitive Processes* 28(7). 1036–1064. https://doi.org/10.1080/01690965.2012.759241.

Coleman, John, Ladan Baghai-Ravary, John Prybus & Sergio Grau. 2012. Audio BNC: the audio edition of the Spoken British National Corpus. *Phonetics Laboratory, University of Oxford*. http://www.phon.ox.ac.uk/AudioBNC. (23 March, 2020).

Collins, Allan M. & Elizabeth F. Loftus. 1975. A spreading-activation theory of semantic processing. *Psychological Review* 82(6). 407. https://doi.org/10.1037/0033-295X.82.6.407.

Dąbrowska, Ewa. 2008. The effects of frequency and neighbourhood density on adult speakers' productivity with Polish case inflections: An empirical test of usage-based approaches to morphology. *Journal of Memory and Language* 58(4). 931–951. https://doi.org/10.1016/j.jml.2007.11.005.

Davies, Mark. 2008. The Corpus of Contemporary American English: 520 million words, 1990-present. http://corpus.byu.edu/coca/. (12 May, 2016).

Davis, M. H., W. D. Marslen-Wilson & M. G. Gaskell. 2002. Leading up the lexical garden path: Segmentation and ambiguity in spoken word recognition. *Journal of Experimental Psychology: Human Perception and Performance* 28(1). 218–244. https://doi.org/10.1037/0096-1523.28.1.218.

Dell, Gary S. 1986. A spreading-activation theory of retrieval in sentence production. *Psychological Review* 93(3). 283. https://doi.org/10.1037/0033-295X.93.3.283.

Draper, Norman R. & Harry Smith. 1998. *Applied regression analysis* (Wiley Series in Probability and Statistics). 3rd edn. Vol. 326. John Wiley & Sons.

Engemann, Marie & Ingo Plag. 2021. Phonetic reduction and paradigm uniformity effects in spontaneous speech. *The Mental Lexicon* 16(1). 165–198. https://doi.org/10.1075/ml.20023.eng.

Ernestus, Mirjam & R. Harald Baayen. 2006. The functionality of incomplete neutralization in Dutch: The case of past-tense formation. *Laboratory Phonology* 8. 27–49. https://doi.org/10.1515/9783110197211.1.27.

Ernestus, Mirjam & R. Harald Baayen. 2007. Paradigmatic effects in auditory word recognition: The case of alternating voice in Dutch. *Language and Cognitive Processes* 22(1). 1–24. https://doi.org/10.1080/01690960500268303.

Fasiolo, Matteo, Simon N. Wood, Margaux Zaffran, Raphaël Nedellec & Yannig Goude. 2021. Fast Calibrated Additive Quantile Regression. *Journal of the American Statistical Association* 116(535). 1402–1412. https://doi.org/10.1080/01621459.2020.1725521.

Fox, John, Sanford Weisberg, Brad Price, Daniel Adler, Douglas Bates, Gabriel Baud-Bovy, Ben Bolker, et al. 2020. car: Companion to Applied Regression. https://CRAN.R-project.org/package=car. (19 May, 2020).

Francis, W. Nelson & H. Kucera. 1971. *A Standard Corpus of Present-Day Edited American*. National Council of Teachers of English. https://doi.org/10.2307/373638.

Frauenfelder, Uli H. & Robert Schreuder. 1992. Constraining psycholinguistic models of morphological processing and representation: The role of productivity. In *Yearbook of morphology 1991*, 165–183. Springer.

Frazier, Melissa. 2006. Output-output faithfulness to moraic structure: Evidence from American English. In *PROCEEDINGS-NELS*, vol. 36, 1.

Fromont, Robert & Jennifer Hay. 2012. LaBB-CAT: an Annotation Store. In *Proceedings of Australasian Language Technology Association Workshop*, 113--117. Australasian Language Technology Associatio. http://labbcat.sourceforge.net/. (6 May, 2019).

Gafos, Adamantios I. 2006. Dynamics in grammar: Comment on Ladd and Ernestus & Baayen* Adamantios I. Gafos. *Laboratory Phonology* 8(4). 51. https://doi.org/10.1515/9783110197211.1.51.

Gafos, Adamantios I. & Angela Ralli. 2002. Morphosyntactic features and paradigmatic uniformity in two dialectal varieties of the island of Lesvos. *Journal of Greek Linguistics* 2(1). 41–73. https://doi.org/10.1075/jgl.2.03gaf.

Gahl, Susanne. 2008. "Time" and "thyme" are not homophones: the effect of lemma frequency on word durations in spontaneous speech. *Language* 84(3). 474–496.

Gahl, Susanne. 2009. Homophone Duration in Spontaneous Speech: A Mixed-effects Model. *UC Berkeley PhonLab Annual Report* 5(5). https://doi.org/10.5070/P784q8q0qn.

Gahl, Susanne & Julia F. Strand. 2016. Many neighborhoods: Phonological and perceptual neighborhood density in lexical production and perception. *Journal of Memory and Language* (Speaking and Listening: Relationships Between Language Production and Comprehension) 89. 162–178. https://doi.org/10.1016/j.jml.2015.12.006.

Gahl, Susanne, Yao Yao & Keith Johnson. 2012. Why reduce? Phonological neighborhood density and phonetic reduction in spontaneous speech. *Journal of Memory and Language* 66(4). 806. https://doi.org/10.1016/j.jml.2011.11.006.

Gelman, Andrew. 2018. Ethics in statistical practice and communication: Five recommendations. *Significance* 15(5). 40–43.

Gelman, Andrew & Eric Loken. 2013. The garden of forking paths: Why multiple comparisons can be a problem, even when there is no "fishing expedition" or "p-hacking" and the research hypothesis was posited ahead of time. *Department of Statistics, Columbia University* 348.

Giegerich, Heinz J. 1992. *English Phonology: An Introduction*. Cambridge University Press. https://doi.org/10.1017/CBO9781139166126.

Goldinger, Stephen D. 1998. Echoes of echoes? An episodic theory of lexical access. *Psychological review* 105(2). 251. https://doi.org/10.1037/0033-295x.105.2.251.

Goldrick, Matthew. 2006. Limited interaction in speech production: Chronometric, speech error, and neuropsychological evidence. *Language and Cognitive Processes* 21(7–8). 817–855. https://doi.org/10.1080/01690960600824112.

Goldrick, Matthew. 2014. Phonological processing: The retrieval and encoding of word form information in speech production. In *The Oxford handbook of language production*, 228–244. Oxford University Press.

Goldrick, Matthew, H. Ross Baker, Amanda Murphy & Melissa Baese-Berk. 2011. Interaction and representational integration: Evidence from speech errors. *Cognition* 121(1). 58–72. https://doi.org/10.1016/j.cognition.2011.05.006.

Gries, Stefan Th. 2013. Elementary statistical testing with R. In Manfred Krug & Julia Schlüter (eds.), *Research Methods in Language Variation and Change*, 361–381. Cambridge University Press. https://doi.org/10.1017/CBO9780511792519.024.

Gries, Stefan Th. 2015. Some current quantitative problems in corpus linguistics and a sketch of some solutions. *Language and Linguistics* 16(1). 93–117. https://doi.org/10.1177/1606822X14556606.

Grieve, Jack. 2021. Observation, experimentation, and replication in linguistics. *Linguistics* 59(5). 1343–1356. https://doi.org/10.1515/ling-2021-0094.

Hanique, Iris & Mirjam Ernestus. 2012. The role of morphology in acoustic reduction. *Lingue e Linguaggio* 11(2). 147–164. https://doi.org/10.1418/38783.

Harrell Jr., Frank E. 2015. *Regression modeling strategies* (Springer Series in Statistics (SSS)). 2nd edn. Springer Cham. https://doi.org/10.1007/978-3-319-19425-7.

Hay, Jennifer. 2001. Lexical frequency in morphology: Is everything relative? *Linguistics* 39(6). https://doi.org/10.1515/ling.2001.041.

Hay, Jennifer. 2003. *Causes and Consequences of Word Structure* (Outstanding Dissertations in Linguistics). Psychology Press.

Hay, Jennifer. 2007. The phonetics of 'un.' *Lexical Creativity, Texts and Contexts* 39–57. https://doi.org/10.1075/sfsl.58.09hay.

Hay, Jennifer & R. Harald Baayen. 2005. Shifting paradigms: Gradient structure in morphology. *Trends in Cognitive Sciences* 9(7). 342–348. https://doi.org/10.1016/j.tics.2005.04.002.

Hayes, Bruce P. 2000. Gradient and well-formedness in optimality theory. In *Optimality Theory: Phonology, Syntax, and Acquisition*. Oxford University Press.

Henry, Molly J. & J. Devin McAuley. 2013. Failure to Apply Signal Detection Theory to the Montreal Battery of Evaluation of Amusia May Misdiagnose Amusia. *Music Perception* 30(5). 480–496. https://doi.org/10.1525/mp.2013.30.5.480.

Hothorn, Torsten, Kurt Hornik, Carolin Strobl & Achim Zeileis. 2020. party: A Laboratory for Recursive Partytioning. https://CRAN.R-project.org/package=party. (20 April, 2020).

House, Arthur S. 1961. On Vowel Duration in English. *The Journal of the Acoustical Society of America* 33(9). 1174–1178. https://doi.org/10.1121/1.1908941.

House, Arthur S. & Grant Fairbanks. 1953. The Influence of Consonant Environment upon the Secondary Acoustical Characteristics of Vowels. *The Journal of the Acoustical Society of America* 25(1). 105–113. https://doi.org/10.1121/1.1906982.

Ioannidis, John P. A. 2005. Why Most Published Research Findings Are False. *PLOS Medicine* 2(8). e124. https://doi.org/10.1371/journal.pmed.1004085.

Jackendoff, Ray S. 2002. *Foundations of Language: Brain, Meaning, Grammar, Evolution*. Oxford University Press. https://doi.org/10.1093/acprof:oso/9780198270126.001.0001.

Jescheniak, Jörg D. & Willem JM Levelt. 1994. Word frequency effects in speech production: Retrieval of syntactic information and of phonological form. *Journal of Experimental Psychology: Learning, Memory, and Cognition* 20(4). 824–843. https://doi.org/10.1037/0278-7393.20.4.824.

Jescheniak, Jörg D., Herbert Schriefers & Ansgar Hantsch. 2003. Utterance format effects phonological priming in the picture-word task: Implications for models of phonological encoding in speech production. *Journal of Experimental Psychology: Human Perception and Performance* 29(2). 441–454. https://doi.org/10.1037/0096-1523.29.2.441.

Johnson, Keith. 1997. The auditory/perceptual basis for speech segmentation. *Working Papers in Linguistics* 50. 101–113.

Jurafsky, Daniel, Alan Bell, Michelle Gregory & William D. Raymond. 2001. Probabilistic relations between words: Evidence from reduction in lexical production. In *Frequency and the emergence of linguistic structure* (Typological Studies in Language, Vol. 45), 229–254. John Benjamins Publishing Company. https://doi.org/10.1075/tsl.45.13jur.

Kemps, Rachel J. J. K., Mirjam Ernestus, Robert Schreuder & R. Harald Baayen. 2005. Prosodic cues for morphological complexity: the case of Dutch plural nouns. *Memory & Cognition* 33(3). 430. https://doi.org/10.3758/BF03193061.

Kemps, Rachel J. J. K., Lee H. Wurm, Mirjam Ernestus, Robert Schreuder & R. Harald Baayen. 2005. Prosodic cues for morphological complexity in Dutch and English. *Language And Cognitive Processes* 20(1–2). 43–73. https://doi.org/10.1080/01690960444000223.

Kenstowicz, Michael. 1995. Base-Identity and Uniform Exponence: Alternatives to Cyclicity. In *European Studies Research Institute, University of Salford*. https://doi.org/10.7282/T34X55VT.

Kenstowicz, Michael J. 1994. *Phonology in Generative Grammar* (Blackwell Textbooks in Linguistics). Vol. 7. Wiley-Blackwell.

Kenstowicz, Michael & Hyang-Sook Sohn. 2008. Paradigmatic uniformity and contrast: Korean liquid verb stems. *Phonological Studies* 11. 99–110.

Kerr, Norbert L. 1998. HARKing: Hypothesizing after the results are known. *Personality and social psychology review* 2(3). 196–217. https://doi.org/10.1207/s15327957pspr0203_4.

Kieslich, Pascal J. & Felix Henninger. 2017. Mousetrap: An integrated, open-source mouse-tracking package. *Behavior Research Methods* 49(5). 1652–1667. https://doi.org/10.3758/s13428-017-0900-z.

Kiparsky, Paul. 2012. Analogical Change as a Problem for Linguistic Theory. *Studies in the Linguistic Sciences Urbana* III(8.2). 77–96.

Kiparsky, Paul. 2015. Stratal OT: A Synopsis and FAQs. In *Capturing phonological shades within and across languages*, 2–44. Cambridge Scholars Publishing.

Kisler, Thomas, Uwe Reichel & Florian Schiel. 2017. Multilingual processing of speech via web services. *Computer Speech & Language* 45. 326–347. https://doi.org/10.1016/j.csl.2017.01.005.

Klatt, Dennis H. 1975. Vowel lengthening is syntactically determined in a connected discourse. *Journal of Phonetics* 3(3). 129–140. https://doi.org/10.1016/S0095-4470(19)31360-9.

Klatt, Dennis H. 1976. Linguistic uses of segmental duration in English: Acoustic and perceptual evidence. *The Journal of the Acoustical Society of America* 59(5). 1208–1221. https://doi.org/10.1121/1.380986.

Klatt, Dennis H. 1979. Speech perception: A model of acoustic–phonetic analysis and lexical access. *Journal of phonetics* 7(3). 279–312. https://doi.org/10.1016/S0095-4470(19)31059-9.

Klatt, Dennis H. & William E. Cooper. 1975. Perception of segment duration in sentence contexts. In *Structure and process in speech perception*, 69–89. Springer.
Kortmann, Bernd. 2021. Reflecting on the quantitative turn in linguistics. *Linguistics* 59(5). 1207–1226. https://doi.org/10.1515/ling-2019-0046.
Kuhn, Thomas S. 1962. *The Structure of Scientific Revolutions*. University of Chicago Press.
Kunter, Gero. 2017a. *Processing complexity and the alternation between analytic and synthetic forms in English*. Düsseldorf, Germany: Heinrich-Heine-Universität Düsseldorf. Postdoctoral thesis ('Habilitationsschrift').
Kunter, Gero. 2017b. Coquery: a free corpus query tool (Version 0.10.0). www.coquery.org. (14 June, 2017).
Kuznetsova, Alexandra, Per Bruun Brockhoff, Rune Haubo Bojesen Christensen & Sofie Pødenphant Jensen. 2020. lmerTest: Tests in Linear Mixed Effects Models. https://CRAN.R-project.org/package=lmerTest. (20 April, 2020).
Labov, William. 1972. *Sociolinguistic Patterns*. University of Pennsylvania Press.
Lahiri, Aditi & William Marslen-Wilson. 1991. The mental representation of lexical form: A phonological approach to the recognition lexicon. *Cognition* 38(3). 245–294. https://doi.org/10.1016/0010-0277(91)90008-R.
Lee, Yoonjeong, Elsi Kaiser & Louis Goldstein. 2020. I Scream for Ice Cream: Resolving Lexical Ambiguity with Sub-phonemic Information. *Language and Speech* 63(3). 526–549. https://doi.org/10.1177/0023830919866870.
Lee-Kim, Sang-Im, Lisa Davidson & Sangjin Hwang. 2013. Morphological effects on the darkness of English intervocalic /l/. *Laboratory Phonology* 4(2). 475–511. https://doi.org/10.1515/lp-2013-0015.
Lehiste, Ilse. 1960. An Acoustic – Phonetic Study of Internal Open Juncture. *Phonetica* 5(s1). 5–54. https://doi.org/10.1159/000258062.
Levelt, Willem J M, Ardi Roelofs & Antje S. Mayer. 1999. A theory of lexical access in speech production. *Behavioral and Brain Sciences* 22(1). 38–75. https://doi.org/10.1017/s0140525x99001776.
Lohmann, Arne. 2017. Phonological properties of word classes and directionality in conversion. *Word Structure* 10(2). 204–234. https://doi.org/10.3366/word.2017.0108.
Lohmann, Arne. 2018a. Time and thyme are NOT homophones: A closer look at Gahl's work on the lemma-frequency effect, including a reanalysis. *Language* 94(2). e180–e190. https://doi.org/10.1353/lan.2018.0032.
Lohmann, Arne. 2018b. Cut (n) and cut (v) are not homophones: Lemma frequency affects the duration of noun–verb conversion pairs. *Journal of Linguistics* 54(4). 753–777. https://doi.org/10.1017/S0022226717000378.
Lõo, Kaidi, Juhani Järvikivi, Fabian Tomaschek, Benjamin V. Tucker & R. Harald Baayen. 2018. Production of Estonian case-inflected nouns shows whole-word frequency and paradigmatic effects. *Morphology* 28(1). 71–97. https://doi.org/10.1007/s11525-017-9318-7.
Losiewicz, Beth. 1992. *The effect of duration on linguistic morphology*. Austin, TX: University of Texas. Doctoral Dissertation.
Mackenzie, Sara, Erin Olson, Meghan Clayards & Michael Wagner. 2018. North American /l/ both darkens and lightens depending on morphological constituency and segmental context. *Laboratory Phonology* 9(1). https://doi.org/10.5334/labphon.104.
Macmillan, Neil A. & C. Douglas Creelman. 2004. *Detection theory: A user's guide*. Psychology Press.

Makowski, Dominique, Hugo Najberg, Viliam Simko & Sasha Epskamp. 2021. psycho: Efficient and Publishing-Oriented Workflow for Psychological Science. https://CRAN.R-project.org/package=psycho. (24 February, 2022).

Marcus, Gary F., Ursula Brinkmann, Harald Clahsen, Richard Wiese & Steven Pinker. 1995. German Inflection: The Exception That Proves the Rule. *Cognitive Psychology* 29(3). 189–256. https://doi.org/10.1006/cogp.1995.1015.

Marian, Viorica. 2012. CLEARPOND: Cross-Linguistic Easy-Access Resource for Phonological and Orthographic Neighborhood Densities. United States, North America: Public Library of Science (PLoS).

Martínez, Ignacio M. Palacios. 2020. Methods of data collection in English empirical linguistics research: Results of a recent survey. *Language Sciences* 78. 101263. https://doi.org/10.1016/j.langsci.2019.101263.

Massaro, Dominic W. 1987. Categorical partition: A fuzzy-logical model of categorization behavior. In S. Harnad (ed.), *Categorical perception: The groundwork of cognition*, 254–283. Cambridge University Press.

Mathôt, Sebastiaan, Daniel Schreij & Jan Theeuwes. 2012. OpenSesame: An open-source, graphical experiment builder for the social sciences. *Behavior Research Methods* 44(2). 314–324. https://doi.org/10.3758/s13428-011-0168-7.

Matthews, Morphology. 1974. *An Introduction to the Theory of Word structure*. Cambridge University Press.

Matuschek, Hannes, Reinhold Kliegl, Shravan Vasishth, R. Harald Baayen & Douglas Bates. 2017. Balancing Type I error and power in linear mixed models. *Journal of Memory and Language* 94. 305–315. https://doi.org/10.1016/j.jml.2017.01.001.

McCarthy, John J & Alan Prince. 1993. Generalized alignment. In *Yearbook of morphology 1993*, 79–153. Springer.

McCarthy, John J & Alan S. Prince. 2001. *Prosodic Morphology: Constraint Interaction and Satisfaction*. Rutgers University. https://doi.org/10.7282/T3B856GM.

McClelland, James L. & Jeffrey L. Elman. 1986. The TRACE model of speech perception. *Cognitive Psychology* 18(1). 1–86. https://doi.org/10.1016/0010-0285(86)90015-0.

Norris, Dennis. 1994. Shortlist: A connectionist model of continuous speech recognition. *Cognition* 52(3). 189–234. https://doi.org/10.1016/0010-0277(94)90043-4.

Norris, Dennis & James M. McQueen. 2008. Shortlist B: a Bayesian model of continuous speech recognition. *Psychological Review* 115(2). 357. https://doi.org/10.1037/0033-295x.115.2.357.

Oller, D. Kimbrough. 1973. The effect of position in utterance on speech segment duration in English. *The Journal of the Acoustical Society of America* 54(5). 1235–1247. https://doi.org/10.1121/1.1914393.

Open Science Collaboration. 2015. Estimating the reproducibility of psychological science. *Science* 349(6251). https://doi.org/10.1126/science.aac4716.

Park, Sunwoo. 2006. *Paradigm uniformity effects in Korean phonology*. Seoul, Korea: Korea University. Doctoral Dissertation.

Pierrehumbert, Janet B. 2001. Exemplar dynamics: Word frequency. *Frequency and the Emergence of Linguistic Structure* 45(137). 10.1075. https://psycnet.apa.org/doi/10.1075/tsl.45.08pie.

Pierrehumbert, Janet B. 2003. Phonetic Diversity, Statistical Learning, and Acquisition of Phonology. *Language and speech* 46(2–3). 115–154. https://doi.org/10.1177/00238309030460020501.

Pinker, Steven & Michael T. Ullman. 2002. The past and future of the past tense. *Trends in cognitive sciences* 6(11). 456–463. https://doi.org/10.1016/S1364-6613(02)01990-3.

Pitt, M.A., L. Dilley, K. Johnson, S. Kiesling, W. Raymond, E. Hume & E. Fosler-Lussier. 2007. Buckeye Corpus of Conversational Speech (2nd release). *Department of Psychology, Ohio State University (Distributor)*. www.buckeyecorpus.osu.edu. (14 June, 2017).

Plag, Ingo & Sonia Ben Hedia. 2018. The phonetics of newly derived words: Testing the effect of morphological segmentability on affix duration. In Sabine Arndt-Lappe, Angelika Braun, Claudine Moulin & Esme Winter-Froemel (eds.), *Expanding the Lexicon: Linguistic Innovation, Morphological Productivity, and Ludicity*, 93–116. De Gruyter. https://doi.org/10.1515/9783110501933-095.

Plag, Ingo, Julia Homann & Gero Kunter. 2017. Homophony and morphology: The acoustics of word-final S in English. *Journal of Linguistics* 53(1). 181–216. https://doi.org/10.1017/S0022226715000183.

Plag, Ingo, Arne Lohmann, Sonia Ben Hedia & Julia Zimmermann. 2020. An <s> is an <s'>, or is it? Plural and genitive-plural are not homophonous. In *Complex words: advances in morphology*. Cambridge University Press.

Pluymaekers, Mark, Mirjam Ernestus & R. Harald Baayen. 2005a. Articulatory planning is continuous and sensitive to informational redundancy. *Phonetica* 62(2–4). 146–159. https://doi.org/10.1159/000090095.

Pluymaekers, Mark, Mirjam Ernestus & R. Harald Baayen. 2005b. Lexical frequency and acoustic reduction in spoken Dutch. *The Journal of the Acoustical Society of America* 118(4). 2561–2569. https://doi.org/10.1121/1.2011150.

Pluymaekers, Mark, Mirjam Ernestus, R. Harald Baayen & Geert Booij. 2010. Morphological effects on fine phonetic detail: The case of Dutch -igheid. (Ed.) C Fougeron, B Kühnert, M D'Imperio & N Vallée. *Laboratory Phonology* 10. 511–531. https://doi.org/10.1515/9783110224917.5.511.

Prasada, Sandeep & Steven Pinker. 1993. Generalisation of regular and irregular morphological patterns. *Language and cognitive processes* 8(1). 1–56. https://doi.org/10.1080/01690969308406948.

Prince, Alan & Paul Smolensky. 2008. *Optimality Theory: Constraint interaction in Generative Grammar*. Wiley-Blackwell.

R Core Team. 2015. R: A Language and Environment for Statistical Computing. (Version 3.2.1). Vienna, Austria. https://www.R-project.org.

Raffelsiefen, Renate. 2004. Paradigm Uniformity Effects Versus Boundary Effects. In *Paradigms in Phonological Theory*. Oxford University Press. http://www.oxfordscholarship.com/view/10.1093/acprof:oso/9780199267712.001.0001/acprof-9780199267712-chapter-9. (10 April, 2019).

Raftery, Adrian E. 1995. Bayesian model selection in social research. *Sociological Methodology* 25. 111–163. https://doi.org/10.2307/271063.

Raphael, Lawrence J. 1972. Preceding Vowel Duration as a Cue to the Perception of the Voicing Characteristic of Word-Final Consonants in American English. *The Journal of the Acoustical Society of America* 51(4B). 1296–1303. https://doi.org/10.1121/1.1912974.

Rebrus, Péter & Miklós Törkenczy. 2004. Uniformity and Contrast in the Hungarian Verbal Paradigm. In Laura J. Downing, T. Alan Hall & Renate Raffelsiefen (eds.), *Paradigms in Phonological Theory* (Oxford Studies in Theoretical Linguistics). Oxford Academic. https://doi.org/10.1093/acprof:oso/9780199267712.003.0010.

Roelofs, Ardi. 1992. A spreading-activation theory of lemma retrieval in speaking. *Cognition* 42(1–3). 107–142. https://doi.org/10.1016/0010-0277(92)90041-F.

Roelofs, Ardi & Victor S. Ferreira. 2019. The Architecture of Speaking. In Peter Hagoort (ed.), *Human Language: From Genes and Brains to Behavior*, 35–50. MIT Press.

Roettger, Timo B. & Dinah Baer-Henney. 2019. Toward a replication culture: Speech production research in the classroom. *Phonological Data and Analysis* 1(4). 1–23. https://doi.org/10.3765/pda.v1art4.13.

Roettger, Timo B., Bodo Winter & R. Harald Baayen. 2019. Emergent data analysis in phonetic sciences: Towards pluralism and reproducibility. *Journal of Phonetics* 73. 1–7. https://doi.org/10.1016/j.wocn.2018.12.001.

Roettger, Timo B., Bodo Winter, S. Grawunder, J. Kirby & M. Grice. 2014. Assessing incomplete neutralization of final devoicing in German. *Journal of Phonetics* 43. 11–25. https://doi.org/10.1016/j.wocn.2014.01.002.

Salverda, Anne Pier, Delphine Dahan & James M. McQueen. 2003. The role of prosodic boundaries in the resolution of lexical embedding in speech comprehension. *Cognition* 90(1). 51–89. https://doi.org/10.1016/S0010-0277(03)00139-2.

Sampson, Geoffrey. 2005. Quantifying the shift towards empirical methods. *International Journal of Corpus Linguistics* 10(2). 15–36. https://doi.org/10.1075/ijcl.10.1.02sam.

Sampson, Geoffrey. 2013. The empirical trend: Ten years on. *International Journal of Corpus Linguistics* 18(2). 281–289. https://doi.org/10.1075/ijcl.18.2.05sam.

Sandra, Dominiek. 2010. Homophone dominance at the whole-word and sub-word levels: Spelling errors suggest full-form storage of regularly inflected verb forms. *Language and speech* 53(3). 405–444. https://doi.org/10.1177/0023830910371459.

Sandra, Dominiek, Steven Frisson & Frans Daems. 1999. Why simple verb forms can be so difficult to spell: The influence of homophone frequency and distance in Dutch. *Brain and language* 68(1–2). 277–283. https://doi.org/10.1006/brln.1999.2108.

Sandra, Dominiek & Lien Van Abbenyen. 2009. Frequency and analogical effects in the spelling of full-form and sublexical homophonous patterns by 12 year-old children. *The Mental Lexicon* 4(2). 239–275. https://doi.org/10.1075/ml.4.2.04san.

Schmitz, Dominic. 2021. mtqgam: Mouse-Tracking Data in QGAMs. https://github.com/dosc91/mtqgam. (1 December, 2021).

Schmitz, Dominic. 2022. *Production, perception, and comprehension of subphonemic detail: Word-final /s/ in English* (Studies in Laboratory Phonology). Language Science Press.

Schmitz, Dominic, Dinah Baer-Henney & Ingo Plag. 2021. The duration of word-final /s/ differs across morphological categories in English: evidence from pseudowords. *Phonetica* 78(5–6). 571–616. https://doi.org/10.1515/phon-2021-2013.

Schmitz, Dominic, Marie Engemann, Ingo Plag & Dinah Baer-Henney. 2021a. Are listeners sensitive to morpho-phonetic differences in English stems and word-final /s/? *17. Phonetik und Phonologie Tagung*. Goethe-Universität Frankfurt, Germany.

Schmitz, Dominic, Marie Engemann, Ingo Plag & Dinah Baer-Henney. 2021b. Subtle morpho-phonetic differences in English stems and word-final /s/ influence listeners' comprehension. *Words in the World International Conference 2021*.

Schmitz, Dominic, Marie Engemann, Ingo Plag & Dinah Baer-Henney. 2022. Subphonemic detail affects morphological processing. *Morphology in Production and Perception: Phonetics, Phonology and Spelling of Complex Words (MPP 2022)*. Düsseldorf, Germany. 7-9 February.

Schmitz, Dominic, Ingo Plag & Dinah Baer-Henney. 2020. How real are acoustic differences between different types of final /s/ in English? Evidence from pseudowords. *19th International Morphology Meeting*. Vienna University of Economics and Business, Vienna, Austria.

Schreuder, Robert & R. Harald Baayen. 1995. Modeling morphological processing. *Morphological aspects of language processing* 2. 257–294.

Schreuder, Robert & R. Harald Baayen. 2015. Modeling morphological processing. In *Morphological aspects of language processing*, 131–154. Psychology Press.

Schuppler, Barbara, Wim A. van Dommelen, Jacques Koreman & Mirjam Ernestus. 2012. How linguistic and probabilistic properties of a word affect the realization of its final /t/: Studies at the phonemic and sub-phonemic level. *Journal of Phonetics* 40(4). 595–607. https://doi.org/10.1016/j.wocn.2012.05.004.

Seyfarth, Scott, Marc Garellek, Gwendolyn Gillingham, Farrell Ackerman & Robert Malouf. 2017. Acoustic differences in morphologically-distinct homophones. *Language, Cognition and Neuroscience* 33(1). 32–49. https://doi.org/10.1080/23273798.2017.1359634.

Seyfarth, Scott, Jozina Vander Klok & Marc Garellek. 2019. Evidence against interactive effects on articulation in Javanese verb paradigms. *Psychonomic Bulletin & Review* 26. 1690–1696. https://doi.org/10.3758/s13423-019-01637-2.

Shatzman, Keren B. & James M. McQueen. 2006. Segment duration as a cue to word boundaries in spoken-word recognition. *Perception & Psychophysics* 68(1). 1–16. https://doi.org/10.3758/BF03193651.

Simmons, Joseph P., Leif D. Nelson & Uri Simonsohn. 2011. False-positive psychology: Undisclosed flexibility in data collection and analysis allows presenting anything as significant. *Psychological science* 22(11). 1359–1366. https://doi.org/10.1177/0956797611417632.

Smith, Rachel, Rachel Baker & Sarah Hawkins. 2012. Phonetic detail that distinguishes prefixed from pseudo-prefixed words. *Journal of Phonetics* 40(5). 689–705. https://doi.org/10.1016/j.wocn.2012.04.002.

Sönning, Lukas & Valentin Werner. 2021a. *The replication crisis: Implications for linguistics* (Linguistics). Vol. 59:5. De Gruyter. https://www.degruyter.com/journal/key/ling/59/5/html. (8 December, 2021).

Sönning, Lukas & Valentin Werner. 2021b. The replication crisis, scientific revolutions, and linguistics. *Linguistics* 59(5). 1179–1206. https://doi.org/10.1515/ling-2019-0045.

Sproat, Richard & Osamu Fujimura. 1993. Allophonic variation in English/l/and its implications for phonetic implementation. *Journal of Phonetics* 21(3). 291–311. https://doi.org/10.1016/S0095-4470(19)31340-3.

Stanislaw, Harold & Natasha Todorov. 1999. Calculation of signal detection theory measures. *Behavior Research Methods, Instruments, & Computers* 31(1). 137–149. https://doi.org/10.3758/BF03207704.

Stein, Simon David. 2022. *The phonetics of derived words in English: Tracing morphology in speech production*. De Gruyter. https://doi.org/10.1515/9783111025476.

Stein, Simon David & Ingo Plag. 2019a. The phonetics of derivation: Segmentability effects on the acoustic duration of affixed words in English. *15. Phonetik und Phonologie Tagung*. Düsseldorf, Germany.

Stein, Simon David & Ingo Plag. 2019b. Lexical storage and morphological segmentability effects on the production of English derivatives. *MoProc 2019 - International Morphological Processing Conference*. Tübingen, Germany.

Stein, Simon David & Ingo Plag. 2022. How relative frequency and prosodic structure affect the acoustic duration of English derivatives. *Laboratory Phonology* 13(1). https://doi.org/10.16995/labphon.6445.

Steriade, Donca. 2000. Paradigm Uniformity and the Phonetics-Phonology Boundary. (Ed.) Michael Broe & Janet Pierrehumbert. *Papers in Laboratory Phonology* 5.

Sugahara, Mariko & Alice Turk. 2009. Durational Correlates of English Sublexical Constituent Structure. *Phonology* 26(3). 477–524. https://doi.org/10.1017/S0952675709990248.

Taft, Marcus & Sam Ardasinski. 2006. Obligatory decomposition in reading prefixed words. *The Mental Lexicon* 1(2). 183–199. https://doi.org/10.1075/ml.1.2.02taf.

Tomaschek, Fabian, Peter Hendrix & R. Harald Baayen. 2018. Strategies for addressing collinearity in multivariate linguistic data. *Journal of Phonetics* 71. 249–267. https://doi.org/10.1016/j.wocn.2018.09.004.

Tomaschek, Fabian, Ingo Plag, Mirjam Ernestus & R. Harald Baayen. 2019. Phonetic effects of morphology and context: Modeling the duration of word-final S in English with naïve discriminative learning. *Journal of Linguistics* 1–39. https://doi.org/10.1017/S0022226719000203.

Tomaschek, Fabian, Benjamin V. Tucker, Michael Ramscar & R. Harald Baayen. 2021. Paradigmatic enhancement of stem vowels in regular English inflected verb forms. *Morphology* 1–29. https://doi.org/10.1007/s11525-021-09374-w.

Torreira, Francisco & Mirjam Ernestus. 2009. Probabilistic effects on French [t] duration. *10th Annual Conference of the International Speech Communication Association (Interspeech 2009)*, 448–451. Causal Productions Pty Ltd.

Tucker, Benjamin V. & Mirjam Ernestus. 2021. Why we need to investigate casual speech to truly understand language production, processing and the mental lexicon. In Gary Libben, Gonia Jarema & Victor Kuperman (eds.), *Polylogues on The Mental Lexicon: An exploration of fundamental issues and directions*, vol. 11, 77–108. https://doi.org/10.1075/z.238.04tuc.

Turk, Alice E. & James R. Sawusch. 1997. The domain of accentual lengthening in American English. *Journal of Phonetics* 25(1). 25–41. https://doi.org/10.1006/jpho.1996.0032.

Van Oostendorp, Marc. 2008. Incomplete devoicing in formal phonology. *Lingua* 118(9). 1362–1374. https://doi.org/10.1016/j.lingua.2007.09.009.

Vasishth, Shravan & Andrew Gelman. 2021. How to embrace variation and accept uncertainty in linguistic and psycholinguistic data analysis. *Linguistics* 59(5). 1311–1342. https://doi.org/10.1515/ling-2019-0051.

Verhaert, Nina. 2015. Rules or regularities? The homophone dominance effect in spelling and reading regular Dutch verb forms. Antwerp, Belgium: Universiteit Antwerpen. Doctoral Dissertation.

Verhaert, Nina, Ellen Danckaert & Dominiek Sandra. 2016. The dual role of homophone dominance. Why homophone intrusions on regular verb forms so often go unnoticed. *The Mental Lexicon* 11(1). 1–25. https://doi.org/10.1075/ml.11.1.01ver.

Walsh, Liam, Jen Hay, Derek Bent, Jeanette King, Paul Millar, Viktoria Papp & Kevin Watson. 2013. The UC QuakeBox Project: Creation of a community-focused research archive. https://ir.canterbury.ac.nz/handle/10092/15635. (20 November, 2018).

White, Katherine K., Lise Abrams & Sarah M. Zoller. 2013. Perception-production asymmetries in homophone spelling: The unique influence of aging. *Journals of Gerontology Series B: Psychological Sciences and Social Sciences* 68(5). 681–690.

White, Katherine K., Lise Abrams, Sarah M. Zoller & Samantha M. Gibson. 2008. Why did I right that? Factors that influence the production of homophone substitution errors. *Quarterly Journal of Experimental Psychology* 61(7). 977–985.
Winter, Bodo & Timo B. Roettger. 2011. The nature of incomplete neutralization in German: Implications for laboratory phonology. *Grazer Linguistische Studien* 76. 55–74.
Wood, Simon. 2021. mgcv: Mixed GAM Computation Vehicle with Automatic Smoothness Estimation. https://CRAN.R-project.org/package=mgcv. (1 December, 2021).
Zimmerer, Frank, Mathias Scharinger & Henning Reetz. 2014. Phonological and morphological constraints on German/t/-deletions. *Journal of Phonetics* 45. 64–75. https://doi.org/10.1016/j.wocn.2014.03.006.
Zimmermann, Julia. 2016. Morphological Status and Acoustic Realization: Findings from NZE. In C Carignan & M.D. Tyler (eds.), *Proceedings of the 16th Australasian International Conference on Speech Science and Technology*, 6–9. Sydney: University of Western Sydney.

Index

annotation, 51–52, 103, 112, 128
articulatory gestures, 4–6, 37, 160

comprehension, 3, 23, 27, 48–49, 123, 138, 154, 162–163, 167
corpus studies, 2, 7, 28, 51–101, 103–104, 155–156, 158, 167
– Buckeye, 2, 37, 51–54, 59, 61–63, 65, 77–100, 155–156, 158–161
– QuakeBox, 1–2, 37, 51–52, 59–77, 100, 120–122, 155–161, 164, 168

decomposability, 1, 28, 31–37, 49
– dual-route model, 32–34, 49
– whole word representation, 20, 32, 49

experiment(s), 1–2, 6–7, 10, 13, 17–20, 22–25, 28, 31, 37, 44–45, 52–55, 57, 59–63, 99, 103–113, 122–124, 126, 130–131, 139–141, 150, 155–160, 162, 165,167
– comprehension task, 109, 123–124, 139–154
– design, 105–106, 123
– participants, 6, 63–64, 105, 110–111, 123–124, 130–133, 135–139, 146, 149–151, 153–154–156
– perception, 2, 24, 28, 123–155, 167
– production, 1–2, 54–55, 57, 60–61, 103–122, 130–131, 140, 155–159, 167
– same different task, 123–138, 146, 149, 162

frequency, 40, 43–44, 72, 83–84, 90–91, 94–95, 99–100, 120–122, 159–160, 167
– bare stem frequency, 27–28, 33–41, 56, 58, 65, 71–76, 79, 82–83, 90–91, 94–95, 98–100, 115, 118–120, 159–161, 167
– frequency band, 74–76, 83, 94–95, 120
– frequency inheritance effects, 43, 45–46
– relative frequency, 6, 27–28, 33–37, 40–41, 54, 56, 62, 71–74, 76, 83, 160
– word form frequency, 2, 33, 40–41, 56, 71–77, 83, 85, 88–91, 94–100, 107, 109, 113, 116, 119–122, 156, 159–161, 167

HPH, 39
homophones, 4, 6, 27, 40–47, 49, 104–105, 107–108, 113, 124–125, 155–158, 160, 163
– homophone dominance, 44–45
hypotheses, 26–28

Independent Network model, 41–42, 157
items, 53, 106, 107, 108, 126, 140
– filler items, 53, 109–112, 126, 130, 140–141, 146, 169–170
– frequency constellations, 57, 105, 107–109, 119, 156
– stimuli, 113, 125, 127–134, 139–141, 160, 162

Levelt model, 37–39, 42–43, 164

mental lexicon, 2, 20, 31–32, 37–38, 40–49, 154, 157, 161–163

OpenSesame, 110–113, 124, 130–131, 141–142
Optimality Theory, 17–18, 31
orthography, 45–46
– heterographic vs. homographic, 46

paradigms, 11–13
– nominal paradigms, 12–13
– verbal paradigms, 12–13
paradigm uniformity, 1–7, 11–22, 26–28, 31–32, 34–41, 49, 51–55, 63, 65, 100, 104–105, 155, 164, 167–168
– categorical paradigm uniformity, 4, 14–16, 27–28, 35, 37, 47, 54, 58, 65–68, 70, 76–77, 79–81, 83, 85–93, 97–100, 104–105, 114–118, 122, 155–158, 167
– gradient paradigm uniformity, 6, 15–16, 27–28, 35, 37, 41, 48–49, 54, 57–58, 65–67, 71, 76–77, 79–81, 83, 85, 89–93, 96, 98–101, 104–106, 108–109, 114–116, 118–122, 158–161, 167

– phonetic paradigm uniformity, 1, 14, 20, 28, 31, 34, 37–38, 45, 77, 101, 155
– phonological paradigm uniformity, 14–19
past tense, 20, 35–38, 53–54, 92–101, 107–108, 156, 158, 160
perception, 1–3, 22–29, 38, 47–50, 123–124, 155, 161–163, 167
– abstractionist models, 48, 162
– exemplar-based models, 49, 162
– eye-tracking, 23
– feature based models, 48, 162
– mousetracking, 24–25, 136, 141–148, 154, 162
– splicing, 23, 25–26, 123, 139–141, 146–147, 154
– uniqueness point, 48
plural, 2, 13, 16, 21–23, 25–26, 28, 35, 37–38, 53–54, 65, 68, 72, 76–80, 84–91, 99–101, 107–108, 110, 123, 125–126, 139–140, 146–148, 154, 156–161
pseudo-stem, 4–6, 27–29, 59, 68, 76, 88, 116-117, 123, 139–140, 155, 167

replication crisis, 2–3, 7–11, 28, 103, 155, 158, 164–165, 167
– confirmatory analysis, 3, 9–10, 27
– cyclical evolution of scientific theory, 8
– exploratory analysis, 3, 9–11, 27, 47, 111, 115, 130–131, 155

– HARKing, 9–10
– multi–method approaches, 3, 28, 103
– *p*-hacking, 9–10
resting activation, 33–34

Signal Detection Theory, 132–138
– a', 135–137
splicing, 23, 25–26, 123, 139–141, 146–149, 152–154
spreading activation, 26, 31, 37–38, 40–41, 49, 164
statistical analysis, 52, 54–59
– beta regression, 135–138
– collinearity, 44, 56–57, 67, 71–73, 83, 94, 116, 118, 159
– linear mixed effects regression, 55–56
– overfitting, 57
– QGAMs, 142–154
syllable weight, 4–5

third person singular, 20, 36–37, 53–54, 79, 81, 86, 89, 90–92, 99, 100, 107, 110, 156–158
type/token ratio, 51, 156, 159

variables, 54–63, 66–67, 79–81, 93, 96, 113–114, 131, 146

www.ingramcontent.com/pod-product-compliance
Lightning Source LLC
Chambersburg PA
CBHW050536300426
44113CB00012B/2125